T0303934

The Core Business Web: A Guide to Key Information Resources

The Core Business Web: A Guide to Key Information Resources has been co-published simultaneously as *Journal of Business & Finance Librarianship,* Volume 8, Number 2 2002 and Volume 8, Numbers 3/4 2003.

The *Journal of Business & Finance Librarianship* Monographic "Separates"

Below is a list of "separates," which in serials librarianship means a special issue simultaneously published as a special journal issue or double-issue *and* as a "separate" hardbound monograph. (This is a format which we also call a "DocuSerial.")

"Separates" are published because specialized libraries or professionals may wish to purchase a specific thematic issue by itself in a format which can be separately cataloged and shelved, as opposed to purchasing the journal on an on-going basis. Faculty members may also more easily consider a "separate" for classroom adoption.

"Separates" are carefully classified separately with the major book jobbers so that the journal tie-in can be noted on new book order slips to avoid duplicate purchasing.

You may wish to visit Haworth's Website at . . .

http://www.HaworthPress.com

. . . to search our online catalog for complete tables of contents of these separates and related publications.

You may also call 1-800-HAWORTH (outside US/Canada: 607-722-5857), or Fax 1-800-895-0582 (outside US/Canada: 607-771-0012), or e-mail at:

docdelivery@haworthpress.com

The Core Business Web: A Guide to Key Information Resources, edited by Gary W. White, MLS, MBA (Vol. 8, No. 2, 2002 and Vol. 8, No. 3/4, 2003). *"The reader will be led to the most relevant resources, thus eliminating much frustration and saving time."* (Bobray Bordelon, MLIS, Economics/Finance Librarian, Princeton University Library)

Library Services for Business Students in Distance Education: Issues and Trends, edited by Shari Buxbaum, MLS (Vol. 7, No. 2/3, 2002). *Explores approaches to providing library services for distance education business students; examines the standards and guidelines for measuring these services.*

The Core Business Web:
A Guide to Key
Information Resources

Gary W. White
Editor

The Core Business Web: A Guide to Key Information Resources has been co-published simultaneously as *Journal of Business & Finance Librarianship,* Volume 8, Number 2 2002 and Volume 8, Numbers 3/4 2003.

Routledge
Taylor & Francis Group

NEW YORK AND LONDON

First Published by

The Haworth Information Press®, 10 Alice Street, Binghamton, NY 13904-1580 USA

Transferred to Digital Printing 2010 by Routledge
270 Madison Ave, New York NY 10016
2 Park Square, Milton Park, Abingdon, Oxon, OX14 4RN

The Haworth Information Press® is an imprint of The Haworth Press, Inc., 10 Alice Street, Binghamton, NY 13904-1580 USA.

The Core Business Web: A Guide to Key Information Resources
has been co-published simultaneously as *Journal of Business &
Finance Librarianship*™, Volume 8, Number 2 2002
and Volume 8, Numbers 3/4 2003.

The development, preparation, and publication of this work has been undertaken with great care. However, the publisher, employees, editors, and agents of The Haworth Press and all imprints of The Haworth Press, Inc., including The Haworth Medical Press® and The Pharmaceutical Products Press®, are not responsible for any errors contained herein or for consequences that may ensue from use of materials or information contained in this work. Opinions expressed by the author(s) are not necessarily those of The Haworth Press, Inc. With regard to case studies, identities and circumstances of individuals discussed herein have been changed to protect confidentiality. Any resemblance to actual persons, living or dead, is entirely coincidental.

Cover design by Brooke R. Stiles.

Library of Congress Cataloging-in-Publication Data

The core business Web : a guide to key information resources / Gary W. White, editor.
    p. cm.
    "Co-published simultaneously as Journal of business & finance librarianship, volume 8, number 2 2002 and volume 8, numbers 3/4 2003."
    Includes bibliographical references and index.
    ISBN 0-7890-2094-7 (alk. paper) – ISBN 0-7890-2095-5 (pbk. : alk. paper)
    1. Business–Computer network resources. 2. World Wide Web. 3. Internet. I. White, Gary W.
II. Journal of business & finance librarianship.
HD30.37.C67 2003
025.06′65–dc21

        2003005541

Publisher's Note
The publisher has gone to great lengths to ensure the quality of this reprint
but points out that some imperfections in the original may be apparent.

The Core Business Web: A Guide to Key Information Resources

CONTENTS

ABOUT THE EDITOR

Gary W. White, MLS, MBA, is Head of the Schreyer Business Library at The Pennsylvania State University in University Park. He will serve as chair of the Business Reference and Services Section of the Reference and User Services Association of the American Library Association in 2003-04. Mr. White is the editor of the Web review column in the *Journal of Business & Finance Librarianship* and is co-author of *Using Microsoft Power Point: A How-To-Do-It Manual for Librarians.* His work has appeared in numerous publications, including *College & Research Libraries, Journal of Academic Librarianship, Reference & User Services Quarterly, The Reference Librarian, Collection Building,* and the *Journal of Marketing Management.*

Introduction

This volume contains a guide to the "best" business Web sites in twenty-five areas of business. The idea for these issues arose from the "Best of the Best Business Web Sites" (http://www.ala.org/rusa/brass/besthome.html), a Web site created and maintained by members of the Education Committee of BRASS (Business Reference and Services Section), a section of the Reference and User Services Association of the American Library Association. Authors, all of whom are active in business librarianship, were asked to explore Web sites in their subject areas and to select what they considered to be the very best. All URLs were working as of the time of publication. Hopefully this guide will aid librarians of all types to pinpoint useful and authoritative resources.

My sincere thanks to the authors, all of whom worked extremely hard on their sections for this volume, and to Christopher D. Greiner for providing excellent editorial assistance.

Gary W. White

[Haworth co-indexing entry note]: "Introduction." White, Gary W. Co-published simultaneously in *Journal of Business & Finance Librarianship* (The Haworth Information Press, an imprint of The Haworth Press, Inc.) Vol. 8, No. 2, 2002, p. 1; and: *The Core Business Web: A Guide to Key Information Resources* (ed: Gary W. White) The Haworth Information Press, an imprint of The Haworth Press, Inc., 2003, p. 1. Single or multiple copies of this article are available for a fee from The Haworth Document Delivery Service [1-800-HAWORTH, 9:00 a.m. - 5:00 p.m. (EST). E-mail address: docdelivery@haworthpress.com].

10.1300/J109v08n02_01

Core Accounting Web Resources

David A. Flynn

SUMMARY. This chapter outlines key Web resources for the accounting field, including sites of professional organizations and associations. *[Article copies available for a fee from The Haworth Document Delivery Service: 1-800-HAWORTH. E-mail address: <docdelivery@haworthpress.com> Website: <http://www.HaworthPress.com> © 2002 by The Haworth Press, Inc. All rights reserved.]*

KEYWORDS. Accounting, Web sites

INTRODUCTION

From the earliest known writings, found near ancient Uruk and etched on 5,000-year-old clay tablets, to MyAccountingPortal.com, accessible from all points around the globe, accounting continues to serve individuals, organizations, and nations as "the language of business." Arguably among the most critical of business functions, this systematic representation of an entity's transactions and financial position is our universal instrument for internal and external scrutiny and decision-making. Because it is the underpinning of our economic dealings and permeates all facets of a business enterprise, the importance of convenient and accurate accounting information cannot be understated.

David A. Flynn is Social Sciences/Business Librarian, University of Hawaii at Manoa (E-mail: dflynn@hawaii.edu).

[Haworth co-indexing entry note]: "Core Accounting Web Resources." Flynn, David A. Co-published simultaneously in *Journal of Business & Finance Librarianship* (The Haworth Information Press, an imprint of The Haworth Press, Inc.) Vol. 8, No. 2, 2002, pp. 3-13; and: *The Core Business Web: A Guide to Key Information Resources* (ed: Gary W. White) The Haworth Information Press, an imprint of The Haworth Press, Inc., 2003, pp. 3-13. Single or multiple copies of this article are available for a fee from The Haworth Document Delivery Service [1-800-342-9678, 9:00 a.m. - 5:00 p.m. (EST). E-mail address: docdelivery@haworthpress.com].

10.1300/J109v08n02_02

Businesspersons, students, librarians, and other interested community members constantly seek timely, exact, and easily accessible information concerning the standards and principles set forth by official boards and recognized professional associations. Additionally, aspiring and veteran bean counters, and others with an interest in unbiased and verifiable beans, desire electronic access to the regulations of related government agencies, current industry news from trade publications and business wires, and career information. The Web sites reviewed below provide the best Internet resources for accounting intelligence known to date. Included are gateway sites, headquarters for organizations and "standards setters," auditing and fraud information, educational resources, industry news, commercial outfits, and more.

It should be noted that, unlike the clay tablets mentioned previously, unearthed and still accurate after five millennia, a number of ambitious accounting Web projects have quickly disappeared after only a brief public engagement. Some projects, infused with loads of cash and a series of facelifts, are still far from my idea of the perfect Web resource. Still, there is already a wealth of information we can employ to help our patrons better understand this "financial information system" called accounting. As described by Strauss (1988), this system "begins with determining the raw data to be collected, proceeds to gathering, recording, analyzing, and verifying them, and culminates in communicating the data to interested parties."[1] Some of those interested parties, perhaps an Enron casualty or two, are inquiring at your reference desk right now. Let's survey the core sites that might help to serve their needs.

FINANCIAL ACCOUNTING STANDARDS AND INTERPRETATIONS

Accounting standards govern the preparation of financial reports. Understanding what these standards are and how they are used is critical for most research endeavors. In describing the standards-setting process and the common set of practices that leads to "generally accepting accounting principles," also known as GAAP, Klopper (1999) explains, "an established and accepted set of accounting standards exists to minimize bias, misinterpretation, inexactness, and ambiguity in financial statements."[2] Much of the background, recent issues, and forthcoming ideas surrounding the standards can be found at the following sites.

Financial Accounting Standards Board
(http://www.fasb.org)

For nearly thirty years, the Financial Accounting Standards Board (FASB) has been the officially designated body for establishing private sector financial reporting standards, recognized as authoritative by the U.S. Securities and Exchange Commission and the American Institute of Certified Public Accountants. As such, this Web site is a leading choice for tracking recently released and forthcoming FASB pronouncements and Emerging Issues Task Force (EITF) activities. Included are summaries of all FASB Statements, as well as status information for each statement and interpretations of potential impacts on financial reporting. Although FASB is still in the business of selling most of their products, this easily navigated site offers a large amount of full-text and downloadable reports about the Board's decisions, statements, interpretations, and emerging issues.

Governmental Accounting Standards Board
(http://www.gasb.org)

Very similar to the FASB site described previously, in both design and offerings, this online home for the Governmental Accounting Standards Board (GASB) provides summaries of standards for guiding the preparation of external financial reports by state and local government entities. Note: For all U.S. *federal* government standards, including access to exposure drafts, newsletters, minutes, and the 1,173-page codification of original pronouncements, visit the Federal Accounting Standards Advisory Board (http://www.fasab.gov).

International Accounting Standards Board
(http://www.iasc.org.uk)

Although the International Accounting Standards Board (IASB) has no authority to enforce compliance, many countries require publicly traded enterprises to prepare reports in accordance with IASB International Financial Reporting Standards. This independent standards setter was formerly known as the International Accounting Standards Committee (IASC) from 1973 to April 2001. All earlier IASC standards were adopted by the Board and are available in summary format on the Web. Also available are IASB Decision Summaries, press releases, exposure drafts, and extensive information on projects in progress.

The Independence Standards Board (ISB), which was the private sector standards-setting body governing the independence of auditors from their public company clients, was dissolved in July 2001. However, ISB standards and interpretations that continue to represent authoritative guidance can be accessed at the old ISB Web site (http://www.cpaindependence.org).

PROFESSIONAL ASSOCIATIONS AND ORGANIZATIONS

American Institute of Certified Public Accountants
(http://www.aicpa.org)

The American Institute of Certified Public Accountants (AICPA) is North America's largest professional association for CPAs with over 328,000 members. As one might expect, their online headquarters is quite suitable for meeting member needs and sharing information with other students, educators, and job seekers. This site is among the most robust, but uses a clean approach for providing access to industry news, educational programs, legal developments, links ranging from international to local interest, and full-text online versions on Institute publications such as the *Journal of Accountancy*. Also of interest are links to AICPA-affiliated projects like the WebTrust (http://www.webtrust.org) and CPA Vision (http://www.cpavision.org) projects. Of strong interest since the collapse of Enron are the offerings of the Professional Ethics Division (http://www.aicpa.org/members/div/ethics/index.htm) and the *AICPA Code of Professional Conduct* (http://www.aicpa.org/about/code/index.htm).

National Association of State Boards of Accountancy
(http://www.nasba.org)

Serving as a forum for the fifty-four U.S. boards of accountancy, the National Association of State Boards of Accountancy (NASBA) provides free access to detailed information for uniform CPA examinations in each state, including deadlines, educational requirements, fees and downloadable application forms. This site also offers links for all state boards of accountancy and state CPA societies. Other sections for continuing professional education and NASBA publications offer large, full-text documents and Microsoft PowerPoint presentations on current topics.

American Accounting Association
(http://accounting.rutgers.edu/raw/aaa/index.html)

The American Accounting Association (AAA) promotes excellence in accounting research, instruction and practice. In addition to providing organizational information, the AAA site offers title and abstract searching for recent issues of its three quarterly journals and the newsletters and journals of the organization's fourteen topical sections.

Although these additional association sites primarily serve their membership, basic organizational information, as well as current news and identification of their recent publications, can be found at the home pages of the Institute of Management Accountants (http://www.imanet.org) and the Association of Government Accountants (http://www.agacgfm. org). For information on international associations, please see the International section following later in this article.

GATEWAYS AND PORTALS

Tax and Accounting Sites Directory
(http://www.taxsites.com)

The Tax and Accounting Sites Directory is a simple but comprehensive approach for identifying selected Web sites by topic. Maintained since 1995 by Dennis Schmidt, Professor of Accounting from the University of Northern Iowa, this directory offers hierarchical access to nineteen main groupings in the accounting section. Here you will find hundreds of links for managerial accounting, financial reporting, career information, regulatory bodies, and certification information for more than twenty designations, such as CPA, CFE, CMA, etc. For similar sites with additional categories, visit CPArunner (http:www.cparunner.com), CPAnet (http://www.cpanet.com), and GASB Links (http://www.gasb. org/rlinks/gasblinks.html).

AccountingWEB
(http://www.accountingweb.com)

AccountingWEB is a well-designed online community for accounting professionals. However, most of the current and archived news, as well as the career and educational resources, are accessible simply as a guest visitor or following a free registration. Among the strongest areas for this site is the community section, where one can find practice ideas, a Q&A forum, and archived transcripts of weekly workshops on a variety of accounting topics.

For additional portals, see My Accounting Portal (http://www.my
accountingportal.com), AccountantsWorld.com (http://www.accountants
world.com) and Rutgers Accounting Web (http://raw.rutgers.edu). Although
Rutgers Accounting Web is considered the grandfather of accounting gateways, it is not featured here because there are several other reliable resources
today with fewer technical errors and additional proprietary content.

U.S. GOVERNMENT

Information for Accountants
(http://www.sec.gov/info/accountants.shtml)

Available from the U.S. Securities and Exchange Commission, Information for Accountants is a very rich full-text resource for accounting interpretation and disclosure issues. Included are complete Staff
Accounting Bulletins back to early 1995, FAQs for corporate financial
accounting, and international reporting and concept releases.

U.S. General Accounting Office
(http://www.gao.gov)

Considered the investigative arm of Congress, the General Accounting Office (GAO) prescribes accounting principles for the executive
branch and issues standards for auditing of government programs. The
GAO publishes thousands of reports each year, including best practices,
executive guides, audit manuals, reform guidelines, and accounting
principles and standards. Full-text access to the reports is usually available within twenty-four hours of release, with full-text archiving back
to 1996. Unfortunately, the search functions and limited online help for
the "Find GAO Reports" section leave a lot to be desired. For publications after 1994, one might also consider searching the GAO reports via
GPO Access (http://www.access.gpo.gov/su_docs/aces/aces160.shtml).
A report of particular interest is *The Accounting Profession: Major Issues: Progress and Concerns* (report number "aimd-96-98").

INTERNATIONAL

IAS Plus
(http://www.iasplus.com)

Produced by Deloitte Touche Tohmatsu, IAS Plus provides easy access to summaries and interpretations of International Accounting Stan-

dards. Also available are country summaries and updates for over thirty nations, archives of the *IAS Plus Newsletter* back to late 2000, well-organized links for international accounting, and chronological access to "reference materials" from a number of in-house and external sources.

International Forum on Accountancy Development
(http://www.ifad.net)

The International Forum on Accountancy Development (IFAD) promotes the value of transparent financial accounting and global financial stability. Of particular interest on this site is the "GAAP 2001 Report." Prepared and backed by the large accounting firms, this report is a survey of national accounting standards for 62 countries benchmarked against International Accounting Standards. For additional information on international standards, please see the entry above for the International Accounting Standards Board (http://www.iasc.org.uk).

International Federation of Accountants
(http://www.ifac.org)

The International Federation of Accountants (IFAC) comprises over 150 national accounting organizations representing two million accountants. Seeking to harmonize standards worldwide, the IFAC publishes a number of handbooks, standards, and studies available for free download.

AUDITING AND FRAUD

Audit and Attest Standards
(http://www.aicpa.org/members/div/auditstd/index.htm)

This no-frills site provides full-text access to the publications of the Audit and Attest Standards Team of the AICPA. Included are emerging issues, exposure drafts, summaries and interpretations of recently issued standards, meeting highlights, and online issues of the Team's *In Our Opinion Newsletter* back to 1996.

AuditNet
(http://www.auditnet.com)

Jim Kaplan, author of *The Auditor's Guide to Internet Resources*, published by the Institute of Internal Auditors (http://www.theiia.org), maintains this massive site of free auditing resources. While it is not the most attractive site, hundreds of useful links are available through his "AuditNet Resource List" and the "AuditNet Virtual Library."

Also of interest are the home pages for the Association of Certified Fraud Examiners (http://www.cfenet.com) and the Government Auditing Standards "Yellow Book" (http://www.gao.gov/govaud/ybk01.htm).

EDUCATION AND EXAMINATIONS

AICPA Student Affiliate Members Home Page
(http://www.aicpa.org/nolimits/index.htm)

Also known as "Accounting: A Career Without Limits," this student-oriented site offers several useful sections for the CPA wanna-be. Of particular interest is detailed information about becoming a CPA, including overview and FAQ sections regarding the CPA uniform examination, as well as sections on the accounting profession and landing a job. For additional information regarding the examination, including recent changes, exam dates, and study courses, visit the Accounting Institute Seminars (http://www.ais-cpa.com).

Additional academic and continuing professional education sites include cpemarket.com (http://www.cpemarket.com), SmartPros (http://www.smart pros.com), Accounting Education (http://www.accountingeducation.com), and the Emanuel Saxe Distinguished Lectures in Accounting (http://newman. baruch.cuny.edu/digital/saxe/default.htm), providing twenty-five years of full-text transcripts.

NEWS FEEDS AND DISCUSSION GROUPS

Several of the sites mentioned in other sections feature current or recent news stories. For example, the portals, standards setters, professional organizations, and "big five" firms provide original content or blurbs siphoned off of the newswires and online trade publications. Selected news providers and discussion groups are listed below.

NewsFlash! AICPA
(http://www.aicpa.org/news/index.htm)

Updated each weekday, NewsFlash! offers recent press releases from the AICPA and summarized news alerts from major publications and wires such as *The New York Times, The Wall Street Journal, Dow Jones News Service,* and *The Associated Press.*

Electronic Accountant
(http://www.electronicaccountant.com)

A very strong free site from the Accountants Media Group of Thomson Corporation, the Electronic Accountant provides several brief articles each weekday from their own Newswire staff, including complete archives back to 1996. From a well-designed main menu, visitors can also access the full-text of several other Thomson publications, including *Accounting Today, Practical Accountant, Accounting Technology,* and several special "top 100" supplement issues that feature products, firms, and professional issues. Also of interest are the active-based discussion groups divided into logical categories, with each moderated by senior editors of Thomson publications or other experts in the field. Both the forums and the publications are easily searchable.

CAREERS, FIRMS, AND DIRECTORIES

"The Big 5" accounting firms produce powerful Web sites that are much more than excellent marketing tools. The following sites provide original content covering areas such as industries and professional topics, current news, risk and tax guides, and more:

Andersen (http://www.andersen.com)
Deloitte Touche Tohmatsu (http://www.deloitte.com)
Ernst & Young (http://www.ey.com)
KPMG (http://www.kpmg.com)
PricewaterhouseCoopers (http://www.pwcglobal.com)

For basic career information, see the entry for "Accountants & Auditors" in the online version of the *Occupational Outlook Handbook* (http://www.bls.gov/oco). For additional career resources and current job listings, visit Careers In Accounting (http://www.careers-in-accounting.com) or the "Career Center" section of SmartPros (http://www.smartpros.com).

CPA Directory
(http://www.cpadirectory.com)

CPA Directory claims to be the largest searchable Web directory of certified public accountants. In addition to state, city, zip code and name searches, CPA Directory offers advice on selecting and hiring a certified public accountant and comments on what kinds of services they may offer for financial planning, tax preparation, and consulting. Other directories include EZ Directory's Accountant Directory (http://cpafinder.com), the List of CPA Firms (http://www.cpafirms.com/Firmlist), and *Emerson's Directory of Leading US Accounting Firms* (http://www.emersoncompany.com/directories/acct_search.asp).

ONLINE PUBLICATIONS AND RESEARCH

Journal of Accountancy Online
(http://www.aicpa.org/pubs/jofa/joahome.htm)

This online version of the century-old standard from the AICPA includes many of the same feature articles and columns; however, AICPA Official Releases and Exposure Drafts Outstanding are omitted. Complete archives are accessible back to January 1997.

CPA Journal
(http://www.cpajournal.com)

Although an embargo period of a couple of months causes a bit of delay with access to the full-text articles, this site eventually offers html versions of selected feature stories and columns. Archives go back to 1989, but some of the older files have problems with images not loading. Also, the earlier years have articles listed alphabetically for the entire year rather than providing a table of contents for each monthly issue.

Accounting Research Network
(http://www.ssrn.com/arn/index.html)

Thousands of full-text working papers and abstracts of already accepted papers are part of the Social Science Research Network's eLibrary, designed to facilitate early dissemination of important research. Papers are primarily theoretical and represent the earliest versions of experts in the field and work from professors at leading universities from around the world. Although browsing of titles is available, recommended access is through the title and abstract keyword search feature.

MISCELLANEOUS

AICPA States
(http://www.aicpa.org/states/stmap.htm)

For quick access to current accounting-related resources for each state, use the AICPA's image map of the United States. A quick click on your favorite state will retrieve a listing of boards and societies, related government offices, tax resources, and student information, including colleges and universities offering accounting degree programs.

Accounting Hall of Fame
(http://fisher.osu.edu/acctmis/hall/index.htm)

Since 1950, The Ohio State University's Accounting Hall of Fame has honored nearly seventy modern accountants who have made significant contributions to the advancement of the field. Biographies and photographs are available for each inductee at this entertaining and educational site. Just a quick read of the biographies helps one build a stronger understanding of the major breakthroughs and seminal publications that impacted accounting practices during the twentieth century.

Accounting Tutor
(http://www.uflib.ufl.edu/cm/business/tutors/acctutor.htm)

The "Accounting Tutor: Ten Steps to Accounting Research" outlines basic steps for tackling topics in the highly technical field of accounting. One of six tutorials offered by the Smathers Libraries of the University of Florida, the Accounting Tutor also provides quick access to an online guide of accounting resources and two interesting case studies about the "Enron debacle" and the impacts of FASB Statement No. 142, "Goodwill and Other Intangible Assets."

NOTES

1. Strauss, D. W. (1988). *Handbook of Business Information: A Guide for Librarians, Students, and Researchers.* Englewood, CO: Libraries Unlimited.
2. Klopper, S. M. (1999, June/July). "Sailing on the accountanSea: Accounting research sources." *Database, 22,* 65-72.

Best of the Web in Banking

James A. Galbraith

SUMMARY. The "Best of the Web in Banking" chapter includes sites for banking regulations, professional organizations, and international banking. *[Article copies available for a fee from The Haworth Document Delivery Service: 1-800-HAWORTH. E-mail address: <docdelivery@haworthpress.com> Website: <http://www.HaworthPress.com> © 2002 by The Haworth Press, Inc. All rights reserved.]*

KEYWORDS. Banking, Web sites

INTRODUCTION

In 1992 Herbert Baer and Larry R. Mote wrote, "The U.S. Financial System is easily the largest in the world . . . and in many respects, the most advanced." Then, they added, "It is also one of the most idiosyncratic financial systems in the world, characterized by an oddly parochial set of laws and regulations that both impair competition and shield inefficiency."[1]

The U.S. banking system is a dual banking system composed of national banks, chartered by the Office of Comptroller of the Currency, and state banks, chartered by state banking agencies. National banks are regu-

James A. Galbraith is Electronic Services & Reference Librarian, Watson Library of Business and Economics, Columbia University (E-mail: Jg2140@columbia.edu).

[Haworth co-indexing entry note]: "Best of the Web in Banking." Galbraith, James A. Co-published simultaneously in *Journal of Business & Finance Librarianship* (The Haworth Information Press, an imprint of The Haworth Press, Inc.) Vol. 8, No. 2, 2002, pp. 15-24; and: *The Core Business Web: A Guide to Key Information Resources* (ed: Gary W. White) The Haworth Information Press, an imprint of The Haworth Press, Inc., 2003, pp. 15-24. Single or multiple copies of this article are available for a fee from The Haworth Document Delivery Service [1-800-342-9678, 9:00 a.m. - 5:00 p.m. (EST). E-mail address: docdelivery@haworth press.com].

10.1300/J109v08n02_03

lated by one or more of the following Federal agencies: the Federal Reserve; the Federal Deposit Insurance Corporation (FDIC); the Office of the Comptroller of the Currency (OCC); and the Office of Thrift Supervision (OTS). State banks are regulated by state banking agencies, often in conjunction with one or more Federal agencies. There are numerous types of banks in the U.S. including bank holding companies, savings and loan associations, savings banks, thrift holding companies, and investment banks. Due to the multiple layers of regulation, the different types of institutions, and the extent to which banking overlaps with economics and finance, banking research can be considerably confusing.

In choosing the best banking resources on the Web, an emphasis was placed on resources concerning commercial banking in the United States. Some key resources on international banking have also been included. A number of criteria were used in selecting these sites: the site's contents; reliability and currency; ease of navigation; and, most importantly, the authority of the publisher.

REGULATORS/SUPERVISORS

Board of Governors of the Federal Reserve System
(http://www.federalreserve.gov/)

The Board of Governors is the guiding authority of the Federal Reserve System. Founded in 1913, the Federal Reserve conducts the nation's monetary policy, supervises and regulates banking institutions to ensure their stability, and provides financial services to the Government, banks, and individuals.

The Board of Governors Web site contains a wealth of information: (1) popular data sets and surveys, including foreign exchange rates, interest rates on commercial and governmental instruments, and consumer credit surveys; (2) an overview of the Federal Reserve's history and organization, testimony, and press releases; (3) the text and interpretations of Federal banking laws and regulations; (4) consumer information on topics ranging from credit cards to vehicle leasing to identity theft; (5) working papers dating back to 1996; (6) major publications such as the *Federal Reserve Bulletin* and the *Beige Book*, a report on current economic conditions published eight times per year.

Navigating this key banking resource can be tricky. Some of its best features are buried. Nevertheless, the content makes the effort worthwhile.

Feds on the Web
(http://minneapolisfed.org/info/sites/)

One of the best ways to navigate the twelve Reserve Banks is via the Federal Reserve Bank of Minneapolis' Feds on the Web. Feds on the Web has links to each Reserve Bank's home page, a clickable map of the twelve reserve districts, and a selection of resources drawn from the Reserves' pages. The site links to gems that are otherwise hidden:

- *The National Information Center* (http://www.ffiec.gov/nic/)
  The National Information Center contains profiles of the banks the Federal Reserve supervises or regulates. Each profile contains information on the bank's history, organizational structure, and finances.
- *FED 101* (http://www.kc.frb.org/fed101/indexflash.cfm)
  The Federal Reserve Bank of Kansas City's FED 101 tutorial is one of the best overviews of the Federal Reserve's history, organization, and monetary activities on the Internet.
- *Fed In Print* (http://www.frbsf.org/publications/fedinprint/index.html)
  Maintained by the Federal Reserve Bank of San Francisco, Fed in Print is an index of the various Federal Reserves' research. Links to the full text of the publications are provided when available.

Federal Deposit Insurance Corporation
(http://www.fdic.gov)

The Federal Deposit Insurance Corporation (FDIC) was founded in 1933 in order to "maintain stability and public confidence in the nation's financial system." The public's faith was understandably low at the time. To this end, the FDIC supervises and insures deposits in most banks and savings institutions.

In the course of its supervisory activities, the FDIC collects a great deal of data. Information on individual banks culled from *Call Reports* (filed by all federally insured banks) and *Thrift Financial Reports* (filed by insured thrift institutions) is available online from 1998 onwards. The FDIC's widely known statistical/analytical publications, *Statistics on Banking, The Quarterly Banking Profile*, and *The Historical Statistics on Banking* are also online, as are a variety of working papers and reports.

One of the appeals of the FDIC Web site is that it is not simply for researchers and bankers. Curious consumers will find information on the history and activities of the FDIC, deposit insurance guidelines, insurance calculators, and consumer rights. One of the fun sections is the "Learning Bank," an FDIC tutorial hosted by "Carmen Cents," an animated piggy bank designed for students, teachers, and parents. The FDIC's Web site is an essential bookmark for anyone interested in banking.

Office of Thrift Supervision
(http://www.ots.treas.gov/)

Founded in 1989, the Office of Thrift Supervision (OTS) is the primary regulator of all federal and many state-chartered thrift institutions (including savings banks and savings and loan associations).

The OTS site is the place to go when looking for information on thrifts. The *Fact Book*, an annual profile of the industry, is an excellent starting point. More current and comprehensive information is provided by four quarterly publications: *Thrift Industry Highlights*; *Thrift Industry Press Releases*; *Thrift Industry Charts*; and *Thrift Industry Selected Indicators*. Coverage of thrift laws and regulations is also strong. The site contains links to the current texts, compliance handbooks, and filing forms and instructions. N.B.–The FDIC, not the OTS, maintains statistics for individual thrift institutions; the FDIC assumed this responsibility in the wake of the S&L Crisis.

The OTS' Web designers have incorporated a site map in the left-hand navigation bar, graciously rendering the search screen (of which the less said the better) unnecessary.

National Credit Union Administration
(http://www.ncua.gov/)

The National Credit Union Administration (NCUA) was created in 1970 to charter and supervise federal credit unions throughout the United States. The NCUA oversees the financial well being of credit unions, which, like banks, are required to file call reports. The NCUA site is a nice mixture of statistical and analytical information.

Both the annual and mid-year issues of *Statistics for Federally Insured Credit Unions* are available in PDF format going back to 1996. The NCUA's online "Find a Credit Union" database contains call report data from 1990 onwards. The database has two search screens. The "basic search" enables users to search for individual credit unions or screen for multiple credit unions using a variety of criteria (city, state, charter type and so on). The "custom report" interface adds Boolean search capabilities, additional search criteria (zip code, assets, total investment, number of members, etc.), and customized reporting; up to ten data items can be downloaded for each result. More ambitious researchers may also download entire call report data files in a spreadsheet-friendly format.

The analytical content of the page includes interesting introductory pieces such as the *History of Credit Unions and the NCUA*. On a separate "Reference" page, the NCUA has compiled a reference library of publications ranging from the *Credit Union Directory*, to the NCUA *Annual Reports*, to suspicious activity report forms.

TRADE ASSOCIATIONS

American Bankers Association
(http://www.aba.com)

The mission of the American Banker's Association (ABA) is "to serve its member banks and enhance their role as pre-eminent providers of financial services." The ABA offers professional and educational services to its members and represents the banking industry's interests in Washington.

The ABA Web site is primarily intended for members of the ABA, but has much to offer non-members. The ABA appears to specialize in position papers. The "Industry Issues" section, for example, offers the ABA's official position on hot topics such as ATM banking fees, deposit insurance reform, and mergers and acquisitions. The "Press Room" contains ABA press releases and quick facts about banking. Users artful in retrieving information will also find value in the proprietary materials. Studies in the "Survey/Statistics Marketplace," such as the ABA's *Bank Card Industry Survey Report*, can run in the $500 to $1,000 range to purchase. Fortunately, the reports' findings are usually included in the highlights of the report.

The layout of the ABA site can be annoying. The non-member site map's subject headings, for example, are not the same as those on the navigation bar. Quirks aside, for members of the ABA, this site is a trove of information, while nonmembers will find enough free information to make the page worth bookmarking.

Conference of State Bank Supervisors
(http://www.csbs.org/)

State banks are often overshadowed by their national counterparts, despite being more numerous. As of 2000, there were approximately 6,086 state banks in the United States versus 2,230 national banks.[2] The Conference of State Bank Supervisors was formed in 1902 to promote cooperation among state bank regulators and to protect the interests of state banking in the United States.

The CSBS Web site is not terribly robust. Many of the CSBS's publications (the biennial *Profile of State Chartered Banking* for example) are in the "members only" section. Nor is quantitative data this Web page's strength. The "Info and Statistics" section has only has a few statistical tables. The CSBS page's main strengths are its public relations, government regulations, and links pages. The "Public Relations" page contains an archive of "The Examiner," the official newsletter of the CSBS, as well as news releases, speeches, and presentations. The "Government Relations" page examines issues such as the Electronic Signatures Act, the FDIC Reform Act of 2002, and predatory lending; each issue is documented with CSBS policy statements, governmental documents, and news reports. The CSBS also provides links to state banking departments (very handy) as well as links to financial organizations at the national, industry, and state level. The Conference of State Bank Supervisors site may not offer endless reams of information and data, but it does effectively offer the state perspective on the banking industry.

PORTALS, META-SITES, AND MISCELLANEOUS RESOURCES

BankersOnline.com
(http://www.bankersonline.com)

The BankersOnline.com banking portal is a joint product of the Gila Group, the principals of which created the bankinfo.com portal, now known as TheBankingChannel.com (see following site), and the Bankers Information Network, publishers of "Compliance Action" and "Bankers Hotline." Despite being a relatively new Web site, BankersOnline is already among the best of the Web.

BankersOnline offers a fresh approach to banking information; the presentation is colloquial and user friendly. Resources include: the "Launch Pad," a comprehensive list of sites related to banking; the "Information Vault," links to information on topics ranging from bomb threats to wire transfers; "Alphabet Soup," federal banking regulations from A-Z; "Web Site Road Maps," a guide to navigating regulators' Web sites; and "BOL Gurus," expert commentary and advice. The best compliment one can give this site is to say that it is both comprehensive and fun to browse. In-depth and user friendly, BankersOnline is an extremely useful banking portal that should continue to improve with time.

TheBankingChannel
(http://www.thebankingchannel.com/)

Maintained by Thomson Financial's Banking, Insurance, & E-Commerce Group, TheBankingChannel portal is intended to "bring together news and data resources to provide banking professionals with a single source for essential industry information."

Thomson Financial owns much of the financial information industry and uses its resources in putting together this portal. TheBankingChannel contains news articles drawn from authoritative sources such as *Dow Jones New Service* and the *Washington Post*, offers full-text access to *American Banker, Bank Technology News*, and *Financial Services Marketing* (all published by Thomson subsidiaries), and compiles bank rankings using Thomson's extensive data bank. Extras include a helpful "Bankers Glossary" and a very comprehensive set of banking links.

TheBankingChannel research vault contains a collection of reports on various aspects of the banking and finance industry. The majority of the reports are proprietary and fairly expensive, but some are free of charge. The site is admittedly an advertisement for Thomson's products. Still, it is hard to begrudge Thomson their advertising when they have provided good, free information on a page that is well crafted and easy to navigate.

Bankrate.com
(http://www.bankrate.com/)

Bankrate.com makes its money by bringing together consumers and financial service providers. First, Bankrate.com collects deposits and loans market data from its client institutions (American Express, Chase Manhattan Bank, Citibank, Wells Fargo, etc.). Then, Bankrate provides portals where consumers can search for competitive rates on financial services. Bankrate's "partner sites" (all of which have portals) include USAToday.com, Yahoo, and The Motley Fool.

Bankrate.com provides current and practical information including interest rates on various types of loans (auto loans, credit cards, mortgages) and deposits (savings, checking, money market rates). Bankrate.com is ideal for looking up Wells Fargo's current interest rate on a $500,000, 20-year fixed, home mortgage loan in California or for comparing your local banks' auto loan rates. In addition to the commercial coverage, Bankrate.com also offers numerous financial calculators, tutorials, and newsletters. The end result is a Web page that is practical, user-friendly, and free.

Visa ATM Locator
(http://www.visa.com/atms/)

ATM locators represent an interesting and ongoing collaboration between mapping and financial companies. There are several good ATM locators on the Web; Visa's system only narrowly edged-out worthy entries from Mastercard and NYCE.

Most ATM locators have similar features. A user enters a street address, city, and state, and the underlying geographical information system locates nearby ATMs and maps their locations. Visa's system adds a couple of features to the industry standard. First, the search is very flexible (city is the only required search field). Visa's locator also allows users to search for ATMs that are handicap-accessible, open twenty-four hours, in airport locations, and have braille instructions. ESRI provides the underlying software. This is an interesting and practical application of mapping technology.

INTERNATIONAL BANKING LINKS

Central Banks

Many countries have central banks that regulate and supervise their financial systems. Central banks are usually the best starting point when exploring banking in other countries. Links to central banks can be found on a number of different pages. The following are comprehensive and current:

- *Central Bank Websites* (http://www.bis.org/cbanks.htm)
  Maintained by the Bank for International Settlements, this regularly updated page has links to most central banks.
- *Central Banking* (http://www.centralbanking.co.uk/)
  A page dedicated to central banking, Central Banking provides a comprehensive set of links to central banks (over 120 are listed).

Bank for International Settlements
(http://www.bis.org)

The Bank for International Settlements (BIS) promotes cooperation amongst central banks by acting as a forum in which its constituents can coordinate monetary policy. The BIS also offers banking services to its members, facilitates the implementation of international agreements, and is a center for financial research.

The BIS Web site contains press statements, speeches, working papers and reports written by the BIS analysts and committees. Moreover, most of the BIS's key reports on international banking from 1996 onwards are available online. These include the *Annual Report, Quarterly Review: International Banking and Financial Market Developments,* and *The BIS Consolidated International Banking Statistics.* The BIS also publishes a variety of international banking, securities, and derivatives statistics and collaborates with the IMF, OECD, and World Bank in releasing the Joint BIS-IMF-OECD-World Bank *Statistics on External Debt.* These statistics are available online in both PDF format and in CSV format. The BIS site is an excellent starting point when doing research on international banking. It contains a wealth of information and is easy to navigate.

World Bank
(http://www.worldbank.org)

The World Bank is the world's foremost development bank; as such, many of its activities fall outside of this article's commercial banking scope. In 2001 the World Bank provided over seventeen billion dollars in loans to developing nations to help nations develop health care and educational systems, build infrastructure, and alleviate poverty. To support its efforts, the World Bank issues bonds and other debt instruments. Last year's issues totaled over seventeen billion dollars in bonds in nine different currencies.

Elegantly arranged, the World Bank's site contains a vast amount of world development information, economics statistics, working papers, and reports. For information about the World Bank's loan programs specifically, consult the World Bank's "Financial Products and Services Page" (http://www.worldbank.org/fps/). For information about its securities issues, consult the "Debt Securities Page" (http://www.world bank.org/debtsecurities).

Global Banking Law Database
(http://www.gbld.org/)

A joint project of the World Bank and the International Monetary Fund, the Global Banking Law Database is a collection of the commercial banking, central banking, and deposit insurance laws of various countries, economic alliances, and financial centers. Although in the early stages of development, the database already contains laws for thirty-seven jurisdictions in both PDF and WORD format.

The Global Banking Law Database allows users to view/download banking laws by jurisdiction or topic and to search by keyword. The jurisdiction search is straightforward. Indicate a jurisdiction (i.e., Switzerland, Kuwait, or the European Union), and the system retrieves the relevant laws. The topical search is similar, but adds a neat twist: users can choose to view laws on a chosen topic for two different jurisdictions at once, displayed side-by-side in separate windows. This function makes it easy to compare banking laws in different jurisdictions. The keyword search is useful, but not very broad. Users have to specify both a country and document prior to searching. It will be interesting to see if multi-jurisdictional searching becomes available in the future. The Global Banking Law Database is an impressive resource that will only become more impressive over time.

NOTES

1. Kaufman, G. G. (Ed.) (1992). Banking Structures in Modern Countries. Boston: Kluwer Academic Publishers.

2. Conference of State Bank Supervisors. (2002). *Commercial Banks By Charter.* [Online]. Available at: http://www.csbs.org/info_stats/banks_by_charter.htm February 18, 2002.

Business Ethics on the World Wide Web

Joseph A. LaRose

SUMMARY. This timely chapter on business ethics includes Web sites of portals, professional associations, and resources on the social responsibility of business. *[Article copies available for a fee from The Haworth Document Delivery Service: 1-800-HAWORTH. E-mail address: <docdelivery@haworthpress.com> Website: <http://www.HaworthPress.com> © 2002 by The Haworth Press, Inc. All rights reserved.]*

KEYWORDS. Business ethics, social responsibility, Web sites

INTRODUCTION

Ethics may be defined as "a set of rules to guide the actions of an individual human being that are consistent with his or her values."[1] In a more general sense, ethics is the study of what is good and right for human beings. It asks what is right and wrong behavior and how it is to be evaluated.[2]

Business ethics is a branch of applied ethics. It examines the moral relationships that exist in the world of business and work. These relationships may be between managers and employees, executives and stockholders, or a corporation and the community (local and global) in

Joseph A. LaRose is Associate Professor of Bibliography and Reference Librarian/Bibliographer, The University of Akron (E-mail: jl@uakron.edu).

[Haworth co-indexing entry note]: "Business Ethics on the World Wide Web." LaRose, Joseph A. Co-published simultaneously in *Journal of Business & Finance Librarianship* (The Haworth Information Press, an imprint of The Haworth Press, Inc.) Vol. 8, No. 2, 2002, pp. 25-34; and: *The Core Business Web: A Guide to Key Information Resources* (ed: Gary W. White) The Haworth Information Press, an imprint of The Haworth Press, Inc., 2003, pp. 25-34. Single or multiple copies of this article are available for a fee from The Haworth Document Delivery Service [1-800-HAWORTH, 9:00 a.m. - 5:00 p.m. (EST). E-mail address: docdelivery@haworthpress.com].

http://www.haworthpress.com/store/product.asp?sku=J109
© 2002 by The Haworth Press, Inc. All rights reserved.
10.1300/J109v08n02_04

which it resides. Indeed, it is an outdated notion that business can be evaluated only on the success of its delivery of goods and services and the making of profits. Most people now believe that every aspect of the business world involves situations that bear examination and evaluation in terms of right and wrong behavior.

The growth of professional literature in the field of business ethics, and the large number of courses and centers at educational institutions dedicated to its study and teaching, testify to a high current interest in this field. Unsurprisingly, information on many aspects of business ethics is currently available freely on the Web. The purpose of this article is to summarize and evaluate the best sites on the subject. I have looked for and selected sites that provide information about business ethics or are gateways to helpful resources, sites that enable users to learn about its important principles, questions, and practices. I have excluded the sites of some major organizations, research centers, and industry services dealing with business ethics because the sites themselves are not intended to disseminate knowledge. I have included a few metasites on the more general subjects of ethics and applied ethics, as these sites are excellent jumping-off points for broadening one's understanding of the ethics of everyday life as well as that of the business world. Other included sites provide case studies, definitions, professional codes of conduct, and general information about business ethics. A final section includes sites that deal with the social responsibility of business.

METASITES

Applied Ethics Resources on WWW–Centre for Applied Ethics
(http://www.ethics.ubc.ca/resources/)

Maintained by the University of British Columbia's Centre for Applied Ethics, this site provides a hierarchical arrangement of extensive Web links to all matter of applied ethics information. Uncluttered and easy to navigate, the main page features twelve categories relating to industry sectors (e.g., "Health Care Ethics" and "Computer and Info-Tech Ethics") or broader topics (e.g., "Business Ethics" and "Professional Ethics"). Each main category is subdivided more specifically on subsequent pages. The subdivisions typically include "Publications" (online newsletters and journals); "Courses" (links to course information and syllabi from various institutions); "Institutes & Organizations" (links to Web sites of organizations); "Topics" (links to resources on a variety of specific topics within the category); and "On-Line Discussion" (newsgroups and listservs). The category "Business Ethics" also includes a subdivision, "Codes of Ethics," with links to company and industry official ethical statements. A brief starting-point bibliography of books and journals in business ethics is provided through a link at the bottom of each page.

This site is a fine starting point for discovering Web information in business ethics, not only for its visual simplicity and ease-of-use, but for the broader view made possible by bringing together many areas of applied ethics.

Ethics on the Internet, Ethics-Related Sites
(http://carbon.cudenver.edu/%7Ejjuhasz/ethiclinks.html#Professional)

Like the Centre for Applied Ethics, this site, hosted by the University of Colorado at Denver, is a basic starting point for finding a broad range of applied and professional ethics sites. Although it uses a primitive Web design (the approximately 100 unannotated links are presented in one long list on a single page), *Ethics on the Internet* helpfully organizes its sites in four major categories: "Metalinks"; "Centers & Institutes"; "Nongovernmental Organizations & Associations" (subdivided into topics such as "Ethical," "Social Justice," "Political," "Human Rights," and "Media Ethics"); and "Professional Codes of Ethics & Conduct." Links to each category are given at the beginning of the list; by clicking on a category, one is taken to the section of the page where the sites in that category begin. While not focused strictly on any one branch of applied ethics (e.g., business ethics), this site affords the user the opportunity to explore the broadest context of moral decision-making, and is especially strong in the areas of human rights and civil liberties. Last updated on June 7, 2001, the site is adequately current as of February 2002.

The EthicalEdge
(http://www.ethicaledge.com/)

In contrast to the simple listing and categorization of the two sites discussed above, *The EthicalEdge*, with a focus on organizational ethics, is a site rich in text and philosophical discussion. Largely a service of ethics consultant Kenneth W. Johnson, *The EthicalEdge* is not easily apprehended at once; rather, it is designed for serendipitous browsing. By following different paths, one can begin to absorb the substantial amounts of information. "The Questions," seven fundamental applied ethics questions such as "What is the role of leadership in organization integrity?" are the heart of the site. Each question is given an essay answer, with links to print and Web resources. The author entreats us to "Begin with whatever question intrigues you most, and see how it opens your vistas."

More structured browsing is possible by perusing the topics at the bottom of the home page: "Principles of Corporate Self-governance"; "Essential Social Responsibility of Business"; "Essential Social Responsibility of Government"; "Global Ethics Resources"; "Organizational Ethics"; "Environmental Ethics"; "Applied Ethics Resources"; and the listed Web sites, each of which is given a brief evaluative annotation. A valuable feature, "Glossary of Ethics and Policy," has lengthy definitions with hyperlinks to key concepts elsewhere in the site or in other sites.

Some topics given space here seem to have a marginal connection to organizational ethics (e.g., Native American Resources Online; UNESCO World Culture Report), but overall, the holistic, interdisciplinary approach makes this site uniquely valuable. You will find things here you will not find at other applied ethics sites.

Center for Ethical Business Cultures
(http://www.cebcglobal.org/)

Affiliated with the University of Minnesota's Carlson School of Management, "the Center strives to be a leading global resource shaping solutions in ethics and corporate citizenship that add value to business" [statement on home page]. While much of the Center's online services to business leaders are under development as of this writing, the site is valuable for its links to business ethics sites at the enterprise, community, and global levels. The links are found under three major categories: "Ethics" (broadly-based) which is particularly good for links to codes of conduct, associations, corporate ethics statements, and business ethics institutes and programs housed at academic institutions; "Work/Life" (work & family issues); and "Corporate Citizenship" (the belief that corporations can make a profound, positive contribution to their communities). The site is clearly organized and easy to navigate. Links to resources under the main categories are found under seven standard subcategories, "Products," "Services," "Research," "Getting Started," "Sample Policies," "Publications," and [Web] "Resources."

GENERAL

Net Impact: New Leaders for Better Business
(http://www.srb.org/default.asp)

Formerly known as Students for Responsible Business, New Leaders for Better Business is an organization of MBAs and new business leaders interested in responsible business practices. The organization focuses on social entrepreneurship, corporate responsibility, and sustainable business. The emphasis of this site is on educational opportunities for its members, with information on programs, chapters, and conferences dealing with this organization. For non-members, much general information on responsible business is to be found in the section entitled "Resources." Included here are links to Web sites of organizations, online newsletters, and articles dealing with socially responsible business practices. A heading, "Curriculum," includes descriptively annotated links to syllabi and course descriptions for business ethics courses taught at academic institutions; many of these are available in full-text as PDF files. Another section provides links to sites where case studies related to business ethics may be purchased. A helpful added value of this site is a standard content coding added to most resources that are listed: CD (Community Development); CR (Corporate Responsibility); ENT (Entrepreneurship); EM (Environmental Management); and OTH (Other). This coding makes it easy for the user to find a broad range of materials that fit his or her research interests.

Carol and Lawrence Zicklin Center for Business Ethics Research
(http://www.zicklincenter.org/)

This center, housed at the Wharton School, University of Pennsylvania, sponsors and disseminates research on business ethics. This site has a unique place on the Web for announcing and disseminating scholarly research in this area. Abstracts for current research projects and an archive of past projects, reprints, and working papers are provided, with links to a small number of the papers online in full-text. Contact information is furnished for requesting full-text copies of all research from the Center. The research found here focuses on topics such as global business ethics, corporate governance, social contracts, deception, disclosure, bribery and corruption.

The site is clearly laid-out and easy to navigate. At the top of each screen are four buttons labeled "Research" (research sponsored by the Center), "Events" (seminars and conferences sponsored by the Center), "Links" (Web links), and "About" (information about the Center). The Web links are further divided into two categories: "Research Links" include links to business ethics organizations, research centers, and metasites; "Academic Journal Links" provide a list (with only a few actual links) of journals that specialize or feature articles in business ethics.

The Free Management Library, Index of Topics
(http://www.mapnp.org/library/topics.htm)

The Free Management Library is a free online collection of resources, created in part by contributions submitted by users and readers. Edited and written by Carter McNamera, MBA, PhD, and hosted by The Management Assistance Program for Non-Profits in St. Paul, Minnesota, this site exists to provide leaders and managers of for-profit and non-profit organizations basic and practical information.

One large general category, "Business Ethics and Social Responsibility," provides extensive links to business and applied ethics organizations, essays, articles, and information resources on the Web. A uniquely valuable part of this site is the "Complete Guide to Ethics Management: An Ethics Toolkit for Managers," an extensive resource in itself which includes fully discussed and annotated lists devoted to many topics. The Toolkit itself is in the form of one very long, but relatively easy-to-navigate document; subject links at the top of the page link the user to the section of the text dealing with the desired subject. The lists deal with thirteen topics, including "10 Myths About Business Ethics"; "10 Benefits of Managing Ethics in the Workplace"; "Ethics Tools: Codes of Ethics"; "8 Guidelines for Managing Ethics in the Workplace"; "Policies and Procedures"; and "Resolving Ethical Dilemmas." Within the lists, full discussions include references to published articles in journals and other periodicals as well as links to other Web resources. All in all, this is an extensive collection of information that, while making only minimal use of Web design for easy navigation, rewards a user's patient browsing with much practical information on a broad range of business ethics issues.

The Ethics Corner, Inc. Online
(http://mothra.inc.com/extra/columns/ethics/)

This site, provided by the magazine *Inc.*, links to the full-text of articles from past issues of the magazine which deal with business ethics issues and situations. Article titles are listed and the subjects are encapsulated on the main page, making it easy for the user to choose articles of interest to read in full-text. Examples of article topics include the ethical considerations in helping a troubled employee, the limits of embellishment to sell a company, the business disaster behind Ben & Jerry's Rainforest Crunch ice cream, and the ethics of walking away from debt after one's company goes bankrupt. Unfortunately, the most recent article included is dated in 1999, suggesting that this site is not being updated. A section entitled "Management Dilemmas," which invites readers to choose the best solution to briefly posed business situations, rounds out the site. They can then immediately check their responses against the percentages chosen by others.

Center for Ethics and Business
(http://www.ethicsandbusiness.org/links/)

The Center for Ethics and Business, housed at Loyola Marymount University, "aims to provide an environment for discussing issues related to the necessity, difficulty, costs and rewards of conducting business ethically" [statement on home page]. The site allows users to view it with or without Flash graphics. Either way, it is clearly laid out and easy to navigate, with all main categories present in a left-hand menu bar on every screen.

This site provides a variety of information and interactivity for students and others interested in ethical business issues. A selection of case studies includes both actual business cases (e.g., case of Oracle Corporation spying on Microsoft) and hypothetical scenarios (e.g., the case of an employee who steals ideas from another). Users can post their own answers and read the accumulated answers of others. A section entitled "Tool Box" provides a variety of resources: an ethics self-quiz, with a link to a description of basic ethical styles; essays on steps in resolving ethical difficulties; and philosophical frameworks for applied ethics. The site also provides a forum where users can post ethical queries and start threads. The forum is current and active, with letters and replies to such topics as "Selling short in the wake of tragedy" and "Ethical advertising." Rounding out the site is an alphabetical list of links to about 100 Web sites of programs and organizations in the areas of business and applied ethics.

SOCIAL RESPONSIBILITY

Business for Social Responsibility (BSR)
(http://www.bsr.org/)

This organization includes 1,400 member and affiliated companies worldwide. Its Web site provides data and sources that help businesses "achieve commercial success in ways that respect ethical values, people, communities and the environment" [statement on Web site]. While members receive some resources that are not available to general visitors to the site, much information is freely available. For example, the site provides news summaries of stories from its *BSR Monitor*, a publication available to members. The news stories typically detail instances of businesses participating in ventures that fill a social need. Editorials and columns fill out the news section of the site.

The heart of the site lies in its "Topic Overviews." Overviews are provided for the general areas: "Corporate Social Responsibility"; "Business Ethics"; "Community Investment"; "The Environment"; "Governance and Accountability"; "Human Rights"; "Marketplace"; "Mission, Vision, & Values"; and "Workplace." Under each of the categories are specific topics. For example, under "Workplace," one finds "Work-life," "Religion in the Workplace," and "Flexible Scheduling." Each of these topics is broken into a standard set of subcategories: "Introduction" (about 200 words); "Business Importance"; "Recent Developments"; "External Standards"; "Implementation Steps"; "Leadership Examples"; "Sample Policies"; "Awards"; and "Links to Helping Resources." These informative summaries of the topics include statistics, recent legislation and government regulation, results of research studies and surveys, identification of socially responsible companies, and other relevant information. They are substantial, well written, and informative. Under "Links to Helping Resources," one finds fully annotated links to sites specifically chosen to apply to that topic.

A bonus of this site is a decent search engine that allows the user to focus their search on the entire site or a specific section. Searching both of the site's two main sections at once, the engine provides a way to find both topic summaries and news reports on one's topic. The search engine works with individual keywords or accepts simple Boolean expressions. Rounding out the site is a helpful site map.

All in all, the site is reasonably well organized and has simple, uncluttered screens. Occasional slow loading of pages detracts from what otherwise is a major Web resource for business social responsibility.

CorpWatch
(http://www.corpwatch.org/)

Subtitled *Holding Corporations Accountable*, this is the official site of a San Francisco-based organization that backs the movement against "corporate-led globalization." The site features signed cautionary articles written about current issues and news events dealing with corporate responsibility in the areas of environment, civil liberties, worker rights, and globalization. Example recent articles review how software companies stand to profit on homeland security, examine corporate abuses in the Enron collapse, and cite un-enforced environmental laws in the wake of the Bhopal disaster.

Two additional features round out the site. The "Issue Library" provides information on twenty-three topics such as money and politics; oil, gas and coal; and pesticides. Each topic is given a 500-800 word summary of issues from the organization's point of view, with links to signed articles from sources such as *The Observer, Prison News,* and political action groups. Several topics were updated one month previous to this writing, which indicates that the site is kept current. A second feature is the "Research Guide," which leads users through a helpful variety of Web-based sources of information on companies. The Guide is subdivided into sections such as "Business & Financial Resources," "Non-U.S. or Private Companies," and "U.S. Government Sources." There are similar sections for doing research on industries and corporate influence on politics. These guides are better than simply lists of links, as they mention which types of information one should expect to find and where to find it. Each source is annotated, and the lists are well organized. A qualm is that the resources are limited to those available freely on the Web, with no mention made of the valuable company and industry resources that can be found in one's local libraries. In summary, this is a worthwhile site for information and opinions from a point of view that favors activism for corporate social responsibility.

CERES
(http://www.ceres.org/)

This is the organizational home page for CERES (Coalition for Environmentally Responsible Economies). CERES is a coalition of organizations and businesses that adopt the CERES Principles, a ten-point code of environmental conduct. The Principles include such values as protection of the biosphere, sustainable use of natural resources, and energy conservation. The site provides a statement of these principles and information about CERES events and conferences. Of perhaps wider interest is a list of the more than fifty CERES member companies. The listing includes each company's statement on its commitment to the Principles in addition to basic information about the company. The visitor might be surprised to find as members venerable corporations such as Coca Cola USA and General Motors, as well as companies like Ben & Jerry's and Timberland, which are more readily identified with social responsibility.

The site is simply but attractively presented and very easy to navigate, with all major links available on the first page and taking up only a single screen (including full contact information for the organization).

Co-op America
(http://www.coopamerica.org/)

Co-op America is a gateway to various pages of sponsored programs, including *Social Investment Forum, Responsible Shopper*, and *Green Pages*. This site makes available a range of information for the person who wishes to consume or invest responsibly, and for businesses that wish to be socially responsible. *Green Pages* is a guide to 10,000 socially or environmentally responsible products and businesses. This guide provides basic information about each company, including contact and products/services information. It can be searched by keyword, a pull-down menu of business categories, or Zip Code. *Responsible Shopper* provides company ratings and report cards on such topics as products, ethics, privacy, and environment. These reports are substantial and detailed. For example, the report on Toys 'R' Us provides information on class action suits and trade law rulings pertaining to the company, sweatshop labor allegations, and labor law violations. Reports can be searched by keyword (company, product, or subject [e.g., "toys"]). *Social Investment Forum* has extensive information on socially screened stocks, shareholder activism, community investment, and socially responsible mutual funds.

NOTES

1. *The EthicalEdge.com Glossary.* [Online]. Available at: http://www.ethicaledge.com/glossary.html February 4, 2002.

2. Hoffman, W., & Moore, J. (1990). *Business Ethics: Readings and Cases in Corporate Morality.* New York: McGraw-Hill.

Best of Law for Business

Kevin R. Harwell

SUMMARY. The business law chapter includes comprehensive Web sites, resources for statues, regulations, and agency decisions, and information on corporate, labor, international and tax law. *[Article copies available for a fee from The Haworth Document Delivery Service: 1-800-HAWORTH. E-mail address: <docdelivery@haworthpress.com> Website: <http://www.HaworthPress. com> © 2002 by The Haworth Press, Inc. All rights reserved.]*

KEYWORDS. Business law, Web sites

INTRODUCTION

All general legal research is ultimately a pursuit of appropriate legal authority on which to base decisions. Authority in this context consists of statutes, regulations, agency adjudications, and judicial opinions. Business questions about law are no different. The answers rest on appropriate authority. Most business law questions can be answered by using general legal resources. However, a substantial portion of law addresses issues raised by people and organizations doing business with each other. Researchers usually find that more focused resources provide much greater efficiency.

Business law is composed of a broad array of subjects. The Web sites listed here are hosted by a variety of law schools, government agencies,

---

Kevin R. Harwell is Business Librarian, The Pennsylvania State University (E-mail: krh@psulias.psu.edu).

[Haworth co-indexing entry note]: "Best of Law for Business." Harwell, Kevin R. Co-published simultaneously in *Journal of Business & Finance Librarianship* (The Haworth Information Press, an imprint of The Haworth Press, Inc.) Vol. 8, No. 2, 2002, pp. 35-53; and: *The Core Business Web: A Guide to Key Information Resources* (ed: Gary W. White) The Haworth Information Press, an imprint of The Haworth Press, Inc., 2003, pp. 35-53. Single or multiple copies of this article are available for a fee from The Haworth Document Delivery Service [1-800-HAWORTH, 9:00 a.m. - 5:00 p.m. (EST). E-mail address: docdelivery@haworthpress.com].

10.1300/J109v08n02_05

publishers, law firms and commercial entities. They were chosen for their relevancy to both business and law generally or to specific subject areas within business law. They provide authorities, interpretation, news or varying combinations of the three. This bibliography is somewhat selective in presenting only seven: antitrust; corporations; international business transactions; labor and employment law; tax and taxation; entrepreneurship; and the Uniform Commercial Code. However, these seven are very broad. Plus, the comprehensive Web sites listed in the first section cover much of what remains.

Readers should be aware that a complete collection of legal authorities cannot be compiled from Internet resources alone. Several states and many municipalities have only begun to place their legal resources on the Web. Materials that are seldom used due to age or ephemeral quality are often unavailable. Some authorities and many interpretive resources are only published commercially and are therefore not available either. Readers should also exercise caution in evaluating legal sources and applying such information to situations involving real world rights and responsibilities, and seek the assistance of a qualified legal professional if legal advice is needed.

COMPREHENSIVE WEB SITES

With the bewildering array of legal information available on the Internet, many Web sites offer good help in sorting it all out. In fact, CataLaw lists about 100 sites that each attempt to organize a sizable number of legal Web sites into directories or indexes. More than sixty of these are hosted in the United States. Each takes a different approach, of course, so the user would benefit by comparing several, first hand, to determine how well they address the current information need.

CataLaw
(http://www.catalaw.com/)

CataLaw (catalog of catalogs of worldwide law on the Internet) is a "metaindex," a searchable index of indexes of legal information on the Internet, attempting to cover all legal and government indexes on the Internet with one search interface. Web site links in CataLaw are organized under three main categories: "Legal Topics"; "Regional Law"; and "Extra Info." Forty-eight legal topics include anti-trust and competition law; contract and remedy law; information technology law; property law; and many others. For added convenience, CataLaw provides keyword searching of the entire Web site and a site map.

"Topical Law" pages use a standard template that presents "see also" references directing users to related pages on CataLaw; "Focused Sites," which are topical sites listed by regions of the world; and "Usual Suspects," which are selected representatives from the 100 Web sites identified by CataLaw as being major Web presences in the area of law. In those instances where several dozen Web sites are listed under a single heading, CataLaw further subdivides the listing into first, second, and third class sites denoting an assessment of the relative quality of the sites with regard to scope, detail, and structure.

"Regional Law" lists twelve nations, six multinational regions, international law, and "legal resources by country." The United States is one of the twelve, but is treated differently in that it receives four listings. Legal resources by country does not list country-by-country, but rather, it lists resources that have their own country lists. "Extra Information" guides the user to non-topical, non-regional resources for continuing legal education, expert directories, law associations, lawschools, pre-law resources, libraries, publishers and the like.

FindLaw
(http://www.findlaw.com/)

FindLaw claims to be the highest-trafficked legal Web site, providing the most comprehensive set of legal resources, which include Web search utilities, cases and codes, legal news, an online career center, and community-oriented tools, such as a secure document management utility, mailing lists, message boards and free e-mail. FindLaw consists of thousands of site listings with editorial descriptions in dozens of practice areas and jurisdictional authorities–state, Federal and international materials. In addition to online codes and case law, it links to sites for legal forms, legal publishers, legal associations, law schools and law reviews, legal experts and continuing legal education courses. Searchers who are familiar with Yahoo! (http://www.yahoo.com) will recognize a similar hierarchical directory approach.

Hieros Gamos
(http://www.hg.org/index.html)

Hieros Gamos (HG) hosts a phenomenal quantity of content and links to legal resources around the world. In addition to extensive links to U.S. law and policy resources, HG provides content and links to laws of 230 countries, the United Nations, the North American Free Trade Agreement, the European Union, and other international governmental organizations. The country-by-country listings present multiple resources for each country, including direct links to government Web sites, U.S. Central Intelligence Agency Factbook entries, entries from the Library of Congress's Global Legal Information Network, Internet Legal Resource Guide, country-specific news sources, and occasional pathfinders from law firms that conduct business in particular countries. HG also hosts seventy primary practice guides, with an additional 130 supplemental guides covering a wide array of subjects. Researchers needing to identify law firms, consultants, or employment opportunities will find helpful directories, as well.

Legal Information Institute–Cornell Law School
(http://www.law.cornell.edu/)

One of the first law schools to embrace the Internet for delivery of legal information to the public was Cornell School of Law. Peter W. Martin and Thomas R. Bruce began the Legal Information Institute (LII) in 1992 on a Gopher server as an attempt to use digital technology to establish a law school publishing center. The Institute does not charge for online delivery of information, nor does it accept advertising. Grants, gifts and consulting work provide funds. More than just a clearinghouse for legal materials, the LII formats all of the material for functionality and creates tools for indexing and sorting documents.

LII receives millions of data requests each week and sends summaries of U.S. Supreme Court opinions to thousands of e-mail subscribers. Its versions of the U.S. Code, Code of Federal Regulations, and Uniform Commercial Code are among the few complete versions available without charge and quite easy to use. LII's Big Ear current awareness service monitors a number of legal discussion lists for information about new Internet resources. Among the most useful features of LII for business law are topical information guides covering over 120 areas, including many business subjects, such as antitrust, commercial law, partnership, and unfair competitions. The guides provide a text overview of the topic and links to specific sections of Federal statutes and regulations, recent court cases on the topic, state law materials, and other references, which may include print, Internet, and fee-based online materials.

MegaLaw.Com
(http://www.megalaw.com)

MegaLaw's main attraction for this survey is another series of guides to finding Internet resources on various legal topics. They tend to offer a wider selection of external links than Cornell's Legal Information Institute. MegaLaw's guides lack a text overview and references to print resources like those found in LII, but they offer far more external links to Internet resources and are more likely to include law firms and other commercial Web sites. Free membership registration provides a means for a user to personalize the Web site to suit his or her interests and needs. Some additional specialized information is available only to registered members.

STATUTES, REGS, AGENCY DECISIONS

United States Code on the Web (Cornell)
(http://www.law.cornell.edu/uscode/)

Although this service is a part of Cornell's Legal Information Institute, previously described, it is noteworthy enough to mention separately because it is one of the easiest to use sources of the U.S. Code on the Web. Users can search by Code title and section, keyword, or a table of acts by popular name, such as the "Library Services and Construction Act." This service is generated from the latest information available from the U.S. House of Representatives and is limited to one recent version of the U.S. Code. Unfortunately, LII does not also offer a public laws service to complement this one.

GPO Access: U.S. Code (1994 and 2000 Editions, plus Annual Supplements)
(http://www.access.gpo.gov/congress/cong013.html)

The U.S. Government Printing Office (GPO) hosts this service of the Office of Law Revision Counsel, U.S. House of Representatives, which is the official agency for codifying all U.S. public laws currently in force. The service can be searched by U.S. Code citation (title and section numbers), Public Law number, keyword or phrase, or by U.S. Statutes at Large citation. Users can select which version to search, from the 1994 edition to the 2000 edition, or any annual supplement in between these editions. The GPO also offers an associated service for public laws. These are the individual laws in the original language as passed by Congress and before codification, covering 1995 to present.

Federal Regulations

Code of Federal Regulations
(http://www.access.gpo.gov/nara/cfr/cfr-table-search.html)

Federal Register
(http://www.access.gpo.gov/su_docs/aces/aces140.html)

Regulations consist of law established by government agencies, as empowered, in order to carry out their respective mandates. Proposed regulations are published in the Federal Register, as are final regulations. Final regulations currently in force are also published in topical order, in the *Code of Federal Regulations* (CFR). Like the United States Code, consisting of statutes, the *CFR* and the *Federal Register* are published electronically by the GPO. This is an invaluable resource for finding current regulations for banking, environment, securities, employment and other business matters.

BusinessLaw.gov–Small Business Administration
(http://www.businesslaw.gov)

This government managed Web site covers legal and regulatory information for small businesses. It offers plain English guides for starting and operating a business, extensive links to state and local business law information sources, Federal regulatory information, sources of legal assistance, news, tools for research, and direct links for research Federal and state laws and regulations.

FirstGov
(http://www.firstgov.gov/)

As the official U.S. Government portal to millions of pages of government information and services, FirstGov is a very busy place on the Internet. It offers multiple avenues for finding one's way to needed information. Users can search among Federal, state and international sources by keyword. They can also browse by branch and agency of the Federal government. The home page also sports quick links to popular government destinations organized under three broad categories: online services for citizens; online services for business; and online services for governments. The services for business include business opportunities, business law and regulations, Federal auctions and sales, tax information, government contracts, and patents and trademarks.

ANTITRUST

A company that monopolizes the market for certain goods or services minimizes competition and undesirably suppresses normal economic functioning. Antitrust laws prevent or reduce the negative impact on the economy of monopolies or trusts, while maintaining economic freedom and minimizing restraints on trade and competition. Activities governed by antitrust law include monopoly, pricing limitations, predatory practices, merger control, and certain aspects of advertising.

American Antitrust Institute (AAI)
(http://www.antitrustinstitute.org)

The American Antitrust Institute is an independent non-profit education, research, and advocacy organization. Taking a centrist position, its mission is to increase the role of competition, assure that competition is fair, and challenge unduly concentrated power in the American and world economy. The Web site is used to electronically publish frequent antitrust news articles authored by AAI, and includes an archive of articles from 1998 to present. It also provides a very good annotated guide to antitrust links on the Web. The "AAI primer on criminal antitrust" is an excellent introduction to the topic. AAI also provides data about the budget, staff and workload of the Federal Trade Commission and the Justice Department. "Who's Who in Antitrust" is a compilation of directories of state and Federal agency officials, congressional contacts, media contacts, and organizations involved in antitrust.

Antitrust Policy
(http://www.antitrust.org/)

This Web site is maintained at the Owen Graduate School of Management at Vanderbilt University, and is designed to resolve the alienation of antitrust academics from practitioners and the difficulty that researchers have in keeping up with recent developments. The site provides news, common-sense guidelines, information about mergers–including news, economics, cases, policy, and research–and information about vertical restraints and price fixing.

Federal Trade Commission
(http://www.ftc.gov/index.html)

The FTC is responsible for enforcing some forty-six Federal laws dealing with competition and consumer protection. The FTC's antitrust arm, the Bureau of Competition, seeks to prevent business practices that restrain competition. Of particular note, the "Antitrust/Competition" page of the FTC Web site offers numerouse public records–opinions, documents, complaints, decisions and orders, final orders, speeches and testimony–reflecting the agency's work in this area. Most record types are on hand from 1995 to present. The Web site also offers a number of guidelines and plain-language resources for researchers who need basic information about this area of law and business.

U.S. Department of Justice–Antitrust Division
(http://www.usdoj.gov/atr/index.html)

Antitrust is one of the few legal issues addressed by more than one agency of the Federal government. In addition to the FTC, the U.S. Department of Justice also has a role. Unlike the FTC, the Justice Department brings criminal actions against violators. The Web site provides guidelines, policy statements, international documents, appellate briefs, business reviews, statistics and budget information.

CORPORATIONS

Forms of Incorporation

Companies can be formed in any of several forms: partnership; limited partnership; joint venture; incorporation; and others. Each form has advantages and disadvantages. Incorporation requires that the company be established in specific ways with appropriate documentation according to state law. It also provides liability protection for the owners and shareholders. A partnership can be as simple to establish as two individuals agreeing to conduct business together, but it offers no liability protection.

Delaware Corporate Law Clearinghouse–Widener University School of Law
(http://corporate-law.widener.edu/)

More businesses incorporate in Delaware than in any other state in the U.S. This site, created and maintained with the cooperation of the Delaware Court of Chancery, offers access to selected filings and opinions in corporate and other business litigation in the nation's premier trial court for corporate law.

Securities Law

Securities laws address an investor's need to have accurate information about the securities he or she is purchasing and the value of the securities. A company that wants to issue publicly traded securities must be registered with the Securities and Exchange Commission, and disclose specific information about the company's securities and finances. This information is made publicly accessible so that investors can make informed decisions before purchasing or selling the securities.

The Securities Lawyer's Deskbook–The Center for Corporate Law, University of Cincinnati College of Law
(http://www.law.uc.edu/CCL/sldtoc.html)

The Securities Lawyer's Deskbook contains the full text of the basic Federal securities laws and regulations, as well as the principal Securities and Exchange Commission forms under those laws and regulations. The Securities Lawyer's Deskbook is designed primarily for use by legal practitioners, scholars, securities professionals, and corporate officers.

State Securities Regulators
(http://www.nasdr.com/3220.htm)

Maintained by the National Association of Securities Dealers, Inc. (NASD), this Web site provides direct links to state securities agencies. Agency Web sites provide information about state securities law, news, forms, guidelines, recommendations for small businesses and other materials.

U.S. Securities and Exchange Commission
(http://www.sec.gov/)

The primary mission of the U.S. Securities and Exchange Commission (SEC) is to protect investors and maintain the integrity of the securities markets. The SEC administers filing requirements for public companies. The Web site provides summaries of Federal securities laws, the EDGAR database of company filings, regulations and interpretations, investor information, news and litigation documents.

Edgar Database
(http://www.sec.gov/edgarhp.htm)

EDGAR is an SEC database that provides access to public company filings. Users can access registration statements, periodic financial reports, annual reports to shareholders, and other electronic documents. This information is available for free download.

Stanford Securities Class Action Clearinghouse–
Stanford Law School
(http://securities.stanford.edu/)

The Private Securities Litigation Reform Act of 1995 addressed the problem of frivolous and abusive suits against companies for unsubstantiated allegations of securities fraud. The Securities Class Action Clearinghouse is a repository of information relating to the prosecution, defense, and settlement of Federal class action securities fraud litigation and maintains copies of complaints, briefs, filings, and other litigation-related materials filed in these cases.

INTERNATIONAL BUSINESS TRANSACTIONS

International business transactions are governed by a combination of national laws and international conventions. Sometimes firms from different countries will form joint ventures in order to accomplish trade. In such situations, one firm may bring new technologies and business approaches to the venture while the other provides access to existing relationships and knowledge of local laws and regulations. Nonetheless, both parties may have to negotiate through cultural and language differences to get to the point of doing business. Treaties to which the two countries are a party may establish protocols for conducting trade and involve specific provisions for the exchange of money and goods, transporting goods, documenting various transactions, financing ventures internationally, transferring technology, recognizing and protecting intellectual property. In some situations, trading partners might not be from countries that have established such agreements. Hieros Gamos, a comprehensive legal Web site previously described, is particularly well suited for research in this legal arena. The resources listed here should also be informative.

Lex Mercatoria
(http://www.lexmercatoria.org/)

Lex Mercatoria claims to be one of the very first law sites on the Web, having begun in 1993. It is a collaborative endeavor among the Law Faculty of the University of Tromsø and the Law Faculty of the University of Oslo, both of Norway, the Institute of International Commercial Law of Pace University School of Law, and by the Australasian

Legal Information Institute. Lex Mercatoria monitors developments in international trade and commercial law and provides extensive international law links and other materials free of charge. The top layers of the Web site lead the user to broad subject areas in international law, such as international economic law, international, finance regulation, and intellectual property. Each of these subsequent pages lists links to more specific resource guides covering subjects such as GATT and the World Trade Organization, alternative dispute resolution, and electronic commerce; or links to external sources, such as the International Monetary Fund and sources for full-text of specific treaties.

Bureau of Industry and Security (BIS)–U.S. Department of Commerce
(http://www.bis.doc.gov/)

BIS, formerly Bureau of Export Administration (BXA), seeks to advance U.S. national security, foreign policy, and economic interests by regulating exports of critical goods and technologies that could be used to damage those interests (while furthering the growth of legitimate U.S. exports to maintain our economic leadership); by enforcing compliance with those regulations; by cooperating with like-minded nations to obtain global support for this effort; by assisting nations that are key exporters or transit points for sensitive goods and technologies to strengthen their own transit and export controls; and by monitoring the U.S. defense industrial base to ensure it remains strong.

Export Administration Regulations
(http://w3.access.gpo.gov/bis/index.html)

Exporters must be licensed and adhere to regulations established by the Bureau of Industry and Security (formerly Bureau of Export Administration). Some commodities are carefully regulated due to national security concerns. They are listed in the Commerce Control List found in Part 744 of the Export Administration Regulations.

International Trade Administration–U.S. Department of Commerce
(http://www.ita.doc.gov/)

International Trade Administration (ITA) coordinates all issues concerning trade promotion, international commercial policy, market access, and trade law enforcement. The Administration is responsible for nonagricultural trade operations of the U.S. government and supports the trade policy negotiation efforts of the U.S. Trade Representative.

U.S. Customs Service
(http://www.customs.ustreas.gov/)

U.S. Customs Service is responsible for collecting revenue from imports; enforcing the customs laws; processing persons, mail, goods and carriers into and out of the U.S.; investigating fraudulent practices designed to circumvent customs laws; and interdicting contraband, including narcotics, along the land and sea borders of the United States. The Web site provides notices, laws and regulations, guidelines, tariff schedules, statistics and other information for travelers, importers and exporters.

U.S. International Trade Commission
(http://www.usitc.gov/)

The USITC is an independent Federal agency that compiles trade information relating to its mission and expertise to both the legislative and executive branches of government. It projects the impact of imports on U.S. industries, and directs actions against certain unfair trade practices, such as patent, trademark, and copyright infringement. USITC analysts and economists investigate and publish reports on U.S. industries and the global trends that affect them. The agency also updates and publishes the *Harmonized Tariff Schedule of the United States* (http://www.usitc.gov/taffairs.htm), which provides the applicable tariff rates and statistical categories for all merchandise imported into the United States.

LABOR AND EMPLOYMENT LAW

Labor and employment law deals with individual employee rights, employment discrimination and labor relations. A host of Federal and state statutes, supported by regulations and case law, address issues which include fair labor standards, safety and health, retirement, leave, social security, other benefits, equal opportunity, affirmative action, and specific working environments, such as mines and railways. Important issues include contracts, right to organize, protection from discrimination, wages and hours, safety and health, retirement, and benefits.

Labor Research Portal
(http://www.iir.berkeley.edu/library/laborportal.html)

The Labor Research Portal is a service of the Institute for Industrial Relations Library, a collaborative effort of The Institute for Labor and

Employment, University of California; The Institute of Industrial Relations, University of California, Berkeley; and The Institute of Industrial Relations, University of California, Los Angeles. The Portal provides original content in the form of Internet guides about government agencies, labor education opportunities, libraries, labor unions, career information, labor culture, union organizing, and many others. It also provides external links to California labor resources, other institutions' finding aids, sources of labor news, and many other items.

National Right to Work Legal Defense Foundation
(http://www.nrtw.org/)

The Foundation is a non-profit organization advocating a worker's right not to be compelled to belong to a union. It provides free legal aid to employees whose human and civil rights have been violated by compulsory unionism abuses. The Web site provides information about workers' rights, issue briefs, news, legal notices, and electronic newsletters.

Workplace Rights–American Civil Liberties Union (ACLU)
(http://www.aclu.org/issues/worker/hmwr.html)

The ACLU is a non-profit organization dedicated to defend and preserve individual rights and liberties guaranteed to all people in this country by the Constitution and laws of the United States. The Workplace Rights Web site provides news, legislative updates, hot topics, resources, and tools.

Federal Agencies

Equal Employment Opportunity Commission
(http://www.eeoc.gov/)

With its headquarters in Washington, D.C., and through the operations of fifty field offices nationwide, the EEOC coordinates all Federal equal employment opportunity regulations, practices, and policies. Its Web site is designed with the interests of employees and employers in mind, highlighting issues and policy frequently requested by them. Users will find announcements of recent developments, information pieces in Q&A format, how-to information on filing charges, and other similar items. Full-text of major EEOC related laws, statistics, and order forms for EEOC publications are also available.

National Labor Relations Board
(http://www.nlrb.gov/)

The National Labor Relations Board administers the National Labor Relations Act (NLRA) which addresses the relationship between employers, unions and employees. In particular, it deals with the rights of employees to form, join or assist a labor organization and to bargain collectively through representatives of their own choosing, or to refrain from such activities. The NLRB's primary objectives are to prevent and remedy unfair labor practices by employers or unions, and hold elections at which employees decide if they wish to be represented by unions. The Web site provides decisions, rules and regulations, manuals, press releases, and other information.

U.S. Department of Labor

Employment Laws Assistance for Workers and Small Businesses–
U.S. Department of Labor
(http://www.dol.gov/elaws/)

This customer-focused service consists of interactive tools that provide information about Federal employment laws. Each interaction simulates a discussion between the user and an employment law expert. It asks questions and provides answers based on the user's responses.

Employment Standards Administration
(http://www.dol.gov/esa/welcome.html)

The Employment Standards Administration (ESA) enforces and administers a large number of laws governing legally-mandated wages and working conditions. The Web site provides full-text to those laws and access to state laws addressing employment standards. Additional information includes minimum wage and overtime pay requirements, Family Medial Leave Act guidelines, press releases, and special reports. Much of the Web site is organized by agency offices, which include the Office of Federal Contract Compliance Programs, the Office of Labor-Management Standards, the Office of Workers' Compensation Programs and the Wage and Hour Division.

Major Laws and Regulations Enforced by the Department of Labor–U.S. Department of Labor
(http://www.dol.gov/dol/compliance/compliance-majorlaw.htm)

The Department of Labor fosters and promotes the welfare of job seekers, wage earners, and retirees of the United States by improving their working conditions, advancing their opportunities for profitable employment, protecting their benefits, helping employers find workers, strengthening free collective bargaining, and tracking changes in employment, prices, and other national economic measurements. In carrying out this mission, the Department administers a variety of Federal labor laws including those that guarantee workers' rights to safe and healthful working conditions; a minimum hourly wage and overtime pay; freedom from employment discrimination; unemployment insurance; and other income support. In addition to the summaries and full-text of the laws themselves, helpful links from this page include "Compliance Tools" to help prevent employment law violations; a "Small Business Handbook," designed to help employers determine which requirements apply to their employees; and "Rulemaking," which links to information about pending regulations proposed by the Department of Labor.

TAX AND TAXATION

Taxes are administered by Federal, state, and local governments, and vary considerably from one jurisdiction to another. Federal tax laws change a bit from year to year and consist of statutes, court cases, regulations and agency adjudications. Interpretive materials include congressional committee reports, revenue rulings, and commercial information services.

Internal Revenue Service
(http://www.irs.ustreas.gov/)

The Internal Revenue Service is the nation's tax collection agency and administers the Internal Revenue Code enacted by Congress. It is responsible for administering and enforcing the internal revenue laws, except those relating to alcohol, tobacco, firearms and explosives. The IRS deals directly with every taxpayer. Despite complaints to the contrary, it also claims to be one of the world's most efficient tax agencies. In 2000, the IRS collected more than $2 trillion in revenue and processed 226 million tax returns.

One look will show that the IRS Web site is organized to deliver information most quickly to individual taxpayers who are not tax professionals. The home page has a trendy, almost commercial look and feel to it. Highlighted links take the user to consumer oriented information such as ways to avoid tax scams and methods for reducing the amount owed for personal income tax. The site also provides a wealth of substantive information on tax issues for individuals, businesses, tax-exempt organizations, government entities, and tax professionals. Nearly every IRS form and publication is available for download. Statistics of Income (SOI) and other data products are available as well. Curiously, the site does not provide the text of the Internal Revenue Code, Federal tax regulations, and other authoritative legal documents. Using this site does not replace the advice of a qualified, experienced tax professional.

Tax.org, Tax Information Worldwide–The Tax Analysts
(http://www.tax.org)

For more than thirty years, The Tax Analysts have published information to stimulate public discussion of tax issues. They are one of the leading publishers of electronic tax information. Much of their output is available only by subscription to print publications, CD-ROM products, WestLaw and Lexis-Nexis. However, their tax.org Web site provides several services without charge. The "Basic World Tax Code" is an attempt by tax experts to provide a framework on which developing and transitional countries can begin formulating a modern tax system for themselves. The Tax Analysts regularly sponsor policy forums featuring panels of recognized experts to discuss various topics like electronic tax filing and European Union company tax issues. The "Tax History Project" presents insightful articles about events and individuals of importance to the history of American taxation. Users can subscribe to several free e-mail bulletins covering various aspects of taxation. The Web site displays a few news stories of the day. It also provides information for subscribing to other Tax Analysts publications.

TaxLinks, Your Online Source for IRS Revenue Rulings
(http://www.taxlinks.com)

IRS Revenue Rulings are pronouncements of the agency that apply law to particular factual situations. Since they address issues of general interest, they differ from letter rulings, which address more private issues. Revenue rulings do not carry the legal authority of Federal tax regulations, but a taxpayer whose situation is similar to that of the ruling can rely upon them. TaxLinks provides a simple service: to provide access to all revenue rulings issued by the IRS since 1954. The rulings are searchable by keyword and by ruling number.

LAW AND ENTREPRENEURSHIP

The Entrepreneurs' Help Page
(http://www.tannedfeet.com/)

This Web site is a moonlighting effort by attorneys of the Chicago law firm of Malven, Powers, and Pasucci, LLC, who recognized that new business owners need legal information most at the beginning, when they can least afford it. The result is nearly 300 pages of original content written to inform entrepreneurs. Major subjects include general business, business strategy, humor, business space, legal issues, finance, and marketing. Legal topics include choice of entity, intellectual property, taxation, and contracts.

Intellectual Property Mall–Franklin Pierce Law Center
(http://www.ipmall.fplc.edu/)

Franklin Pierce Law Center is one of the top intellectual property law schools in the United States. This Web site links to a very broad and unique collection of intellectual property resources offered by the Law Center and others on the Internet. It is intended to offer "one stop shopping" for patent, trademark, copyright, trade secret and related professionals in academia, business and science, as well as for inventors and entrepreneurs. The Web site provides links to hundreds of external Web sites, organized by topic, such as laws, search resources, practitioner associations, news sources, U.S. and foreign government agencies, international governmental organizations, articles, and other discussion pieces. Original content is extensive and includes compilations of laws, regulations, and cases; invited articles by renowned experts; legislative histories; information guides and many more.

The Upstart Small Business Legal Guide–2nd ed. by Robert
Friendman for Business Week Online
(http://businessweek.findlaw.com/sblg/)

Designed for the small business owner, or someone who wants to start a small business, this guide consists of twenty chapters covering attorneys, form of incorporation, franchises, record keeping, employees, and other topics. This electronic book includes forms, worksheets, tips, warnings, and references to additional sources of information.

UNIFORM COMMERCIAL CODE

The Uniform Commercial Code is a comprehensive work that addresses most aspects of commercial law. It is not law, per se, until at least one state enacts it as law, but nearly every state has enacted the UCC with local variations. The UCC was written by experts in commercial law and submitted to the National Conference of Commissioners on Uniform State Laws.

Uniform Commercial Code
(http://www.law.cornell.edu/ucc/ucc.table.html)

The UCC is available on a couple of Web sites. The Cornell site offers the text of current proposals and enacted proposals only. This is coupled with the *Uniform Commercial Code Locator* (http://www.law.cornell.edu/uniform/ucc.html), which links to state statutes that correspond to articles of the Uniform Commercial Code.

National Conference of Commissioners on Uniform State Laws
(http://www.nccusl.org/)

The National Conference of Commissioners on Uniform State Laws (NCCUSL), also referred to as the Uniform Law Commissioners, has been in operation for more than a century. Membership is made up of lawyers, judges, and law professors, appointed by the states as well as the District of Columbia, Puerto Rico, and the U.S. Virgin Islands. The task is to draft proposals for uniform and model laws on subjects where a difference in law between states creates difficult tangles. Where uniformity is desirable and practical, they develop recommendations and work toward their enactment in legislatures. The Web site provides the text of drafts and proposed acts as well as state-by-state status information for each proposal. Users will also find links to alternative and working drafts. Press releases, other news, and contact information are also provided.

**National Conference of Commissioners on Uniform State Laws,
Drafts of Uniform and Model Acts–Official Site**
(http://www.law.upenn.edu/bll/ulc/ulc_frame.htm)

The Uniform Law Commissioners are committed to making draft
and final recommended acts available to the public. To this end, they
work with the University of Pennsylvania Law School to place these
texts on the Web. The site is not limited to UCC draft and final recommendations, but includes all uniform and model acts developed by or
for the Uniform Law Commissioners.

Business Research Platforms: Selected Academic Business Library Web Sites

Glenn S. McGuigan

SUMMARY. The "Business Research Platforms" chapter describes the Web sites of business libraries at ten top business schools, ranked on research output by faculty. Highlights of each site are included. *[Article copies available for a fee from The Haworth Document Delivery Service: 1-800-HAWORTH. E-mail address: <docdelivery@haworthpress.com> Website: <http://www.HaworthPress. com> © 2002 by The Haworth Press, Inc. All rights reserved.]*

KEYWORDS. Business libraries, Web sites

INTRODUCTION

Academic business libraries and business collections possess Web pages that are used in various ways to promote or provide library services. The variety of business library Web pages reflects the diversity of Web development within these institutions and the evolution of these sites from simple promotional tools, posting information about library hours or location, to resources that deliver access to a wide range of information, such as information about library collections and services, links to proprietary databases and listings of selected Web resources. The fol-

Glenn S. McGuigan is Business Reference Librarian, Penn State Harrisburg (E-mail: gxm22@psu.edu).

[Haworth co-indexing entry note]: "Business Research Platforms: Selected Academic Business Library Web Sites." McGuigan, Glenn S. Co-published simultaneously in *Journal of Business & Finance Librarianship* (The Haworth Information Press, an imprint of The Haworth Press, Inc.) Vol. 8, No. 2, 2002, pp. 55-62; and: *The Core Business Web: A Guide to Key Information Resources* (ed: Gary W. White) The Haworth Information Press, an imprint of The Haworth Press, Inc., 2003, pp. 55-62. Single or multiple copies of this article are available for a fee from The Haworth Document Delivery Service [1-800-HAWORTH, 9:00 a.m. - 5:00 p.m. (EST). E-mail address: docdelivery@haworthpress.com].

10.1300/J109v08n02_06

lowing annotations provide a sampling of the high quality and diverse library Web pages that promote and support academic business research.

Houghton declares that there are essentially two kinds of Web page users: hunters and gatherers. "Hunters are users who need information quickly and rely on easy to follow links; gatherers are users who need material to read on screen and digest slowly."[1] Taking into account these two approaches, these annotations derive more from the hunter than the gatherer perspective. My aim is to comment on features of the Web pages that may be apparent to someone scanning a site quickly looking for information. In observing electronic resources and applications, it is useful to address the factors of task support, usability, and pleasant aesthetics.[2] The following annotations are made with that fact in mind and arise from my experience as a business librarian. Features of the business library Web pages that are observed include such items as access to commercial electronic resources, listing of Web sites, research guidance, and information about library services.

SELECTION OF BUSINESS LIBRARY PAGES

The selection of business library Web pages arises from a recent study published in the *Academy of Management Journal* that offers a novel approach to examining the rankings of business schools within the United States. Rather than basing the rank of business schools upon forms of criteria relating to various factors within the business school experience (including job placement, facilities, alumni relations, etc.), the study produced a ranking based on the research productivity of faculty members within business schools.[3] Based on an overall research rank of per/page production by faculty within the business schools from 1986-1998, the authors rank the top ten business schools as: Pennsylvania, Michigan, Stanford, New York, Chicago, Columbia, Minnesota, Texas, Harvard, and Northwestern. Considering the nature of this ranking based on research activity, it appears appropriate to use this as a basis for this brief selection of academic business library Web sites.

This descriptive list of Web sites does not intend to rank or rate the quality of these sites, although in general the quality is extremely high. Rather, this brief overview aims to provide a glimpse into some of the features and functionalities of selected business academic library Web sites that support the most active business schools in the country based on faculty research production.

University of Pennsylvania Lippincott Library
(http://www.library.upenn.edu/lippincott/)

An impressive Web site, the University of Pennsylvania Lippincott Library provides a wealth of information regarding resources and services to the Wharton School. A video "tour" of the building and services of the Lippincott Library includes a reference encounter between a business student and a librarian. A unique and extremely useful feature of the library is "The Business Database Wizard." This simple electronic form enables a user to select a particular topic within business, such as company financials, industry information or economics journals, and then submit the query that results in a list of the relevant links to Penn's subscription databases.

Highlight. The selection of business Web sites contains thirty-two categories. The outstanding link of *Finance & Investment* is two-tiered in its categorization, providing links within sub-topics to such categories as corporate financials, stock exchanges, and mergers and acquisitions.

University of Michigan–Ann Arbor Kresge
Business Administration Library
(http://eres.bus.umich.edu/)

On the top banner of the page, authorized users may link to the M-Track Intranet system of the School of Business Administration. This "virtual community" system is a communications tool for the students and faculty as well as a job recruitment tool, which enables students to post their resumes for corporate recruiters.

The research guide feature of the site provides access to eight individual pages that indicate appropriate electronic resources and print library resources for the various subject areas. An especially strong selection of guides focus upon international business research strategies including various documents that one may print out in MS Word format.

Highlight. An impressive feature of the site includes a link to full-text working papers of faculty within the University of Michigan Business School, the Department of Economics, and research institutes within the university, including the Center for International Business Education and the National Quality Research Center and those of other institutions. The working papers are available in PDF format.

Stanford University–Jackson Library
of the Stanford Business School
(http://wesley.stanford.edu/library/)

A site designed with simplicity and ease of navigation in mind, the Jackson Library pages provide access to the essentials of an academic business library page: the catalog, databases, selected business Web pages, and research guides.

The research guides are available in the PDF format, and this contributes to a visually appealing handout that one may print out. Subjects of research guides include business history, company information, industry information, and international information.

Highlight. Within the research guide page is a link to a description of the Jackson Library's "Trader's Pit," which is a part of the library where patrons may access stand-alone machines that provide access to financial services data delivered through Bloomberg, DataStream, Reuters 3000, and other business information services.

New York University Bobst Library
(http://www.nyu.edu/library/bobst/)

While New York University does not have a separate business library apart from the main Bobst Library, the Business, Social Science and Documents Collection within the main library supports the Stern School of business. There is a separate library of real estate, The Jack Brause Library supporting NYU's Real Estate Institute. The real estate library has a useful in-house index of real estate periodicals searchable from the Web.

Highlight. The undisputable highlight of the Bobst Library's Web pages concerning business topics is the NYU Virtual Business Library collection of pages. A template arranges links to business databases by subject, such as industry, company, country or marketing information. Many of the subject pages contain links to selected Web sites dealing with that particular topic. The Web based research guides linked here are particularly strong and provide access to and information about electronic resources as well as paper business resources within the Bobst Library.

University of Chicago Library
(www.lib.uchicago.edu/e/)

The Business & Economics Resource Center of the Regenstein Library of the University of Chicago provides the platform for business research within these pages. The subject guides are quite detailed and provide links to subscription databases and bibliographic information regarding resources held within the library. The links to working papers are particularly valuable.

The main page also links to the Kenneth G. Fisher Library of the Graduate School of Business. The primary purpose of this library is to provide services to alumni and part-time MBA students and serves as the "center for career and job related research at the University of Chicago Graduate School of Business." The library provides access to career electronic career guides within many fields, but requires a user ID and password to retrieve these documents.

Highlight. Extensive industry guides list relevant databases, indexes, periodicals and Web sites for particular industries.

Columbia University Thomas J. Watson Library of Business and Economics
(www.columbia.edu/cu/lweb/indiv/business/)

The Web page communicates the fact that the scope of the library's collection is quite broad. "Special focus is placed on the topics of accounting, business economics, business history, management of organizations, management science, operations management, corporate and international finance, international economics, corporate relations, security analysis, marketing, money and financial markets and labor." With that much to address, the Watson Library's page does an admirable job of delivering access to a wide range of resources.

Regarding databases, a link to each database description includes a template that describes the scope of the resource (subject description, date of coverage, content type), the publishing information (such as the databases provider and access restrictions), and search methods (such as by company, keyword, industry, etc.). The Business & Economics Library page also provides access to Prometheus, a Web-based courseware application that allows students to access course-related information online.

Highlight. Research guides are divided into fifteen subject areas. This includes an extensive listing of entertainment industry directories and resources, international company information sources and nonprofit organization resources. A separate section of Internet resources provides links to Web sites and an e-resources link connects users to a well-constructed page of Internet search engines and directories.

University of Minnesota Libraries–Business Reference
(http://busref.lib.umn.edu/about/about.html)

Serving the Carlson School of Management, the Business Reference pages include links to various topics on the opening page, including security analyst report resources, company information and corporate reports, and sources for marketing information. The Minnesota pages deliver extensive research assistance in the form of a university-wide tool called "Research Quick Start." This electronic form enables one to select a subject area, such as business finance, and produce a vast list of databases, Web sites, and print resources.

Highlight. The "Biz Quick Links" of selected Internet resources are divided into more than forty categories. The page also includes very useful links to guides from the University of Minnesota Law Library concerning tax research. Convenient links in the left hand frame provide access to tax forms and tax help links.

University of Texas, Austin–Business Reference
(http://www.lib.utexas.edu/)

Resources within the Perry-Castañeda Library support the undergraduate and graduate programs of the McComb's School of Business. Two main pages compose the business platform: business reference and business resource pages. The Business Reference page is divided into two main sections: a list of databases available in the subject area and a collection of subject links divided into categories. The Business Research page delivers access to information concerning the search process, such as particular course guides, searching tips, and a useful link to full-text career resource books delivered via Net Library.

Highlight. The site provides access to an extremely useful information literacy tutorial entitled TILT (Texas Information Literacy Tutorial). This tutorial enables a user to engage in an interactive experience and to customize a tutorial session to a particular research area, such as Internet business.

Harvard Business School Baker Library
(http://www.library.hbs.edu/)

The home page of the Baker Library of the Harvard Business School is an extremely content-rich site that delivers access to the resources and services of this venerable institution. An excellent feature of the Baker School Library collection of resources is that proprietary databases are combined with Web pages by subject to provide access to business resources based upon research need rather than format or subscription restrictions.

The main page is categorized into various subject areas including company information, economics and statistics, and career resources.

The template for the career resources subject area provides annotations of each Web site, instead of just providing a link without any explanation. Selected database links include descriptions as well, which facilitate selection of the appropriate resource.

Highlight. The links to the historical collections of the Baker Library, Baker publications and the Baker Books list all combine to make this a unique site on the Web. The new Web-based study guides are attractive and user-friendly resources that enable access to the Business Manuscripts collection of the library. Links within the various topics include an introduction to the collection, indexes, bibliographies, and notes on the collections. Beautiful scanned images of documents are selectively available at this site.

Northwestern University
(http://www.library.northwestern.edu/)

The Northwestern University Library houses the collections that support the Kellogg School of Management. Selecting a collections icon leads the searcher to a page of subject links that includes the categories of "management" and "economics." The subject pages deliver access to lists of databases and selected Internet resources. A link to "Electronic Handouts" provides access to PDF files that concern various areas of business research, such as locating company information (both U.S. and international), industry information, and marketing information. Certain guides contain an initial section entitled "Questions to Answer Before Beginning." In addition, beside the usual list of types of sources, such as electronic, statistical, or consumer, there is a listing of "Other Leads" that includes access to citations or links of sources that a researcher may often turn to in order to find relevant information or as a last resort. These sources include items such as the *Encyclopedia of Associations*, the *Encyclopedia of Business Information Sources*, and selected Internet sites.

Highlight. Each subject area contains a collection development policy statement that communicates the collection development scope of each area. This is particularly useful if one is interested in the breadth and depth of the library collection.

List of Academic Business Library Links

http://www.lib.washington.edu/business/abl.html
http://web.bryant.edu/~canderso/buslib.html
http://dir.yahoo.com/Reference/Libraries/Business_Libraries/

NOTES

1. Houghton, D. (2000). "Building an Academic Library Website: Experiences at De Montfort University." *Program,* 34 (3), 271.

2. Battleson, B., Booth, A. and Weintrop, J. (2001). "Usability Testing of an Academic Library Web Site: A Case Study." *The Journal of Academic Librarianship,* 27 (3), 188.

3. Trieschmann, J.S.; Dennis, A.R.; Northcraft, G.B.; and Niemi Jr, A.W. (2000). "Serving multiple constituencies in business schools: M.B.A. program versus research performance." *Academy of Management Journal,* 43 (6), 1130-1141.

A Brief Primer
for Business Statistics Web Sites

Steven Greechie

SUMMARY. This chapter outlines key sources for business statistics, including governmental sites and resources from private companies. *[Article copies available for a fee from The Haworth Document Delivery Service: 1-800-HAWORTH. E-mail address: <docdelivery@haworthpress.com> Website: <http://www. HaworthPress.com> © 2002 by The Haworth Press, Inc. All rights reserved.]*

KEYWORDS. Business statistics, Web sites

INTRODUCTION

We need to define what is being referred to as a business statistic. A *statistic* is a measurement–quantitative information. For the purpose of this study, a *business statistic* is defined as any measurement that is useful in business. But is there any measurement that would not be useful to the businessperson under the proper circumstances? The reach of the business world is so broad, and its research so probing, that no area of knowledge can be categorically excluded.

In defining the parameters of our examination, we will limit this study to resources that offer quantitative information. But not necessarily *exclusively* quantitative; it is often necessary to examine a text document to

Steven Greechie is Research Associate, McGraw-Hill Companies (E-mail: steven_greechie@mcgraw-hill.com).

[Haworth co-indexing entry note]: "A Brief Primer for Business Statistics Web Sites." Greechie, Steven. Co-published simultaneously in *Journal of Business & Finance Librarianship* (The Haworth Information Press, an imprint of The Haworth Press, Inc.) Vol. 8, No. 2, 2002, pp. 63-70; and: *The Core Business Web: A Guide to Key Information Resources* (ed: Gary W. White) The Haworth Information Press, an imprint of The Haworth Press, Inc., 2003, pp. 63-70. Single or multiple copies of this article are available for a fee from The Haworth Document Delivery Service [1-800-HAWORTH, 9:00 a.m. - 5:00 p.m. (EST). E-mail address: docdelivery@haworthpress.com].

find the needed measurement. Further, we will limit the scope of the examination to those Web sites that are not restricted to a specific industry.

It is important to remember that not all areas of a Web site are equally useful. We might be impressed with a site's data on U.S. finance, while its coverage of international data may be scant or even unreliable. We do not feel obliged to comment on every area of a Web site, or even on a Web site as a whole.

While the primary concern in examining a Web site is its content, another major consideration must be the interface. The development of search engine technology has not kept pace with the accumulation of material on the World Wide Web. It is common for a Web site to contain an abundance of useful information that is inaccessible to any researcher who has not learned its idiosyncrasies. In many cases, we do not use the resource often enough to maintain the specific search skills it demands and we need to relearn with each use. We do not reject a resource, however arcane its search technology may be, but it is not possible to assess a Web site thoroughly without considering the interface.

We note there is a vast difference between free information and information that has a price. We cannot expect free data to have the depth or the reliability of priced data. This does not imply that free data is useless; indeed, we often could not do without it.

PRIVATE WEB SITES

DialogWeb
(http://www.dialogweb.com)

DialogWeb (fee-based) is the most straightforward of the comprehensive options for accessing the more than 600 Dialog databases. This Dialog aggregator offers data in an enormous range of areas, including industry, market, and product information. There is company information available for U.S. and international firms that are both public and private. DialogWeb is one of the resources most likely to help in research for private company data. More technical data is available in the various areas of reference, such as science and technology.

Happily, the "Guided Search" option does not demand the infamous, esoteric Dialog search language.

One of the relevant databases, TableBase, contains tabular information regarding industries, markets, and products. With the Dialog databases, indexing is an invaluable tool. The various output options in DialogWeb allow you to identify the characteristics of the search results before purchasing the entire documents. Dialog's content has always been of primary importance to the researcher; now the interface is updated, and the enhancement is invaluable.

DRI-WEFA
(http://www.dri-wefa.com)

The U.S. Macro database (fee-based) on the DRI-WEFA site gives a ten-year forecast of the U.S. economy, updated monthly. It also offers a twenty-five year forecast, updated semi-annually. The data items here would satisfy the most specialized economist. They include a long list of financial indicators, such as GNP, GDP, imports and exports, CPI, etc. It looks at consumer markets, housing and construction, investment, government, inflation, and labor. It offers projections, as well, of GDP for global regions. The researcher can retrieve packages of data or the entire forecast. It takes specialized training, and patience, to utilize this resource, but this is the definitive source for dependable projections.

Dun & Bradstreet
(http://www.dnb.com/)

There are few resources available for the researcher looking for information on private companies. It is here that Dun & Bradstreet (fee-based) is uniquely useful. The *Business Information Reports* give the financial information on private companies that is not usually available elsewhere. The various areas of the report are updated on different schedules. It is not comprehensive because it only has figures that private companies choose to give them. Still, we could not do without it for basic data and the interface cannot be faulted.

Hoover's
(http://www.hoovers.com/)

The free material on this site is impressive, with basic company financials, corporate affiliations, and number of employees on each company page. American and foreign public companies are covered, and even some private companies. It is not in-depth material but it is designed to quickly meet common needs. There is also an area for IPO's.

The fee-based material goes into considerably more detail for public companies, with financial ratios, company history, key personnel, leading brands, competitor comparisons, and other information. This is very processed data, a thorough introduction to a company. For free or for a fee, searching is easy.

LIVEDGAR
(http://www.gsionline.com/info.htm)

The "Company Filings" area of this fee-based database offers material that the SEC offers for free. So why pay? Because the material has been reformatted, so it is more palatable for the user. The nasty tags on Edgar documents are gone, and you can link to the various areas of the document. The functionality is also improved so the financial information may be viewed in Excel.

This Web site makes electronic filings available as soon as the SEC receives them. Many paper filings are also available, and the database reaches back farther than the Edgar database on the SEC site. It is also easy to search. In this fee structure, the user accumulates charges by the minute; many researchers will find this preferable to paying by the document.

S&P NetAdvantage
(http://www.netadvantage.standardandpoors.com/netacgi/netadv)

The eleven (fee-based) Standard & Poor's databases that form this resource contain data on a range of business topics focusing on investment. Company information covers stocks, bonds, directors and officers, dividends and the various financials figures; the well-known S&P tear-sheets are available. In addition, there is material covering mutual funds and security dealers, as well as information from the S&P Industry Reports.

The interface is clear, and the information is designed so that links appear for data related to whatever is on the screen. The supple search mechanisms allow you to search by parameters such as measures of size and location. This is an indispensable resource for company or investment research.

TradStat
(http://www.tradstatweb.com/)

TradStat, one of the specialized (fee-based) products from Thomson Dialog, uses data from the governments of twenty-six countries to produce trade information. It often identifies trading partners. The report options are designed to present various types of data for products, countries, or aggregate data for the EU as a whole. There is a specialized report identifying trends.

This search tool is supple, and there are various personalization options, including options for currency and formatting. Some yearly data goes back twenty years, and it is possible to create alerts. TradStat claims to record ninety percent of world trade, but then it also claims to be "the only way to obtain trade statistics online." For those who need information regarding international trade, this site should not be overlooked.

U.S. GOVERNMENT

FedStats
(http://www.fedstats.gov/)

The site is the portal to statistics, largely free, from over 100 federal agencies. The straightforward home page immediately gives a choice of access tools. "Topic Links," the index, is perhaps the most direct way to maneuver. There are a couple of ways to access statistics by geography. Data for a range of disciplines may be found by state, county, political division, or by other geographic entities. The data may be from FedStats itself or from other agencies. Users can link to a small collection of federal statistics publications available online, and there is an amazing search engine that can search across all federal agencies.

It is noteworthy that we find here a list of federal agencies with statistical programs, their coverage, and even key statistics. The site, on whole, is a terrific tool for researchers exploring the federal statistical terrain. It makes locating government data surprisingly straightforward.

U.S. Bureau of Economic Analysis
(http://www.bea.gov/)

The Bureau of Economic Analysis is the agency of the U.S. Department of Commerce that profiles the economy through a wide span of data (largely free) on income, output, wealth, flow of products, etc. It measures personal income as well as the Gross Domestic Product. This is all broken down by industry, state and region. It also offers, "on a reimbursable basis," the regional economic multipliers that calculate the effect of change in one industry to another.

International figures are included as well. It is here that you will find the definitive information regarding U.S. direct investment abroad and foreign direct investment in the U. S. as well as the international balance of payments. Material regarding international accounts is detailed by its various elements. The data also covers U.S. affiliates of foreign companies and U.S. multinationals. The site is not difficult to use and for a detailed economic assessment it cannot be faulted.

U.S. Bureau of Labor Statistics
(http://www.bls.gov/)

The Bureau of Labor Statistics is the agency of the U.S. Department of Labor that compiles data on the myriad facets of the economy. Its most widely known product, the Consumer Price Index, from which the inflation rate is calculated, is published online monthly; the Web site offers a handy inflation calculator that does the computation. There are a host of other free stats available here in areas from productivity and wages to unemployment and industry data, often by state or metropolitan area. It is not only U.S. data on the site; a surprising amount of foreign data is online here, including international comparisons of such data as the Consumer Price Index, Gross Domestic Product, and productivity. Data may be selected to create a customized report and accessing the information is straightforward. This data could answer many researchers' needs directly or by inference.

U. S. Census Bureau
(http://www.census.gov/)

The U.S. Census is an agency of the Department of Commerce and an enormously important resource for free and fee-based information. The home page along with its family of linked pages has enormous value. There is a lengthy and useful "Subjects Index," as well as a page with several tools for searching the site. A page labeled "Data Access Tools" offers "Interactive Internet Tools" (which refers to sub-areas of the site) and downloadable software for specialized use.

Labeled links on the page lead to the enormous wealth of census data, notably those links labeled "People," "Business" and "Geography." Even a relatively minor area such as that labeled "State and County Quick Facts" can be enormously useful when needed. "American Fact Finder" is a portal for population, housing, economic and geographic data. It is a universe of information.

U.S. Census: 1997 Economic Census Data
(http://www.census.gov/epcd/www/econ97.html)

The 1997 Economic Census is the heart of census data for many researchers. There is an astounding amount of information available and the organization of the data is complex to the point of being arcane, but we could not do without it.

It includes industry data for all sectors including summary statistics by industry, and industry statistics by state and zip code, as well as data for businesses without paid employees, and a section for "Minority- and Women-Owned Businesses." There are nineteen sector-specific reports, each of which is actually composed of digital documents. The heart of these is the set of documents comprising the "Subject Series," where the pithy information regarding receipts and companies is to be found.

There is an important page called "Consolidated List of PDF's" that disentangles the documents by categorizing them into series: "Core Business Statistics Series"; "Subject Series"; "Industry Series" (a nascent area); and "Geographical Area Series." To use a single example of the valuable material here: a document called "Company Summary" has aggregate information with U.S. businesses categorized by many characteristics such as form of organization, industry sector, race, etc.

U.S. Securities and Exchange Commission
(http://www.sec.gov/)

The Securities and Exchange Commission, of course, is the regulatory organization for the securities market. All American public companies with assets of ten million dollars or more and with 500 or more shareholders are required to file statements electronically. These documents include many of the common financials: annual reports, quarterly statements, proxy statements, etc.

Companies began filing electronically between 1993 and 1996. Users can retrieve all these filings directly and easily from this Web site. The required filings of foreign companies traded in the U.S. are also available. Users can also search mutual fund filings and prospectuses. All of the material is free.

INTERNATIONAL ORGANIZATIONS

Eurostat
(http://europa.eu.int/comm/eurostat/)

It is not clear from the site's confusing home page (in English) that it is the statistics page of Europa, "The European Union Online." Beneath its over-designed interface there is a wealth of economic indicators regarding the E.U. Users get an impression of its overall depth through the labels of the up-front data tabs: "General Statistics"; "Economy and Finance"; "Population & Social Conditions"; "Industry Trade & Services"; "Agriculture & Fisheries"; "External Trade"; "Transport"; "Environment & Energy"; and "Science & Technology."

Much data regarding trade, economics, and demographics is available for free; other data is priced. It is not the easiest site to use, but the information is valuable and highly specific. Researchers focusing on European information would do well to master its intricacies.

Organisation for Economic Co-operation and Development
(http://www.oecd.org)

The OECD functions over a huge range of concerns (economic, trade, social, scientific, etc.). The topics are arranged in the index on the home page. The researcher may start with the statistics link at the top of the page and choose an area of study. Or users may select the "Search" option, which will allow for the screening of results by theme. Either way, it is a unique system, providing the researcher with a means of retrieving the data.

Note that economic and social indicators are available by country and region. Much free data is imbedded in the OECD reports, but for a direct avenue to the data, users are recommended to choose the *statistics* link whenever one is available. It is possible to personalize the Web site and to receive e-mail alerts. The researcher may not find this data anywhere else.

World Bank
(http://www.worldbank.org)

The World Bank is concerned with development assistance. In its work, it produces databanks of free indicators resulting in an enormous trove of information. This site offers development indicators for over 200 countries. These fall into the more familiar business areas of labor, economic growth, and debt and trade, but they extend to a great many other fields, such as health, education, environment and gender issues.

There is hardly a global issue that is not represented here. General and specialist researchers alike will find the World Bank databases useful. In fact, they may well find unexpected aggregate data. For example, topic indicators of the site's various subjects are designed to provide such figures as aggregate GDP for chosen regions. As global economic research engages more attention, this site will become increasingly popular.

World Trade Organization
(http://www.wto.org/)

The business of the WTO is the analysis of global trade, and it naturally produces the definitive data in this area. Its latest publication, *International Trade Statistics 2001*, is in itself an invaluable free resource. In assessing world trade, it gives detailed analyses by region and sector, identifying key trends. Much of the data is specified at the country level.

The site's historical series presents aggregate data back to 1980 and specifies the goods and services information by country, region, and economic sector. All of this information can be downloaded into Excel format. It may take time to find your data, but it would be difficult to research import-export business comprehensively without the help of the WTO.

Career Information and Salary Surveys

Matthew J. Wayman

SUMMARY. The "Career Information and Salary Surveys" chapter provides an overview of important resources for locating career and salary information. Also included are comprehensive career Web sites. *[Article copies available for a fee from The Haworth Document Delivery Service: 1-800-HAWORTH. E-mail address: <docdelivery@haworthpress.com> Website: <http://www. HaworthPress.com> © 2002 by The Haworth Press, Inc. All rights reserved.]*

KEYWORDS. Careers, salaries, Web sites

INTRODUCTION

There are many Web sites that provide information on careers and salaries. As with any popular topic, both good and bad sites exist. My intent, of course, is to filter out the "bad" and retain only the "good." Hopefully, I have made the lives of those seeking high-quality career/salary Web sites a little easier.

This article is divided into four separate sections. The first lists metasites, or sites that simply provide links to other sites, but do not necessarily provide a great amount of career-oriented information themselves. The second section lists sites that contain information on both careers and

Matthew J. Wayman is Reference Librarian, Penn State Abington (E-mail: mjw13@psu.edu).

[Haworth co-indexing entry note]: "Career Information and Salary Surveys." Wayman, Matthew J. Co-published simultaneously in *Journal of Business & Finance Librarianship* (The Haworth Information Press, an imprint of The Haworth Press, Inc.) Vol. 8, No. 2, 2002, pp. 71-79; and: *The Core Business Web: A Guide to Key Information Resources* (ed: Gary W. White) The Haworth Information Press, an imprint of The Haworth Press, Inc., 2003, pp. 71-79. Single or multiple copies of this article are available for a fee from The Haworth Document Delivery Service [1-800-HAWORTH, 9:00 a.m. - 5:00 p.m. (EST). E-mail address: docdelivery@haworthpress.com].

10.1300/J109v08n02_08

salaries. The third and fourth sections list sites that provide only career information and only salary surveys, respectively.

Some sites provide general information on careers and/or salaries in a large number of fields of employment, and still many others focus on one specific field (or a very small number of focused and related fields). Some sites contain information that is not specific to one geographic region of the United States, and many others are location-specific. This article focuses on only those sites that both contain information on many fields and are not location-specific. There is one exception to these rules: Web sites containing information on military careers have been included, and are listed in the appropriate section depending on whether they include information about military careers, salaries, or both. Military careers are often not included in other career and/or salary Web sites. Further, only sites that have information on careers in all branches of the military are listed here; sites providing information on careers in only some branches have not been included.

A few sites I have included are those of college/university career centers and placement offices. These sites can prove extremely useful, especially for recent graduates or those planning to graduate soon, and are often the most creative and innovative. Although each college or university, by design, tends to help its own students most, much of the information provided should prove useful to any job seeker. Information typically provided includes average starting salaries, often listing the minimum, maximum, and average, and often divided by major. Some excellent examples are available from the placement offices at Texas A&M University and the Massachusetts Institute of Technology.

Many Web sites containing information on careers and salaries provide a very small amount of information up front, then require purchase or the payment of subscription or membership fees for more detailed information. These sites, for the most part, have not been included in this article. A small number of sites listed do contain some documents that may be purchased, but every site present should have a decent amount of information available free.

A recurring problem with metasites is that they tend to contain many dead links. I have made an attempt to limit the inclusion of metasites to only those that have very few dead links. It seems that it is nearly impossible to find any metasites with no dead links whatsoever.

Anyone interested in finding career-specific Web sites may find them listed in some of the metasites included below. Those searching for location-specific information should try looking at the Web sites of local newspapers, and will often find useful information in the Web sites of local (and sometimes state) government agencies that deal with labor and employment.

METASITES

Career Adviser
(http://www.careeradvisor.com)

Either enter an occupation in the search box or select the appropriate field from the bottom of the page. Resulting pages will provide links to a variety of Web sites for associations and organizations associated with that profession which provide relevant information. Look specifically at sites listed under the "Perspective" section, with the subset of "Job Outlook and Salaries."

Exploring Occupations, Student Counselling and Career Centre, University of Manitoba
(http://www.umanitoba.ca/counselling/careers.html)

This site provides a long list of occupations. Clicking on any occupation brings up a page with links to relevant Web sites providing further information. Sites listed for each occupation generally include those of professional organizations and other career-based sites with entries for each occupation.

CAREERS AND SALARIES

America's Career InfoNet
(http://www.acinet.org)

There are a number of valuable resources available on this Web site. The user can search for jobs by employability and required level of education from the home page, select a job family and then an individual occupation and state from the "Wages & Trends" tab, find further resources from the "Career Exploration" link, or go directly to the "Resource Library." A unique feature is the presence of brief, narrated, one-minute, twenty-second videos displaying each occupation in practice (RealPlayer required).

Armed Forces Careers.com
(http://www.armedforcescareers.com)

A great source for information on military careers, click on either "Enlisted Careers Options" or "Officer Careers Options" for lists of career tracks. Clicking on any career will provide a table with brief descriptions of those careers and information on which branches employ people in those fields. The "Plan Your Military Career Today!" link also provides relevant information, such as benefits, pay, and rank insignias (necessary in order to understand the pay chart).

Bureau of Labor Statistics
(http://www.bls.gov)

The two portions of this site that are most relevant to the topic at hand are "Career Guides" and "How Much People Earn." The former contains the current, online editions of the *Occupational Outlook Handbook* and *Career Guide to Industries*. Both are searchable by career or industry, and are appropriately cross-referenced. The "How Much People Earn" section provides a wide variety of data through several sub-sections, including salary by occupation and by geographic area, hourly wage earnings, and employee benefits, to name a few. The "Occupational Employment Statistics" home page provides useful national, state, and metropolitan area wage information by occupation (available at http://www.bls.gov/oes/).

Career Chase
(http://www.careerchase.net)

The most relevant section is the "Career Center." Under "Interviews" is a list of fields; clicking on a field generates a list of available "Informational Interviews." Each interview provides a profile of that profession, and has answers to several questions, such as why that person entered the profession, what the application requirements were, what his or her daily tasks are, what the salary range is, etc. Each interview also lists the age and gender of the interviewee.

CareerJournal.com
(http://www.careerjournal.com)

From the Wall Street Journal, this site provides career-related articles and information. Click on the "Salary & Hiring Info" tab and select a career to view relevant articles and salary tables, or select one of the other options from that tab's drop-down box. The salary calculator is a great feature which shows the relative cost of living between two cities selected by the user. Most other information on this site provides career-related advice, such as tips for interviewing and "Career Killers" to watch out for in planning a strategy.

CareerPlanit: Resource Mining
(http://www.careerplanit.com/resource/profile.asp)

Either select a field of study under "To search by major . . . " or select a specific job under "To search by job title . . . " Searching by major provides a list of potential jobs, linked to any available profiles, for people pursuing study in that subject. Similarly, selecting a career provides a list of majors that people working in that career are likely to have studied. One interesting feature in each profile is the "Types of employers" section, which lists types of companies and business sectors likely to employ people in that profession.

College Grad. Job Hunter
(http://www.collegegrad.com)

"Career Info" can be selected from the navigation menu on the left side of the page. Users may do a keyword search, browse by category, or view all listings. Each entry provides a rather lengthy description of that occupation, along with sections on working conditions, chances for employment, training and/or qualifications required, and earnings, to name a few. The included salary calculator links to that on Salary.com.

CollegeBoard.com: Career Browser
(http://www.collegeboard.com/apps/careers/index)

After selecting one of the available occupation groups, a list of specific careers will be available. Select a career, and a lengthy description will appear. Each section of every job description is thorough, with detailed information on required education, earnings, and job outlook. Related occupations are appropriately cross-referenced. Worthy of note are the "Sources of Additional Information" sections found at the end of each profile.

JobProfiles.org
(http://www.jobprofiles.org)

Select a job category on the left side of the page, then select a specific career from the resulting list. The amount of information about the job provided in a profile depends upon the individual contributor, but all profiles have some standard elements. Those elements include type of college degree(s) required, size of organization, salary, and job description. Other interesting inclusions are the stresses and rewards of each listed profession. Note that less than 1% of profiles are unsolicited, and only favorable profiles are posted.

JobStar
(http://jobstar.org)

The two sections most relevant are "Career Guides" and "Salary Info." Each section simply provides links to other Web sites providing information on each topic. Many of the resources are very general, and some are included in this bibliography, but others are extremely location- or career-specific.

The Princeton Review: Career Assessment
(http://www.review.com/career/index.cfm)

The "Investigate Careers" section allows the user to select a career, then see a page-long profile of that career. Other sections of particular interest are "Tools," which provides a "Career Assessment Quiz" and information about college majors and what career options are available for graduates with those degrees, and "Advice," which has a "Myth vs. Reality" test for a number of careers and "Professional Profiles" of several figures (both current and historical) with interesting careers.

Quintessential Careers
(http://www.quintcareers.com)

The most useful portion of this site is the "Career Resources Toolkit," available from the "Open Our Career Toolkit" link. Some items contained within are career- and job-related articles, quizzes, and assessment tools. It's interesting to note that articles are divided into three different sections—for teens, for college/graduate students, and for experienced job seekers and career changers.

SalaryExpert.com
(http://www.salaryexpert.com)

From the home page, select a career and geographic location (U.S. or Canada), then click on "Get Free Report." The resulting page will display salary information for the selected career in that location, plus a brief description of what someone in that profession would normally do. Links to position descriptions for related jobs are provided, but viewing them often requires the input of personal information and/or the payment of a fee.

WetFeet.com: Career Profiles
(http://www.wetfeet.com/asp/careerlist.asp)

Select a career from the list of profiles. Each profile provides the standard information for that career, such as general description, requirements, job outlook, and compensation. To the right of each profile is a list of "Recommended Resources," which has hyperlinked Web sites of organizations and associations that can provide further information.

CAREERS ONLY

The Career Key
(http://www.careerkey.org/english)

The most relevant section is "You," available from the top right side of the page. After entering some personal information, the site provides a list of options. If the user starts with "take the Career Key measure," the site will help the user to determine his/her personality type and personal interests, then provide advice on potential careers and suggest relevant majors in college. All job profiles provided link to the online version of the *Occupational Outlook Handbook*, available through the Bureau of Labor Statistics Web site, listed elsewhere in this bibliography.

CareerZone
(http://www.nycareerzone.org/)

Select one of six different fields, then select a specific career. Note that lists of careers are very long, and there are several sorting options. Each career has a rather lengthy entry including a description, required skills, abilities, knowledge, and education, and a job outlook. The "Similar Jobs" section cross-references to other available entries. Many jobs listed also have a RealPlayer video of someone at work in that profession.

Military Career Guide Online
(http://www.militarycareers.com)

There are many ways to get started from this site's home page. The user can select "Intro to the Armed Forces," "Search the Guide," "How to Get Started," or scroll down in the page to select more information on "enlisted occupations" or "officer occupations." Each occupation contains a summary, lists of "Civilian Counterparts," "Helpful Attributes" for those interested in that occupation, "Physical Demands," and "Special Requirements," to name just some of the information provided. Icons at the top of each page denote which branches of the Armed Forces employ people in those occupations.

Monster.com: Career Center
(http://content.monster.com)

Under "Resources" in the right-hand navigation bar are links to sections for "Career Changers" and "Salary Center." "Career Changers" contains a variety of resources providing information on non-profit careers and making the transition from military to civilian life, and the "Job Q&As" section provides interviews with people holding a number of different jobs. The "Salary Center" simply links to other Web sites.

SALARIES ONLY

BestJobsUSA.com
(http://www.bestjobsusa.com)

For salary information, click on the "Salary Survey 2001 Exclusive" link in the navigation bar on the right. There is a brief article about salaries and a list of professions. Each profession has a separate PDF document (requiring Adobe Acrobat Reader) which lists average salaries for each level within that profession. Under "Best Jobs University," there is further salary information from the "Starting salary ranges for college grads" link, which lists average salary by major. The rest of the Web site deals mostly with resume writing and has databases for job fairs and job postings.

Defense Finance and Accounting Service: Military Pay
(http://www.dfas.mil/money/milpay)

This site provides current and past pay information on military careers and other financial and benefits information for military personnel. Note that in order to understand the salary tables, the user must know the E-, W-, and O-systems that designate military ranks (see the

Armed Forces Careers site at http://www.armedforcescareers.com for excellent tables displaying ranks and insignias). Users interested in military careers should also be sure to look at the Basic Allowance for Subsistence (BAS) and Basic Allowance for Housing (BAH), which often supplement military incomes.

Economic Research Institute: Career Planning
(http://www.erieri.com/freedata/career_planning/index.cfm)

ERI provides salary information with a twist. Select a career, and ERI provides you with a free report indicating estimated annual salary for the year 2015. Further information is available to paid subscribers or in the form of actual survey results which may be purchased.

Salary.com
(http://www.salary.com)

The most useful resource on this site is the "Salary Wizard," which many other career and salary sites link to or incorporate in their own pages. It allows the user to select a career and geographic location, then determine what the average salaries and salary ranges are for the various ranks within that profession. "Salary News," "Salary Advice," and "Salary Talk" are also useful salary resources on this site, but the "Career Resources" section is actually a job posting board, and does not contain any information about working in various careers.

WageWeb
(http://www.wageweb.com)

WageWeb simply provides national average salary data for a number of professions (170) within eight different business fields. Also listed are the average minimum and average maximum, average bonus, and the numbers of companies responding with the number of employees in each position. More information on geography and industry is available to subscribing members.

Company Information on the Web

Stacey Marien

SUMMARY. Company information is a fundamental area of business research. This chapter covers Web sites for company research tutorials, annual reports, company directories, and SEC filings. *[Article copies available
for a fee from The Haworth Document Delivery Service: 1-800-HAWORTH. E-mail
address: <docdelivery@haworthpress.com> Website: <http://www.HaworthPress.com>
© 2002 by The Haworth Press, Inc. All rights reserved.]*

KEYWORDS. Company information, annual reports, company research,
Web sites

INTRODUCTION

The Web sites reviewed for this section were chosen from a variety of
sources. The Education Committee of the Business Reference and Services
Section (BRASS) of the Reference and User Services Association (RUSA)
of the American Library Association (ALA) maintains a "Best of the Best
Business Web Sites" (http://www.ala.org/rusa/brass/besthome.html). Sites
were selected from their "American Corporations" section. Some sites
were selected from browsing through the Business and Economy section
of Yahoo!

Most of the sites were chosen from the author's personal business
Web page. Over the years, the author has maintained an extensive list of

Stacey Marien is Business Librarian, American University (E-mail: smarien@
american.edu).

[Haworth co-indexing entry note]: "Company Information on the Web." Marien, Stacey. Co-published simultaneously in *Journal of Business & Finance Librarianship* (The Haworth Information Press, an imprint of
The Haworth Press, Inc.) Vol. 8, No. 2, 2002, pp. 81-94; and: *The Core Business Web: A Guide to Key Information Resources* (ed: Gary W. White) The Haworth Information Press, an imprint of The Haworth Press, Inc.,
2003, pp. 81-94. Single or multiple copies of this article are available for a fee from The Haworth Document Delivery Service [1-800-HAWORTH, 9:00 a.m. - 5:00 p.m. (EST). E-mail address: docdelivery@haworth
press.com].

business Web pages, many of them gathered from the Internet Scout Report's *Business and Economics Newsletter*. Sadly, the Scout Report for Business and Economics was discontinued due to lack of funding.

The following reviews are arranged by types of company information. The first section is on Web sites that offer tutorials on how to do company research using the Internet. The second section lists sites where annual reports may be obtained; the third section lists company directory sites. The fourth section contains links to sites that offer SEC filings, and the last section is company research sites.

COMPANY RESEARCH TUTORIALS

Many students do not know where to begin when researching a company or industry. The following three Web sites provide information on how to get started with the research.

Company Research
(http://iws.ohiolink.edu/companies/)

This Web site was put together as a collaborative project between Youngstown State University, Bowling Green State University and Kent State University librarians. It details a step-by-step approach to researching companies and industries. Print and electronic resources are recommended throughout the guide. The "Company Research" section begins with suggestions on how to determine a company's ownership status. Once the ownership is established, the user can choose the appropriate category such as "Public," "Private," "International" or "Subsidiaries" to explore for information. The "Industry Research" section is divided into four segments: structure (SIC/NAICS); industry profiles; current development; and statistics. The authors have also included sample business course syllabi, library assignments and class assignments to further help students with their research.

Researching Companies Online
(http://home.sprintmail.com/~debflanagan/index.html)

Debbie Flanagan, a Training and Development Manager for a medical equipment manufacturer in Fort Lauderdale, Florida, has put together this site on using free Internet sites for business research. Some of the topics covered are "High-Level Company Information," "Sales Prospects," "Telephone and Addresses," "Financial Information," "Professional Associations," "Industry Information" and "Non-Profit Organizations." While the site does not go into great depth on how to do the research like the previous site, one nice feature is the tutorial that accompanies the user when an Internet resource is selected. When an Internet resource is chosen, two frames are opened. One frame contains the actual site, while the second frame has instructions on how to search the site and suggestions as to terms to use to do the search.

Stock Naked: Uncovering a Company History
(http://www.sls.lib.il.us/reference/por/features/99/comphist.html)

Stock Answers: Finding Historical Stock Prices
(http://www.sls.lib.il.us/reference/por/features/99/stock.html)

Nell Ingalls, a research librarian for the Illinois Suburban Library System Reference Service, has written two articles on using old stock certificates to research a company and how to find historical stock prices. In *Stock Naked*, she gives a step-by-step approach on how to proceed in researching a company's history when presented with an old stock certificate. The site provides information on print resources, fee-based services and scripophily (collecting old commercial paper) sources. In *Stock Answers*, Ingalls outlines the steps to take to find historical stock prices for a company and provides print and electronic resource suggestions.

ANNUAL REPORTS

Most annual reports can be found on the company's home page. It is usually located under the "Investor's Information" area. There are several Web sites that provide access to annual reports.

PRARS
(http://www.prars.com)

The Public Register Annual Report Service (PRARS) provides company financials, including annual reports, prospectuses or 10k filings on over 3,600 public companies. The annual reports are free but need to be ordered through the site. One can search by company name, ticker symbol, industry or state. There is a guide available that gives an introduction to reading annual reports. The Online Annual Report Service (http://www.annualreportservice.com/) is PRARS's online access to annual reports and provides reports for over 2,000 companies. The reports are provided in PDF format while some selected companies have had their reports converted to HTML file format.

Annual Reports Service
(http://wsjie.ar.wilink.com/)

This is a free service provided by World Investor Link and Wall Street Journal Interactive. Reports can be accessed by company name or industry. Hard copies of the reports can be requested and are mailed within twenty-four hours. Some reports are available in PDF format.

CAROL–Company Annual Reports Online
(http://www.carol.co.uk/)

Annual reports for Asian, European and U.S. companies can be found through this free site. Companies are listed by region, then in alphabetical order by name. Searching can also be done by choosing a sector such as "Banks," "Entertainment," "Insurance" and "Pharmaceuticals." The financial information is organized by area: "Profit & Loss"; "Cash Flow"; "Balance Sheet"; "Chairman"; "Shareholder"; "Five Year Review" and "Highlights"; as well as the actual annual report. The level of financial information available for each company varies. The "IR Links" area provides a list of Web sites for foreign stock exchanges, investment sites, professional bodies, vendors and media. The "News Source" section (which requires registration) provides merger, acquisition and takeover news. It is often difficult to find financial information for foreign companies and CAROL provides a useful service.

AReport.com, Annual Reports of the World's Biggest Companies
(http://www.areport.com/)

The only information available about the authors of this site is a contact link that shows photographs and e-mail for three people. There is no information on who they are or what is their background. This site offers free annual reports although there are fee-based compilation packages that provide reports on a CD or can be downloaded from the site. Reports may be searched by company name or ticker symbol and there is an index to the company names. Advanced searching allows reports to be chosen by industry, geographical area (foreign companies are included), revenues, and stock exchange or ranking index. There are four indexes available to search: "Rank 1000 USA"; "World 500"; "E 50";

and "Eurostoxx 50." The "Rank 1000" is the top 1000 companies in the U.S. by revenue, the "World 500" is the top 500 companies in the world by revenue, the "E 50" consists of fifty representative U.S. companies of the new economy, and there is no definition given for the "Eurostoxx 50" index. There is a link on the home page to a list of companies that fell off the Rank 1000 list and the reason for the disappearance. The results list may be displayed by revenue (largest to smallest and vice versa), company name or industry.

Once a company is selected, a table appears with the company's name, industry type, ticker symbol and stock exchange, a link to the annual report on the company's home page, country of origin, revenues, and their ranking in the four indexes. Even though there is no author or currency information on the site, it has user-friendly searching capabilities, links to current reports, results sorting options and the various ranking lists to choose.

COMPANY DIRECTORIES

Businesses in numerous categories may be searched by using Yahoo!'s Commerical Directory (http://dir.yahoo.com/Business_and_Economy/Business_to_Business/). The following sites provide information on businesses in specialized categories.

Nonprofits

GuideStar–The National Database of Nonprofit Organizations
(http://www.guidestar.org/)

Guidestar, a project of Philanthropic Research, Inc., contains information on over 850,000 nonprofit organizations based in the United States. If you know the name of the organization, you can use the quick search option. If you want to browse organizations, then the advanced search must be used. You can search by organization name, keyword, city, state, zip, category, nonprofit type, income range, EIN (Employer Identification Number) and NTEE (National Taxonomy of Exempt Entities) Code. The information supplied for each company includes missions and programs, goals and results, financial filings (if required by the IRS), leaders and a Web site if available. Supplemental information such as an analyst report is available for subscribers. A list of Web sites of interest to nonprofits is listed. GuideStar is an excellent site for otherwise hard to find nonprofit information.

Idealist.org
(http://www.idealist.org/)

Idealist.org provides information on over 24,000 nonprofit and community organizations in 153 countries. Searching can be done by name, mission, location and area of focus. There is an index of organizations by country. Information on each organization includes mission statement, contact person, phone number, e-mail contact and Web site address if available. While the company information on this site is not as extensive as Guidestar, Idealist.org does provide job and volunteer listings for opportunities around the world. There is an extensive list of materials and resources for topic areas. The strength of this site is its global coverage of nonprofit organizations.

Manufacturing

Thomas Register
(http://www.thomasregister.com)

This is the free online version of the well-known Thomas Register of American Manufacturers. The user must register in order to access the information. There are over 168,000 companies included in the site with 68,000 product and service categories. Searching is done by keyword within the chosen categories of products and services, company name or brand name. A sample search for food equipment yielded a results list of forty-nine companies. A company profile is given and depending on the availability, an online company catalog, a Web site address, an online order form, a CAD drawing and an e-mail contact. Once the initial keyword search is done, the results may be limited by state. There is an online form for those companies who wish to be listed at the site.

General

Corporate Information
(http://www.corporateinformation.com/)

Corporate Information seems to be test driving a new site that requires registration. When the URL is chosen, a pop up menu advises users to register at the new site in order to continue to have access to the information. Once registered, an easy to use search menu is available. Drop down menus allow searching to be done by company name, industry and country. The "Company Research" section contains company profiles from a variety of sources, research reports and sales, and price and earnings information. The "Country Research" section contains a list of companies by country and a list of general links to other Web sites related to that country. The "Industry" section lists companies by the selected industry category, sorted by country, and includes links to other relevant industry Web sites. There is a "Research Exchange Rates" search menu and an option to search for the Top 100 companies in a variety of categories. There is no help screen to give any hints on how the searching capabilities work. Quotations are required for phrase searching but that was found out by trial and error. There is a wealth of information available on this site and it remains to be seen how the new registration requirement will differ from the old site.

Kompass
(http://www.kompass.com)

This is a subscription site but some information is offered for free. When searching on a product, you get a company list. A directory listing for some companies is available, otherwise you must subscribe to access the information. A search is done by geographic region, then by product category. For example, contact information for gas production companies in Africa is available. Kompass provides a business-to-business search engine with over 1.6 million companies and twenty-three million product and service references listed.

SEC FILINGS

Sites that previously provided free access to SEC filings such as 10K Wizard (http://www.tenkwizard.com/) and Free Edgar (http://www.freeedgar.com/ or http://www.edgaronline.com) have now become subscription-based services. The following sites offer SEC filings for free.

Security and Exchange Commission's Edgar database
(http://www.sec.gov/edgar.shtml)

According to their site, "the SEC requires all public companies (except foreign companies and companies with less than $10 million in assets and 500 shareholders) to file registration statements, periodic reports, and other forms electronically through EDGAR." The dates for filings covered in this site are from 1993 to the present and the information is free to access and download. A tutorial for newcomers is offered along with a description of the various SEC forms. A separate search menu is available to find the more common filings such as the 10K, 10Q and 8K. There is a search help section. Searches for special purpose filings such as mutual funds and prospectuses can also be done. Interestingly, there is a link on the home page to other sites that provide free real-time access to EDGAR filings and the one listed is http://sec.freeedgar.com/. This is a section of the previous mentioned Free Edgar site. There are documents available for free here but only for the current day's filings.

SEC Info
(http://www.secinfo.com)

Finnegan O'Malley, a software development company, created the SEC Info database. It searches both the SEC's Edgar database and the Canadian equivalent, SEDAR, and only lists electronic filings. The information on the site is free although registration is required to access the full range of documents available. The simple keyword searching may be done by company name, industry, business, SIC code, area code, topic, zip code, CIK (Central Index Key), accession number, file number or date. The search terms are then scanned through five areas: "Registrants"; "Group Members" (non-registrant filers such as subsidiaries); "Names" (directors, officers, accountants, etc.); "Industries" (2-4 digit SIC codes); and "Businesses" (5-6 digit SIC codes). A sixth area, "Topics," is not automatically searched. All of the areas may be searched individually.

A sample search was done for the company Amgen. Four records under "Registrants" were produced. For each company, the first and last filing dates are given along with the company name, ticker symbol and the regulator (such as the U.S. SEC or Canada CSA). Four group members were listed, all subsidiaries of the parent company, Amgen. No other categories produced results. A separate search under "Topics" produced fifty-three records. Each of these records represented filings where the word "Amgen" appeared. Once the company name is chosen from the "Registrants" results list, the full range of filings is listed. For Amgen, filings from 1994 to February 2002 were available. An e-mail notification option for all future filings of the company is on this page as well as a keyword text box that allows searching over the filing pages.

Alternative categories for documents are available from the home page such as "Today's Filings," "IPO Filings," "M&A Deals," "Insider Trading," "Proxies," "Late Filing Notices" and "SEC Deleted Filings." There is a help screen that contains information on how to contact the SEC, CSA or individual companies as well as a FAQ about the SEC Info database. SEC Info is an easy database to use and is an excellent way to search both U.S. and Canadian company filings.

EdgarScan
(http://edgarscan.pwcglobal.com/servlets/edgarscan/)

Developed by PricewaterhouseCoopers Technology Centre, EDGAR SCAN reads and analyzes SEC EDGAR documents, primarily 10K (annual) and 10Q (quarterly) filings. Data may be searched by company name or ticker symbol although the day this reviewer looked at the site, this function was not working properly. A list of company names was obtained but when a company was selected, the search screen reappeared. Companies were found more successfully through the "Initial Public Offering" link and the "Standard Industrial Classification" link. When SIC is chosen, a list of companies per SIC code is listed. A company name is selected and then a list of financial tables from its filings is available in an Excel friendly format.

COMPANY RESEARCH

There are too many company research sites to come close to reviewing them all. Some of the sites provide up to date financial news stories such as Corporate Financials Online (http://www.cfonews.com/). Some of the sites focus on regional companies such as SiliconValley.com (http://www.siliconvalley.com/) or industry specific companies such as Tech Investor (http://content.techweb.com/investor/). There are many sites that focus on Internet companies such as Dotcomscoop (http://www. dotcomscoop.com). The Web sites that follow are just a sample of what is available on the Internet to do company research.

AmericanCompanies.com
(http://www.americancompanies.com/)

For a change from the usual company research resources, visit www.americancompanies.com. It is the brainchild of John Newbegin who decided to take a cross-country trip and photograph the office buildings of the Fortune 500 companies. He took two months to finish the trip and photographed 350 companies. There are a total of 525 companies listed on the site, including previous company photos Newbegin had taken in New York City. Newbegin is also the author of New York

City Skyscrapers (www.nycskyscrapers.com) that "takes a look at all those tall buildings in New York City."

The site is arranged by location and industry. For location, the sites are divided by region: West; Midwest; South; East; and New York City. Under "Industry," the companies are arranged in the broad categories of "Manufacturing," "Service," "Financial" and "Information Technology." Each of these areas is further divided into individual industries such as "Automotive," "Clothing," "Drug Stores," "Hotels," "Banks" and "Internet."

The information for each company includes their address, Web site, year 2000 sales and earnings, a description of their business and a photograph of their headquarters. The featured company when this site was reviewed was Enron and it included a stunning photograph of their headquarters in Houston. This is a fun site to visit to see where all those Fortune 500 companies conduct their business.

Business.com, The Business Search Engine
(http://www.business.com/)

This Web directory and search engine was "developed by a team of industry experts and library scientists and contains more than 400,000 listings within 25,000 industry, product and service subcategories." The twenty-five categories range from accounting to transportation and logistics. Searching may be done by keyword; the search function automatically "ands" the terms and allows for stemming. The search results produce a list of sites within the subject categories. Each of these sites is briefly annotated and at the end of the list are other suggested categories to try for information.

Searching may also be down by company name or ticker symbol. There are a wide variety of information sources available for each company when the Google search option is used. A search for "K Mart" produced a link to their home page, news articles, an encyclopedia entry and their Team Kmart NASCAR site.

The searching capabilities were tested by using "Kmart." When searched as one word, the business.com categories came up. At the end of the category list, there is an option to search for Web sites using Kmart. When searching by company name and using Kmart as one word, a company profile is available as well as brief financial information. When either search option is used with K Mart as two words, the results list is produced by Google and doesn't include any of the site's categories. One needs to use all variations of a name in order to get a more complete list of resources.

This is an excellent resource for business searching. The site is easy to navigate and loads quickly. The site has strict editorial criteria as all potential listings must be business oriented and are reviewed by the editorial staff.

Business 2.0
(http://www.business2.com/)

Business 2.0 was started by Imagine Media in 1998 as a business magazine that covered the people and companies involved in the "New Economy." The magazine and corresponding Web site was acquired in June 2001 by the FORTUNE Group and merged with its eCompany Now publication. A new Web site was introduced a month later and combined the information from the former Business 2.0 site and the eCompany Now site. The content of the site includes over 11,000 business and technology topics, editorial archives, a searchable database of articles from Business 2.0, eCompany, Fortune, Money, FSB and C/Net, and a networking area for people to expand their contacts. The site is updated daily.

One may search the site by keyword and resource (Business 2.0, eCompany, Fortune, CNET, Money and FSB). A search was done for the company JDS Uniphase and the results list contains two information areas. The first area is the "Web Guide Search Results" and the second area is "Article Search Results." When the company name is selected from the "Web Guide" area, a list of Web sites is produced which include links to the company's home page, a company capsule by Hoover's, SEC filings, and articles from other sources such as the *Motley Fool* and *The New York Times*. Other links under the "Web Guide" include a list of players in the telecommunication industry, players in the optical network industry, company career pages for the telecommunication industry and business listings for networking and devices. There were 252 articles listed under the "Article Search Results" area that came from the original six resources searched. There is an option to format the articles for printing or e-mailing them.

There are other subject listings available for browsing on the home page. These listings include "Magazine," "Archives," "Newsletters," "E-Business," "Marketing," "Technology" and "Talent Pool." There is a "Web Guide" that is described as an "annotated directory of the best e-business links selected by research experts." The directory topics include "Acronyms," "Building an E-Business," "Careers," "Internet Economy" and "Security." Registration is required in order to be a part of the "Talent Pool" networking feature and to receive e-mail notification for future articles. Business 2.0 is an easily searched site that provides an extensive amount of free information.

Hoover's Online
(http://www.hoovers.com)

Hoover's is well known for its business directories and their online site provides some business information for free. There are over 17,000 companies in Hoover's proprietary database (they provide premium access to over twelve million public and private companies). Company capsules include address, Web site, a brief snapshot, subsidiary locations, corporate hierarchy, competitors and links to news stories. Company financials are provided when available. The industry snapshots provide information for twenty-eight sectors. When a sector is chosen, a list of companies within that industry is listed, an industry profile is given, and links to resources about the industry as well as associations and organizations are provided. Hoover's makes available on their home page different business lists such as the S&P 500 and the Fortune 500.

A nice feature is "IPO Central," which provides links to IPO filings, pricings, news and a directory of all companies that have filed for an initial public offering of common stock since May 6, 1996. There is an IPO scorecard that gives statistical data on offerings, a list of the best/worst returns, a list of biggest first day jumps and drops and a list of CEOs who profited nicely from their IPOs. There is a beginner's guide to IPOs and an SEC document primer. Under the "News Center," "Company News" is divided into several categories including "Mergers & Acquisitions" and "Internet News." The "News Center" also includes "IPO News," "Market News" and "Industry News." There is a wealth of free information available on this site.

Three other sites where IPO information may be found are Investquest (http://www.investquest.com/), IPO.com (http://www.ipo.com/) and IPO Maven (http://www.123jump.com/ipomaven.htm/).

Investquest is a subscription service; however, they do offer a section that lists recently filed IPOs. A search may be done for recently filed S-1 and S-11 registration statements for companies with public offerings. Companies are searched by clicking on the corresponding letter of the alphabet. The results list for the companies lists the document name and filing date. The document link goes directly to the SEC's Edgar database. Investquest provides an option to request e-mail notification for recent filings.

IPO.com's mission is that "all investors should have access to quality news and analysis surrounding the IPO market." Some of the resources covered on their site include news analysis, IPO calendar, pricings and filings, company profiles, after market performance, and withdrawals. Much of the information is free although analysis reports may be purchased for a fee. A drop down menu allows searching to be in a number of areas such as "IPOs," "Secondaries," "Underwriters," "Law Firms," "Executives" and "Quotes." A search for PayPal produces a company profile that includes a link to the home page, company vitals, executives, a business description and a list of competitors. Other information available on PayPal is SEC filings, final price of the offering, total shares, underwriters, shareholders, news stories and current status of stock.

There are several resource guides on the home page to help users such as an "IPO Glossary," "IPO Guide" and "Venture Capital Guide." A sidebar offers quick statistics on IPOs and includes IPOs filed in 2002, IPOs postponed or withdrawn in 2002, and IPOs priced in 2002 using Arthur Andersen as their consultant.

IPO Maven offers similar information as IPO.com and is a section of 123jump.com. Under the "IPO Center" area are links to "This Week's IPOs," "IPO Calendar," "Recently Priced," "IPO Reports" and "Sector Watch." Searching may be done by ticker symbol, company name or state. Free registration is required to access some information such as the archives and to receive a selection of IPO related newsletters. The "IPO Reports" cover financials, competitors, business environment, company strategy, and product/services portfolio.

Wall Street View
(http://www.wallstreetview.com)

This site is a "financial portal that provides access to a wide range of news and information on stocks, bonds, mutual funds, futures, options and personal finance." The directory topics include "Today's Market" (e.g. "IPO" and "Market Overview"), "Mutual Funds," "Research," "Reference" and "Editorial." The categories may be browsed or company information may be searched by ticker symbol. Once a company has been searched, a tool bar appears with the possible information available such as profile, news, opinions, performance, ownership and sec filings. Subscription is required to access some of the real-time data.

Wall Street Research Net
(http://www.wsrn.com)

WSRN is an extensive research site that provides information on over 29,000 companies, mutual funds and indexes. There are eleven sections such as "Company Research," "Market Data," "Historical Download," and "IPOs" under the "Stocks" heading and four sections ("Sector Stats," "Internet stocks," "Industry News," and "Economic Calendar") under the "Industries" heading. Companies may be searched by name or ticker symbol (there is a ticker symbol lookup feature). Once a company is selected, the results list is presented in several sections. The "Key Links" includes the company's home page, SEC filings, earnings estimates, broker recommendations, competitors and partners. All of this information is free. The next several sections provide fee-based information (denoted by a $) such as annual financial statements, stock price and volume history and company profiles. WSRN also provides a data center for its subscribers. Other free information includes stock graphs and charts, news stories and links to what WSRN calls value added sites. A search was done for Amgen Inc. and its value added links included Clinical Laboratory News, FDA home page, World Health Organization and National Center for Health Statistics.

A nice feature under the Company Research is the inclusion of Canadian stocks that are traded on the Toronto, Vancouver, Montreal and Alberta exchanges. There are several other sections under the "Features" heading. "Economics" provides links to resources such as the U.S. Department of Commerce, National Bureau of Economic Research, Bureau of Labor Statistics, and Resources for Economists on the Internet. "Resources" provide links to "Equity Publications," "Market Resources" and "Trade Associations." Although premium data is only available through subscription, there is plenty of free information provided by this site to satisfy researchers.

Consumer Information on the Web

Ken Johnson

SUMMARY. The consumer information chapter covers important Web sites for consumer protection, advocacy, and awareness as well as sites reviewing specific products and services. *[Article copies available for a fee from The Haworth Document Delivery Service: 1-800-HAWORTH. E-mail address: <docdelivery@haworthpress.com> Website: <http://www.HaworthPress.com> © 2002 by The Haworth Press, Inc. All rights reserved.]*

KEYWORDS. Consumer information, consumer protection, Web sites

INTRODUCTION

Power to the people! Well, maybe. The information purporting to represent consumer interests has never been more readily available on the Web than now. However, the amount of consumer information pales in comparison to the staggering amount of commerce related Web sites that want consumers to spend their hard earned dollars. Proponents of commerce argue convincingly that consumers have never before had such "perfect" information on countless products and services available on the market. Company Web sites and online retailers provide product descriptions, photographs and performance data for their product lines, and increasingly, the consumer is one click away from a live customer service representative available to answer any lingering questions. While "per-

Ken Johnson is Reference & Instruction Librarian, Business Specialty, Appalachian State University (E-mail: johnsnkw@appstate.edu).

[Haworth co-indexing entry note]: "Consumer Information on the Web." Johnson, Ken. Co-published simultaneously in *Journal of Business & Finance Librarianship* (The Haworth Information Press, an imprint of The Haworth Press, Inc.) Vol. 8, No. 2, 2002, pp. 95-101; and: *The Core Business Web: A Guide to Key Information Resources* (ed: Gary W. White) The Haworth Information Press, an imprint of The Haworth Press, Inc., 2003, pp. 95-101. Single or multiple copies of this article are available for a fee from The Haworth Document Delivery Service [1-800-HAWORTH, 9:00 a.m. - 5:00 p.m. (EST). E-mail address: docdelivery@haworth press.com].

10.1300/J109v08n02_10

fect" information may be available (assuming you take it with a grain of "perfect" salt) consumers are still left with the decision of how best to spend their money. Which product is most reliable? Where can I find recall information on this manufacturer? To whom do I complain when things go awry? Even with perfect information, consumers must still make a decision that could impact their health, safety and finances.

A larger issue related to consumer information regards consumer advocacy, protection and awareness. Numerous sites, many government authored, address the privacy and safety concerns of the consumer. These sites do not compete with product review Web sites, which evaluate a product or service; instead, they seek to inform consumers on issues. Consumer advocacy sites answer questions such as, "Where can I find information on Internet privacy rights in the workplace?" Is a business in my town acting legally? At the charity to which I contribute, how much money goes to administrative costs? Who do I contact in my state on consumer issues? Consumer advocacy sites can answer each of these questions and more. Sometimes, one will be surprised as to which site holds the answer.

Bearing in mind the above statements, the following reviews relate to these two aspects of consumer information available on the Web. The first section covers protection, advocacy and awareness of consumer issues. The second section regards evaluation of products and services. To varying degrees, each site acts as a meta-site that will link a user to other possibly valuable sources of information.

PROTECTION, ADVOCACY, AND AWARENESS

Consumer.gov
(http://www.consumer.gov)

Consumer.gov functions as a meta-site with links to other government agencies, and departments on specific issues of consumer importance like food, health, product safety, technology and transportation. An image-based menu bar at the top of the site takes a user to the desired sections of the site. In addition, the site provides links to issues of current importance to consumers. Part of the FirstGov collection of Web sites.

Consumerworld.org
(http://www.consumerworld.org)

This meta-site, founded by consumer advocate/attorney Edgar Dworsky, combines information on consumer advocacy and protection with links to product and service reviews. As a non-governmental Web site, Dworsky addresses the issue of objectivity and authority by stating, "Consumer World contains no banner advertising, and in over 99% of the cases, receives no compensation directly or indirectly from the sites listed." The site is arranged by topic and is easily navigable.

U.S. Consumer Product Safety Commission
(http://www.cpsc.gov)

As an Independent Federal Regulatory Agency, the CPSC conducts research, collects statistics, recommends and enforces standards, issues product recalls, and informs the public on problems with consumer goods sold in the U.S. The site provides links to current and archived recall information and has an online full-text library of nearly 400 CPSC publications on product safety and warnings and approximately fifty current and historical statistical reports on injuries. In addition, the site includes a current pressroom and a section for individuals, doctors and businesses to report unsafe products. Also the CPSC provides links and other information for the businessperson seeking product safety compliance.

Better Business Bureau
(http://www.bbb.org)

The BBB has been around since 1912. Before the Web, one could call the local BBB and check out complaints against a business or discover past complaints, then the BBB would help resolve the dispute between customer and business. With the current Web site, one may research complaints on a business nationally, file a complaint and enter into the dispute resolution process all with a few clicks. The site offers full-text online publications that seek to educate consumers on issues ranging from making wise purchase decisions to recognizing scams to dealing with natural disasters. Another valuable service provided by the Web site is the ability to research the giving patterns of a charity.

Give.org
(http://www.give.org)

A BBB companion site, Give.org provides detailed reports on the charitable giving and organization of over 300 national and international charities with a pie chart that shows the percent of giving for each charity compared with administrative costs. The site also includes tips on giving, a service to inquire or forward complaints to a charity, and a detailed explanation of the *Standards of Charitable Solicitations* developed by the Council of Better Business Bureaus.

Consumer Information Center
(http://www.pueblo.gsa.gov)

Home of the famous *Consumer Information Catalog*, this Web site provides the full-text of the publications included in the catalog as well as a way to order, for a minimal fee, the printed version of the document. For those unfamiliar, the publications usually are brief guides on consumer issues. Broad categories include cars, computers, children, education, federal programs, food, health, housing, money, small business, travel, and more. The site also includes an online version of the *Consumer Action Handbook*, a 148-page guide that provides leads to direct assistance with consumer problems.

Federal Trade Commission
(http://www.ftc.gov)

The FTC enforces a broad spectrum of consumer protection laws to ensure fair competition in the marketplace. This site provides links to useful information for consumers, but mainly offers information on a larger scale than the individual consumer may need. However, one may register a complaint with the FTC using the online complaint form. One unique feature of the FTC site is the Registered Identification Number (RN) lookup. From the site, a registered identification number is a number issued by the Federal Trade Commission, upon request, to a business residing in the U.S. that is engaged in the manufacture, importing, distribution, or sale of textile, wool, or fur products. Such businesses are not required to have RNs. They may, however, use the RN in place of a name on the label or tag that is required to be affixed to these products. Take a look on the tag of your favorite shirt and you are likely to see the RN number listed. Search the RN database and find out who manufactured that garment.

Find It! Consumer (Washington State)
(http://finditconsumer.wa.gov)

Find It! Consumer is a search engine of more than 100 consumer related Web sites. A searcher can limit to Washington State or search sites of national interest. One may also browse by topic and see a list of top searches. Search results are ranked by relevancy. This site is a joint project with select government agencies of Washington State and the State Library.

Public Citizen
(http://www.citizen.org)

Ralph Nader founded the Public Citizen in 1971 as a consumer advocacy organization dedicated to represent consumer interests in Congress, the executive and legislative branches of government. This site allows one to track legislation important to consumers, contact elected representatives and take action on issues considered important to the organization. The national divisions of Public Citizen provide links and advocacy information in their areas of concern. These divisions include auto safety, Congress watch, critical mass energy and environment program, global trade watch, and the litigation group. As a political group, users may not agree with positions taken by the Public Citizen.

Privacy Rights Clearinghouse
(http://www.privacyrights.org)

The PRC is a nonprofit consumer advocacy organization founded in 1992 at the University of San Diego Center for Public Interest Law. The site includes over thirty "Fact Sheets" that provide sensible tips on protecting personal privacy and Web links to deal with specific problems. Areas covered include Internet privacy, identity theft, workplace privacy, email security, telemarketing, junk mail, and financial privacy.

Direct Marketing Association
(http://www.the-dma.org)

While not a consumer advocacy site, the DMA site provides an example of useful consumer information in a site dedicated to increasing commerce. Members of the Direct Marketing Association are responsible for sending most of the junk mail, national telemarketing calls and national email solicitations. Knowing that many consumers do not wish to receive these mass mailings and telephone calls, the DMA provides a method to have a name removed from the mass marketing lists of its member organizations and businesses. The page at the following address (http://www.the-dma.org/consumers/consumerassistance.html) provides step-by-step instructions on how to remove a name from mailing, telemarketing, and e-mail lists. This site also provides an interesting perspective on the scope of direct marketing in the U.S.

PRODUCT/SERVICE EVALUATION AND OPINION

Consumer Reports
(http://www.consumerreports.org)

CR, the most well known source of consumer product and service reviews, also includes articles on consumer advocacy and issues. The Consumers Union started the magazine in 1936 with the stated mission to test products, inform the public and protect consumers. The Consumer's Union accepts no outside advertising and supports itself on print and online subscriptions to *Consumer Reports* and related publications, and through noncommercial donations, grants and fees. The online *Consumer Reports* costs $4.95 monthly or $26 annually. A price break is given for print subscribers. Although not free, the reputation of *Consumer Reports* magazine warrants inclusion in any list of consumer information Web sites. The site is well organized and searchable by broad topic or keyword. Reports are included for about the last four years.

Consumer Guide
(http://www.consumerguide.com)

Consumer Guide magazine has been published for thirty years and its "Best Buy" and "Recommended" designations are well known to consumers. The site is searchable by broad subject, brand name and keyword. The product reviews are understandable, but often times the editor's review criteria are not explained which questions the authority of the reviews. This site does accept outside advertising.

Epinions.com
(http://www.epinions.com)

Here is a site where the consumer rules. Epinions.com collects actual owner reviews of over two million products, claims the Web site. The site maintains about one million reviews, which means that almost one half of the available products are not reviewed. Anyone can contribute a review either positive or negative, and the Epinions.com editors provides as much information as possible about the reviewer in order to assure a level of authority. Users then rate the reviews for helpfulness, which allows Epinions.com to place the most helpful reviews at the top of a results list. Epinions.com blurs the lines between product reviews and commerce by providing a best prices list of online retailers, but the practice of ranking actual owner reviews works well. This site does accept outside advertising.

Consumersearch.com
(http://www.consumersearch.com)

This site takes a different approach than most product review sites, and the results are top notch. Instead of reviewing products, Consumersearch. com ranks and reviews the reviewers. For a given product, a user will likely find an analysis of the reviews by *Consumer Reports, Consumer Guide* and other online or print publications. The site covers the full spectrum of consumer products, and includes fast facts, where to buy information and the full story on the reviews. The site does accept outside advertising.

What'sTheBest.net
(http://www.whatsthebest.net)

Started in 1998 by a group of management consultants from Straight Path Management, What's The Best began with one product review on lawn mowers. They have since expanded to forty-nine different products. Each product review provides advice on how to shop for the product, reviews of specific items, and a reader's forum where consumers can ask for advice from other product owners and share their own experiences. The site claims to be unaffiliated with any commercial interests and their reviews are based on their own experience and research. What's The Best contains hard to find buying guides like mattresses, motorcycles, hot tubs, and hair loss remedies in addition to more standard products like kitchen appliances and home electronics. This site does accept outside advertising.

ConsumerReview.com
(http://www.consumerreview.com)

This site primarily reviews sporting goods and consumer electronics. The executives of ConsumerReview.com have designed "product communities" which provide user submitted reviews and comments with links to experts. The review content from ConsumerReview.com has been sold to other sites including eBay and iWon.com. Product communities include audio, auto, videogames, mountain and road biking, outdoor products, and others. The site does accept advertising.

A Guide to the Best Demography Web Sources

Peter Linberger

SUMMARY. This chapter on Web sites for demographic data covers sources from the government, international organizations, and universities and research centers. *[Article copies available for a fee from The Haworth Document Delivery Service: 1-800-HAWORTH. E-mail address: <docdelivery@haworth press.com> Website: <http://www.HaworthPress.com> © 2002 by The Haworth Press, Inc. All rights reserved.]*

KEYWORDS. Demography, demographics, Web sites

INTRODUCTION

Demography can be defined as the study of human populations. Demographic information includes data on births, deaths, age, race, income, education, occupation, and distribution. According to Pol, demography and demographics are terms used interchangeably; although they do not really mean the same thing. He goes on to say "demographics is translated as static characteristics of a population such as average or median family income. These data are used to describe markets or settings and have intuitive appeal because it is known that buy-

Peter Linberger is Business Librarian, The University of Akron (E-mail: pl@uakron.edu).

[Haworth co-indexing entry note]: "A Guide to the Best Demography Web Sources." Linberger, Peter. Co-published simultaneously in *Journal of Business & Finance Librarianship* (The Haworth Information Press, an imprint of The Haworth Press, Inc.) Vol. 8. No. 2, 2002, pp. 103-116; and: *The Core Business Web: A Guide to Key Information Resources* (ed: Gary W. White) The Haworth Information Press, an imprint of The Haworth Press. Inc.. 2003, pp. 103-116. Single or multiple copies of this article are available for a fee from The Haworth Document Delivery Service [1-800-HAWORTH, 9:00 a.m. - 5:00 p.m. (EST). E-mail address: docdelivery@haworthpress.com].

10.1300/J109v08n02_11

ing patterns, for example, vary from one demographically defined group to another. The demographic perspective, however, emphasizes a more in-depth understanding of the connection between demographic characteristics and behavior. That is, demographic perspective connects ongoing demographic changes such as increase in population size with continued alterations in the business environment. Demography, or population study, provides understanding of the population processes, for example, why birth rates fluctuate or why people move."[1]

The use of demographic data and methods in business planning has a relatively long history. As business strategy in general, marketing in particular, began to move away from a mass-market approach to new systems of segmenting and targeting populations during the 1960s, demographic data proved useful in the identification of distinct market segments.[2] Demographic methods, data, and theory have been used primarily in marketing for site analysis, market area assessment, sales forecasting, target marketing, advertising, strategic planning, as well as new product introduction.

Traditionally, demographic information is gathered by various government agencies, or from market research surveys and reports. Today, social scientists, managers, and marketers are turning to the Internet to access demographic data. In addition to official government Web sites, other institutions, organizations, and individuals are providing Web access to various data. Having this data available and easily accessible can lead to better decision-making, an advantage in the competitive business world.

This article lists and describes Web sites that contain demographic data, along with sources of information to assist in demographic research. Criteria for inclusion included the authority of the author; the quantity of information and data; organization of information; ease of use; and currency. In addition to the Web sites given here, it should be noted that commercial sites are available for demographic information. Some sites provide free data, and all provide products or generation of specific reports for users for a fee (www.esribis.com; www.connect. claritas.com; www.easidemographics.com).

Census and Demographics, Mansfield University
(http://www.mnsfld.edu/depts/lib/census.html)

This is probably one of the best Web resources for demographic research and a good place to start when searching for information due to the large number of links made available. Most of the listed sites are annotated and are arranged in alphabetical order in the following categories:

"Census 2000"; "Databases and Data"; "Demographic Miscellany" (non-data reference sources); "Economic Data"; "International Statistics"; "Local Data"; "Pennsylvania Data"; and "Statistical Resources Pathfinder." The site begins with a "Starting Points" section which provides links to mega-sites such as American Factfinder, Government Information Sharing Project, University of Michigan's Statistical Resources on the Web and the U.S. Bureau of the Census Homepage. The concise, well-written, and evaluative annotations can help users in determining which Web sources to consult and may help users narrow down their search from the numerous sources available. Other links from this site include various Census Bureau pages, *County and City Data Book*, *Statistical Abstract of the United States*, economic census data, historical data, international data, a glossary, and links to state data centers. The large number of sites included, along with the annotations, makes this site one of the best for finding demographic information.

CIESIN–Center for International Earth Science Information Network
(http://www.ciesin.org)

CIESIN–U.S. Demography Home Page
(http://www.ciesin.columbia.edu/datasets/us-demog/us-demog-home.html)

CIESIN–Socioeconomic Data and Applications Center
(http://sedac.ciesin.columbia.edu)

CIESIN's mission is to "provide access to and enhance the use of information worldwide, advancing understanding of human interactions in the environment and serving the needs of science and public and private decision-making." Established in 1989 as an independent non-government organization, CIESIN is currently a part of Columbia University's Earth Institute and continues "to focus on applying state-of-the-art information technology to pressing interdisciplinary data, information, and research problems related to human interactions in the environment." From the "Data & Information" section, users can browse, by subject, all data and information products and resources developed by CIESIN and CIESIN projects indexed by thematic area; access data conversion tools, database query applications, and online mapping tools; download data free of charge from FTP servers; access metadata catalogs numerous data centers, government and international organizations.

The "U.S. Demography Home Page" contains a collection of applications and detailed descriptions of various data sources. It also identifies and describes sources of demographic information and provides links to national data resources, online supporting documentation, and extraction tools for data access. These resources include *Current Population Survey*, Economic Census data, *County and City Data Book*, *Statistical Abstract of the United States*, *County Business Patterns*, and STF3A Census data.

The "SEDAC" (Socioeconomic Data and Applications Center) gateway provides links to various data resources such as the Global Population Database and U.S. Census data. The "Demographic Data Viewer," a unique feature of this site, allows for interactive mapping of U.S. Census data at various geographic levels. Users can also access the attribute data once the map has been created online. Users can map and view 1990 census data at the regional, state, county, census tract, and block level. Generated maps can be viewed and downloaded in a number of formats including ASCII, Excel, dBase, and SPSS Portable. Hopefully, the 2000 census data will soon be available from this site. This is a good place to find what data is available, for accessing data, and for generating thematic maps.

Current Population Statistics
(http://www.bls.census.gov/cps/cpsmain.htm)

The Current Population Survey (CPS), conducted by the Bureau of the Census for the Bureau of Labor Statistics, is a primary source of information for the U.S. labor force. The Bureau conducts monthly surveys of approximately 50,000 households. Estimates obtained from the samples include employment, unemployment, earnings, and hours of work. These figures are available by demographic characteristics such as age, sex, race, and by occupation, industry, and class of worker. From the "Data" section users can choose from a number of publications including *Basic Monthly Survey, Annual Demographic Survey*, and supplemental reports such as *Computer Ownership, Work Schedules*, and *Employee Tenure*. Searching by keyword is available across publications and documentation; however, data searching is done by using FERRET (Federal Electronic Research and Review Extraction Tool). Once data is chosen at the variable level, custom data tables are created then sent via e-mail to users. Links to other labor and related surveys are provided under the Related Surveys section. This is a good source for those interested in examining characteristics of the U.S. labor force.

Data on the Net, University of California, San Diego
(http://odwin.ucsd.edu/idata/)

Over 800 Internet sites dealing with social science statistical data, data catalogs, data libraries and social science gateways are available from this site from the University of California, San Diego. Users can conveniently browse through the extensive listing of Web sites in the following categories: "Data," "Data Archives," "Searchable Catalogs of Data," and "Distributors and Vendors of Data." The "Data" category alone lists over 400 sites of numeric data. The Web sources within each category are arranged in alphabetical order and most have detailed annotations. New and updated sources are available under a separate category. Keyword searching across the database is available and that can be a great advantage for users not knowing which category to choose. For example, a search for "religion" will produce a list of Web resources containing religion statistics. These include the American Religion Data Archive (Purdue University), and the International Data Base from the U.S. Census Bureau International Programs Center. And finally, the "Social Science Gateways" category provides an extensive, annotated list of sites covering both U.S. and international social science related data. The extensive collection of Web links, the annotations, and the keyword searching capability, make this site an excellent research tool for accessing demographic data.

FedStats
(http://www.fedstats.gov)

This site, developed by the Federal Interagency Council on Statistical Policy, provides easy access to a full range of statistics produced by over seventy U.S. government agencies. Federal agencies reporting expenditures of at least $500,000 are included. Users can access statistical data from various government Web sites by topic, program/subject area, geographic area, keyword, and can also choose specific data listed under each agency thereby saving time and bypassing the agency's main page. Information and summaries of major statistical programs and data available include the areas of agriculture, education, energy, environment, health, income, labor, safety, and transportation. All of the statistical information available through FedStats is maintained and updated solely by Federal agencies on their own Web servers. The agencies reporting demographic related data include the Bureau of the Census, Agency for International Development, Office of Population

Affairs, Department of Housing and Urban Development, and the Social Security Administration. From the "Statistical Reference Shelf" section, users can access the full text of the *Statistical Abstract of the United States, State and Metropolitan Area Data Book, Health United States, Digest of Education Statistics,* and the *Report on the American Workforce.* The MapStats section of this site allows users to access a profile of a state, county, Federal judicial district, or congressional district. This is a fairly comprehensive and easy-to-use site for accessing demographic information.

GEOSTAT: Geospatial and Statistical Data Center, University of Virginia Library
(http://fisher.lib.virginia.edu)

According to their home page, GEOSTAT "supports a wide range of academic and scholarly activities through access to extensive collections of numeric and geospatial data files; computing facilities and software for data manipulation, research, and instruction; and a suite of Internet-accessible data extraction tools." There is much information available from this site; however, the most useful for researching demographics are the links to the U.S. Census page, ICPSR page, CIESIN's page, *County Business Patterns* data, electronic versions of the *County and City Data Book,* and links to some of the other sites covered in this article. While not as comprehensive as some, this site is valuable for providing access to the *County and City Data Book* data, and for anyone needing to obtain geospatial information or data for mapping purposes.

Government Information Sharing Project, Oregon State University
(http://govinfo.kerr.orst.edu)

This Oregon State University site provides easy access to demographic, educational, and economic data from various U.S. federal government agencies. From the Demographic section of the site, users can access statistics from USA Counties 1998, 1990 Census of Population and Housing, Population Estimates by Age, Sex, and Race 1990-1998, and Equal Employment Opportunity File, 1990. Users can also select geographic regions from a map or scroll down menu, and then select sets of data for display. Data can be provided at the national, state, county, metropolitan area, city, town, or place level. The "Other Government Web Sites" section provides access to government resources by subject and also gives a listing of major sites. A note of the home page alerts users that "some data may not be available . . . we are creating a new, more powerful version of this service, please bear with us." Data from the most recent U.S. Census is not yet available, and the new and more powerful version of the site will most likely include year 2000 statistics. All of the information provided on this site can be found elsewhere on the Web; however, the Government Information Sharing Project is an example of a user-friendly site, and a good place to see some of the types of demographic data that are available. Until this site is updated, researchers will have to look elsewhere for recent demographic data (i.e., 2000 Census).

ICPSR–Inter-University Consortium for Political and Social Research
(http://www.icpsr.umich.edu)

The Inter-University Consortium for Political and Social Research (ICPSR), based at University of Michigan's Institute for Social Research, is a membership-based, not-for-profit organization serving colleges and universities in the U.S. and abroad. It is the largest repository of machine-readable data in the world. ICPSR contains many resources for researchers in the social and political sciences, but is best known for its large archive of data files. Users can browse the files by broad categories, or can search using a basic search engine. Results are generally provided by tables with the study title and date, principal investigator, and study number. Links are provided for users to read the abstract or to retrieve the dataset. ICPSR is normally available to members of registered institutions, however non-affiliated individuals can contact ICPSR for access information. The site is valuable for anyone trying to find statistical information and also to determine what studies have been done on a given topic.

Internet Crossroads in the Social Sciences
(http://dpls.dacc.wisc.edu/newcrossroads/index.asp)

The Data and Program Library Service (DPLS) of the University of Wisconsin at Madison has developed a site that provides access to over 650 annotated links to data-related Internet resources. Categories are listed in boxes, a nice user-friendly feature, and include these four categories: "U.S. Government Links"; "U.S. Non-Government Links"; "International Government Links"; and "International Non-Governmental Links." Information is subdivided further within each box into "General," "Economic/Labor," "Education," "Geographic/Historical," "Political," and "Sociological/Demographic" categories. Direct links are provided to widely used sites such as Census Bureau, FEDSTATS, CIESIN, ICPSR, and Council for European Social Science Data Archives (CESSDA). Keyword searching is also available. Another nice feature is the availability of dataset user guides such as the *United Nations Statistical Yearbook* User Guide, and other resource guides to census data, international data, and a FAQ section. This is another well organized, and worthwhile site for finding demographic information.

Internet Resources for Demographers
(www.access4cheap.com/~tdgryn/demog.html)

Thomas Gryn of the Ohio State University's Department of Sociology has assembled a site with pertinent links to resources in demography. Links are assorted into six categories: "North American Demography"; "International Demography"; "General Demography"; "Health"; "Geography"; and "Other Link Collections." Links to popular Internet sites such as the U.S. Census Bureau, CIESIN, Current Population Survey, United Nations, and other demographic-related megasites are all available, some including brief annotations. A separate section lists Census 2000 sites as well as a site describing 2000 data access and usage. Although this site is not a comprehensive listing of demographic resources, it does cover all the basic and most popular sites.

Penn State Population Research Institute, Population and Demography Information
(http://www.pop.psu.edu/Demography/demography.htm)

According to the mission statement posted on the Penn State Population Research Institute's site, "the institute encourages, organizes, and supports innovative research and training in the population sciences." This well organized site provides a large number of links dealing with demography and begins with an alphabetical listing of Association of Population Centers. These sites often provide links to other demographic resources. The categories continue with the "North American Demographic, Population, and Social Science Data Servers" section, which include links to CIESIN, and other academic population and data centers. Other links are categorized and listed in the following categories: "U.S. Census and Government"; "Extractable Datasets on the Web"; "International Data Sources"; "Country Studies"; "Professional Associations"; and "Related Fields" such as anthropology, economics, education, geography, health, and sociology. Users also have the option of searching for data by using the search function. Although the links provided are not annotated, the arrangement and completeness makes this site a valuable tool for accessing demographic information.

PopNet
(http://www.popnet.org)

PopNet is produced and maintained by the Population Reference Bureau with funding and assistance from the U.S. Agency for International Development. Founded in 1929, the Population Reference Bureau is the leader in providing timely and objective information on U.S. and international population trends and their implications. "PopNet presents information on population topics such as demographic statistics, economics, education, environment, gender, policy, and reproductive health. Its resources include Web sites produced by government and international organizations, non-governmental organizations, university centers, associations, and listservs." In addition to browsing by category, users can also find relevant data and information by keyword searching, and listings by topic, by region, and by type of information including graphs, maps, datasheets, lesson plans, teacher guides, and newsletters. Links to the various sites include annotations. From the "Datafinder" section of the site, users can choose selected population and health variables by region, country, and data for the U.S. by state. Data for the U.S. comes from the Population Reference Bureau's 2000 United States Population Data Sheet. This is a good source for finding demographic information by topic for U.S. and the world.

Population Studies Center, PSC, University of Michigan
(http://www.psc.isr.umich.edu)

Established in 1961, the Population Studies Center (PSC) at the University of Michigan is one of the oldest population centers in the United States. "The PSC is comprised of independent researchers who pursue their own agendas with the support of the PSC cores." A large portfolio of both domestic and international research is supported by the Center. Key areas of demographic research are grouped into several major areas: "Fertility, Family Planning, Health and Sexual Behavior"; "Marriage, Family, Children, and Links Between Generations"; "Inequality, Social Mobility, Race, and Ethnicity"; "Aging and Disability"; "Education and Training." Users can access the Center's publications by keyword or author searching. From the "Data Archive and Data Support" section of this site, users can choose "Data Home Pages Available on the Internet." Links to various demographic data sites are accessible for both U.S. and international researchers. From the "Library" section, users can access more demography sites by choosing "Demography Resources by Subject." Direct links to U.S. Census data, National Institute of Health data, and population centers are made available. Users can also search for resources by format such as demographic agencies, population centers, country statistics, journals/newspapers, or by subjects such as aging, demography, fertility, immigration, ethnicity, health, and economics and poverty. Links to Web sites are not annotated, but the quantity, arrangement, and searching capabilities make this site a valuable resource for demography and population research.

Statistical Resources on the Web, University of Michigan Documents Center
(http://www.lib.umich.edu/govdocs/statsnew.html)

This site, developed and maintained by the University of Michigan's Document Center, is a fairly comprehensive and very well organized resource for all sorts of data. Web resources are arranged into twenty-four broad categories, which include demographics, health, labor, housing, economics, cost of living, foreign trade, energy, environment, and sociology. Each category has its own box and icon making this a very user-friendly site. Within each category are links to statistical sites arranged alphabetically by title and most links are annotated which helps users quickly evaluate content. Links found in the "Demographics" category are arranged by "types" of data and include Census 2000 data, various search engines and mega-sites for demographics, geography and mapping, demographic profiles, access to and description of census summary tape files, 1990 census information and data, and historical census data. The site also includes a sidebar with a main index; an alphabetical list of over 100 subjects such as abortion, ancestry, census, population, marital status, literacy, etc. A click on one of these subjects will take users directly to links within one of the twenty-four categories. This is one of the best places for finding demographic information due to its ease of use and exhaustive list of data links. Users will understand why this site has won a number of Web awards once they begin to access this site.

Statistics.com
(http://www.statistics.com)

The home page to this site has a similar look to the Yahoo! home page, in that it gives a list of categories from which users can choose. The categories, however, are all listings and links to statistical information. These categories include "Agriculture," "Business," "Crime," "Education," "Health," "Sports," and "Transportation." The category for demographics is found under "Market Research & Demographics," and within this category users can choose from business, geography, homes, language, population, and religions. Choosing the "population" link gives users the choice of connecting to eighty-six Web sites relating to population information and statistics. Most of these sites are official census Web sites for various regions and nations of the world. This site also allows for keyword searching; a definite asset when searching for any information. A link to a statistical terms and glossary dictionary is also provided. A unique feature to this site is the free downloadable software for statistical analysis, and the discussion board that is available to users of this site. This is a good site to consult for international data, and for those interested in improving their knowledge and understanding of statistical methods and analysis.

Statistics and Statistical Graphics Resources
(http://www.math.yorku.ca/SCS/StatResource.html)

"This page provides an annotated, topic-based collection of available resources for statistics, statistical graphics, and computation related to research, data analysis and teaching, now containing over 580 links." This site, created by Michael Friendly of the University of York, not only includes access to statistical data, but also to journals, statistical software packages, data visualization and statistical graphics resources, online statistical courses, and other analysis tools. The "Data" section provides links to Web sites such as ICPSR, Bureau of Justice, and other social science data. The real value of this site is not the availability of demographic data, although some is available, but the accessibility of an extensive list of statistical analysis resource tools valuable to researchers in a variety of disciplines.

United Nations Statistics Division
(http://www.un.org/Depts/unsd/statdiv.htm)

The United Nations gathers and disseminates demographic data in a number of categories. Data sources and links are provided under the following categories: "Demographic and Social Statistics"; "Statistical Databases On-Line"; and "National Data Sources and Links." The most useful section for researchers interested in finding international data is the "National Data Sources and Links." Here, users can link to official Web pages of national statistical agencies by country, and to Web pages of international statistical organizations. Information from various UN publications on statistics, statistical methods, international trade, demography and population, social indicators, energy, environments, and human settlements are given.

U.S. Census Bureau
(http://www.census.gov)

No guide to demographic Web sources would be complete without the inclusion of the United States Bureau of the Census home page. The 2000 data can be accessed as soon as it is tabulated and users have a number of search options available. To access data by geography, users can use "American FactFinder" and obtain maps and tables of year 2000 data for all geographies down to the block level. Keyword searching is also available for accessing data and census publications. Summaries of the most requested data for individual states and counties are also available. In addition to the "American FactFinder" search engine, users have access to the following interactive tools to find information: "CenStats"; "MapStats"; "QuickFacts"; "TIGER Map Service"; "US Gazetteer"; "1990 Census Lookup"; "Data Extraction System (DES)"; and "Ferret Data." Links to an overview of the 2000 Census, summary files, news releases, data release schedule, questionnaires, briefs and special reports, geographic and mapping products information, and historical census data are found under the "Your new Gateway to Census 2000" section of the home page. This site best serves researchers wanting the most recent Census data, projection data, or information about the Census.

U.S. Census International Programs Center (IPC)
(http://www.census.gov/ftp/pub/ipc/www/)

This site, produced by the U.S. Bureau of the Census, provides access to a wide variety of international demographic data. The most useful section for demographic research and data is the "International Data Base" or IDB. The IDB is a source of demographic and socio-economic statistics for 227 countries and areas of the world. The IDB combines data from country sources with the IPC's estimates and projections to provide information from as far back as 1950 and as far ahead as 2050. Amount of information by country varies. Major types of data available include: population by age and sex; fertility; migration; ethnicity; religion; language; literacy; labor force; income; and households. Sources of the data come from the U.S. Bureau of the Census and from official country and national statistics offices. Direct links to these offices is available from an alphabetical list of nations.

World-Wide Web Virtual Library,
Demography and Population Studies
(http://demography.anu.edu.au/VirtualLibrary)

Provided by the Demography Program of the Australian National University, this site keeps track of leading information in the field of demography, and provides an extensive, up-to-date list of Web resources. The site is divided into six categories: "Associated Virtual Libraries"; "Census and Data Servers"; "Electronic Journals"; "Historical Demography Resources"; "Demography and Population Conferences"; "Other Demographic and Population Servers"; "Electronic Mailing Lists"; and "Other WWW Servers of Use to Demographers." Links to data centers, servers, population centers, research institutes, archives, journals, academic programs and departments, and government institutions are all available from these categories. There is no keyword searching or annotations to resources, but the most important links are listed. This site is not only useful for finding data, but also valuable for population studies, immigration, geography, sociology, and multicultural studies. Essential for researchers who want to find a comprehensive look at demographic information on the Web.

World Wide Web Virtual Library: Statistics
(http://www.stat.ufl.edu/vlib/statistics.html)

This site from the University of Florida's Department of Statistics includes an extensive list of links to numerous departments and schools of statistics. While on the surface this would not seem useful for finding demographic data, the home pages of these institutes often include a vast collection of links to this type of information. The "Statistical Archive and Resources" section to this site provides links to popular statistics sites such as the U.S. Bureau of the Census, U.S. Bureau of Labor Statistics, and Department of Commerce. Listed sources are international in scope. The "Statistical Software Vendors and Software FAQs" section links users to a large number of vendors and information on statistical methods and analysis. The large collection of links to statistics departments and schools worldwide might seem to be overwhelming at first, but demographic researchers should consult this exhaustive list of resources for both domestic and international demographic information.

White House Briefing Room
(http://www.whitehouse.gov/news/fsbr.html)

The White House Briefing Room is a good source for locating popular economic and demographic information from various federal government agencies. This site contains three major sections: "Economic Statistics Briefing Room (ESBR)"; "Social Statistics Briefing Room (SSBR)"; and "Federal Interagency Council on Statistical Policy" (FEDSTATS). The "SSBR Demography" category is divided into four sections: Crime; Demography; Education; and Health Statistics. Data on income, poverty, housing characteristics, school dropout rates, and college enrollment can be found. Even though the data tables provided are general and not always available by geographic region, links to the home pages of the issuing agency is available. The last section, "FEDSTATS," is probably the most useful as this would put users directly in the FEDSTATS search page.

NOTES

1. Pol, L. G. (1987). *Business Demography: A Guide and Reference for Business Planners and Marketers.* Westport, CT: Quorum Books.

2. Pol, L. G. & Thomas, R. K. (1997). *Demography for Business Decision Making.* Westport, CT: Quorum Books.

Best of the Web in Economics

Kristi Jensen

SUMMARY. The economics chapter covers key resources from government, international, and working papers sites. There are also sections on reference sites and collections of economics links. *[Article copies available for a fee from The Haworth Document Delivery Service: 1-800-HAWORTH. E-mail address: <docdelivery@haworthpress.com> Website: <http://www.HaworthPress.com> © 2003 by The Haworth Press, Inc. All rights reserved.]*

KEYWORDS. Economics, Web sites

INTRODUCTION:
ECONOMICS INFORMATION AND THE INTERNET

Government Data and Reports

The Internet provides an ideal environment for the distribution of economics information for several reasons. First, and perhaps most importantly, government agencies produce much of the economics information and have traditionally, at least in the United States, made it freely available to the public. In the past, there was considerable delay in the distribution of this information in print publications. With the advent of the Internet, government information can now be easily distributed as soon as agencies choose to make it available. Another advantage

---

Kristi Jensen is Earth Sciences Librarian, The Pennsylvania State University (E-mail: kjensen@psu.edu).

[Haworth co-indexing entry note]: "Best of the Web in Economics." Jensen, Kristi. Co-published simultaneously in *Journal of Business & Finance Librarianship* (The Haworth Information Press, an imprint of The Haworth Press, Inc.) Vol. 8, No. 3/4, 2003, pp. 117-131; and: *The Core Business Web: A Guide to Key Information Resources* (ed: Gary W. White) The Haworth Information Press, an imprint of The Haworth Press, Inc., 2003, pp. 117-131. Single or multiple copies of this article are available for a fee from The Haworth Document Delivery Service [1-800-HAWORTH, 9:00 a.m. - 5:00 p.m. (EST). E-mail address: docdelivery@haworthpress.com].

10.1300/J109v08n03_01

of the Web for the distribution of government information relates to the dissemination of data and statistics. The Web environment allows agencies to provide data in a downloadable digital format, thereby enabling users to import and manipulate data in various software programs. Not only can some of the most important economics information be provided in a more timely fashion; it can also be found in a more useful format than in the past.

Working Papers

A second reason for the prevalence of economics information on the Web relates to one of the most popular means of distributing information related to current research in economics, the working paper. Prior to the advent of an extensive networked environment, information about working papers was included in the same print, and later CD-ROM, resources responsible for notifying researchers about recent articles and papers in this field. After identifying papers of interest, researchers next had to contact the writer or distributing organization in order to access a copy. The networked environment of the Internet has provided for the distribution of information about these papers via several online databases and numerous organizational Web sites. Furthermore, the Internet environment allows researchers to directly download many online economics papers.

Reference Resources

The Internet also provides a venue for the dissemination of economics information through traditional "reference resources," including economics glossaries, statistical abstracts, and biographical resources. As with any topic, the Web is an excellent location to provide access to historical information; a great deal of historical information is provided on the Web for both important figures and schools of thought within the field of economics.

Collections of Links

Finally, one of the most important functions of the Web is the ability to link users to other resources by creating collections of links on a particular topic. Since this article is necessarily limited to only a handful of resources, a selection of the best "collections" of economics links is also provided. These "lists of lists" selectively gather the most interesting and important resources together in one location and help users navigate to important economics resources available online.

These four broad categories, Government Data and Reports, Working Papers, Reference Resources, and Collections of Economics Links, provide the framework for the "Best of the Web" resources described in this article. Entries under each category are organized alphabetically by the title of the Web site rather than in order of importance.

Selection Measures: Identifying the "Best"

Due to the plethora of economics Web sites available, choosing only a handful to represent the "best" proved challenging. After reviewing hundreds of sites, nineteen were selected for inclusion. In general, the resources are meant for an academic audience, but they may be of interest to other parties as well. Furthermore, the focus of items selected is on general economics resources rather than those providing information about a specific sub-field or aspect, e.g., agricultural economics, environmental economics, or Victorian economics. Numerous valuable subject specific resources are available; however, those appealing to the broadest possible audience were included here. Besides adhering to these general guidelines, several evaluative measures were utilized to determine the "best" online economics resources.

Substantial Content

First, the resources selected contain a substantial amount of important information. The most important resources were identified not only by an evaluation of the content provided but also by the frequency of referral from various Web resources, especially referral from selective and highly touted resources. Despite the fact that all sites selected include substantial content, they do not necessarily contain the "most" content. Often the resources that allowed users to most easily navigate to useful online economics resources were selective rather than encyclopedic.

Organization

Second, another important measure utilized to evaluate economics Web resources, especially those resources containing collections of links to other resources, was organization. Organizational considerations evaluated included descriptive categories chosen, consistent application of categories, and inclusion of the major or important resources in each category.

Free Content

Third, in most cases, the sites selected provide users access to information freely available via the Web. Although many subscription resources provide valuable economics data and reports, some of the most important sites are freely available to everyone. Rather than describing or reviewing sites some users may not be able to examine, only those resources available to everyone were chosen for this "Best of the Web" list.

Current Content

Fourth, a malaise associated with many Web resources is outdated content or links. Most reputable sites include information about the most recent update or the frequency of updates. Beyond examining sites for this basic update information, link checking software was also utilized in order to determine the percentage of active and functional links for various sites. Only those sites with a small percentage of "bad links" were included here.

Web Functionality–Design and Navigability

Finally, resources were selected that best utilize the functionality of the Web to format and develop the content of their site or resources. Although substantial, reliable content was an important factor, each resource also had to be well designed and easily navigable. Resources consisting of a long list of barely legible items or data were not considered for inclusion. Rather, sites providing easy linking between similar content or data displayed in formats allowing for the immediate interpretation of data were selected. In other words, sites were evaluated not just on the information they provided, but also on how well the online resources functioned in providing access to the information.

BEST OF THE WEB–RESOURCES IN ECONOMICS

U.S. Government Data and Reports

Beige Book
(http://www.federalreserve.gov/FOMC/BeigeBook/2002/)

The Beige Book is an anecdotal report on the state of the U.S. economy provided by the Federal Reserve Board eight times a year. The report is generated based on feedback from "Bank and Branch directors and interviews with key business contacts, economists, market experts, and other sources." A summary for the entire U.S. for various sectors of the economy is provided first; following the summary detailed reports for each of the twelve regions of the Federal Reserve are given. An archive of the reports from 1970 to the present is available at the Federal Reserve Bank of Minneapolis site (http://minneapolisfed.org/bb/index. html).

United States Bureau of Economic Analysis
(http://www.bea.gov/)

The United States Bureau of Economic Analysis (BEA) provides both gross domestic product (GDP) and economics account data related to the U.S. economy. The BEA site provides access to a wealth of current and historical online information.

First, National Income and Products Accounts Data (NIPA) can be accessed from a number of entry points: an alphabetical keyword index of products and industries; a list of all sections and tables included in the National Accounts Data; a list of the most frequently requested tables; or a list of selected NIPA tables. Once a section or product has been selected, utilizing the enhanced data viewer provides data in a table format for a number of years for each variable. Users can choose particular years of coverage, ranging from 1929 to the present, and refresh the table to reflect their changes. Data can be displayed as annual or quarterly summaries for most variables, although monthly summaries are provided in some instances. Researchers can also download comma separated data for selected years or for all available years. Advanced downloading options allow users to choose Excel formatted files or comma separated values; either format can also be downloaded in a zipped format if desired.

Another key resource on the BEA site is the Regional Accounts data providing state and local area economic information. Data can be accessed, viewed and downloaded in the same manner as the National Accounts Data. If the interface at the BEA is not to your liking, feel free to access the same data at the Regional Economic Information System available at the University of Virginia (http://fisher.lib.virginia.edu/reis/) or at Oregon State University (http://govinfo.kerr.orst.edu/reis-stateis.html).

Finally, other valuable resources can be accessed on the BEA site as well. The U.S. International Transactions Accounts provide data related to transactions between U.S. and foreign residents. Areas covered range from import and export of goods to direct or portfolio investments. The monthly publication, *Survey of Current Business*, is also published online and contains recent updates of data, reports and analysis articles.

United States Bureau of Labor Statistics
(http://www.bls.gov/home.htm)

The United States Bureau of Labor Statistics (BLS) Web site contains an overwhelming amount of economic information. The site is divided into major sections, including "Inflation and Consumer Spending," "Employment and Unemployment," and "Wage, Earnings and Benefits." Users can link to a description or overview of each area or link directly to a sub-section of interest. For example, from the main page, users can link to an overview of the "Inflation and Consumer Spending" section, including a description of each of the areas contained therein, or jump directly to the "Consumer Price Index" information included in this section.

Data and information is also summarized in specialized resources like the "Economy at a Glance" tables. Current data is displayed for a number of variables for a particular geographic location or industry. However, historical data can also be displayed and reformatted based on user preferences. Flat files containing the data can also be accessed and saved from the BLS Data page.

In addition to these valuable data resources, the BLS site contains other important information sources. Subscribers to the print journals produced by the BLS, including the *Monthly Labor Review* and *Occupational Outlook*, can access the online versions and archives of these resources via the BLS site. A variety of BLS research and discussion papers can be easily browsed or searched directly from this resource. Finally, links to recent BLS economic news releases are also provided.

United States Economic Census
(http://www.census.gov/epcd/www/econ97.html)

The United States Economic Census provides a profile of the U.S. economy every five years with well over 1000 reports on specific industries and areas. Despite the fact that reports are given for different geographic areas, including states, counties, and metropolitan areas, the most detailed information is provided for the U.S. as a whole.

The most recent Economic Census data from 1997 is available online for various economic sectors, for example, mining or manufacturing, and in some cases for all sectors combined. All reports for a particular state can also be easily located from the census site utilizing a simple drop down box. Among the most recent information released by the economic census is a section allowing users to access information based on a particular zip code. Reports are downloadable in PDF format and, and therefore can be viewed immediately from any location. One of the few disadvantages of this site is the lack of downloadable data for use in various software programs.

Economic Report of the President
(http://w3.access.gpo.gov/eop/)

Prepared on an annual basis, this report on the state of the economy is prepared by the Executive Branch for the U.S. Congress. Details on the current administration's economic programs and a review of the economy's past performance and outlook are provided. The annual report of the Council of Economic Advisers is also included. Two-thirds of the *Report* is narrative; the remaining third consists of 100 statistical tables covering the major economic indicators, with some series going back to 1929.

Online access to this report allows users to view the entire report in PDF format for any year since 1995. Files containing the statistics from Appendix B of the report are also available from 1997 to the present. All tables can be downloaded in a zipped file or individual tables can be downloaded in a spreadsheet format; the spreadsheet format varies depending on the year of the report. The full-text contents of the *Report* from 1996 forward may also be searched for particular words and phrases.

Federal Deposit Insurance Corporation
Regional Economic Conditions (RECON)
(http://www2.fdic.gov/recon/)

Originally designed to assist the Federal Deposit Insurance Corporation in the analysis of financial risk for institutions in various geographic locations, RECON now allows any user to depict economic conditions for several different geographic levels, including state, county or metropolitan statistical area (MSA). RECON provides access to data for over twenty-four economic variables in three categories: "Industry Activity"; "Employment and Income"; and "Real Estate Activity." Data, however, is not available for every variable at every geographic level.

RECON has utilized the Web to produce a simple interface providing access to maps, charts, and tables. In some cases more than one output format is provided for the same data. Navigation is based on geographic areas. A drop down box allows users to choose a particular state leading to a display of available statewide data; if statewide data is not of interest, users can utilize one of two drop down boxes to move forward to county overviews or particular MSA data. Viewing charts or tables for one of twenty economic variables is as easy as clicking on the links provided within the list of available data. A "shopping cart" option allows users to select data to view and print together at the end of their RECON session. Users can also access a search interface to focus their search.

United States Congress–Economic Indicators
(http://www.access.gpo.gov/congress/eibrowse/broecind.html)

Economic Indicators, a monthly publication bringing together a wide array of economic data from various U.S. government agencies, is produced for the Joint Economic Committee of Congress by the Council of Economic Advisors. Online reports are available from 1998 to the present. The report includes tables of both current and historic data from numerous government agencies and covers all aspects of the U.S. economy. A report can be viewed in its entirety or one page at a time in either PDF or text format.

INTERNATIONAL DATA

Penn World Table
(http://pwt.econ.upenn.edu/)

The Penn World Table provides access to twenty-nine economic data variables for approximately fifty countries. Historic data is provided for the time period of 1950-1992. It is important to note, however, that not every variable is available for every country and year. One important enhancement provided by the Penn World Table is expenditure entries "denominated in a common set of prices in a common currency so that real quantity comparisons can be made, both between countries and over time."

The Penn World Table data can be accessed from multiple entry points: an alphabetical list of countries; a geographical or regional list of countries; or a list of all variables. Another access alternative, the PWT Online Retrieval Service, allows users to generate more complex queries. This more advanced request form allows users to choose multiple countries and multiple variables, all at the same time. Once a user has selected the variables, countries, and time period a table is generated displaying the requested data. Although manipulable data cannot be downloaded directly, users can download a zipped version of the table to install on a personal computer. Data can then be extracted and exported to various software programs.

Although it is difficult to find one resource to provide country level economic data for the world in the online environment, the Penn World Table provides a great place to get started.

WORKING PAPERS

Although numerous Web sites providing access to economics working papers exist, one of the most important free resources linking researchers to economic papers is included here. The disadvantage of using a working paper consolidator like the resource mentioned below is that there may be a delay between the time the paper is actually available on the organization Web site and the time it appears in the consolidated database. Keep this in mind when searching for working papers and do not hesitate to visit an economics organization or institution's Web site to view the content of their online resources for the most current content.

RePEc (Research Papers in Economics)
(http://repec.org/)

RePEc is a cooperative effort of volunteers from around the world working to "enhance the dissemination of research in economics." The primary work of the volunteers is the creation and maintenance of a database containing information on economics working papers, journal articles and software components. RePEc has an extensive list of highly regarded participating institutions and authors and is organized into several different components allowing users to access all content or a subset of the database.

The complete RePEc database can be accessed from two entry points. IDEAS (http://ideas.uqam.ca/ideas/search.html) and EconPapers (http://econpapers.hhs.se/) both allow users to search and browse the working papers, journal articles, software components, and authors found in the RePEc database. Lists of working papers series, journal titles, software by language, registered authors and participating institutions create a means for browsing, and in some cases downloading, contributed content.

In addition to browsing the RePEc content, users can also search for content on a topic of interest. Both IDEAS and EconPapers provide a search interface allowing users to search within one of the individual sections (working papers, journal articles, software components, or authors) contained within the RePEc database. An advanced search also allows users to perform a search on all sections at the same time.

Additional resources can also be found on the RePEc Web site. NEP (New Economics Working Papers) provides an e-mail alerting service informing subscribers of new additions to the literature within specific sub-fields. WoPEc provides access to only those papers and journal articles available full-text online. BibEc provides information about papers and journal articles exclusively available in a print format. Author contact information is provided to facilitate access to a print copy. Finally WebEc provides information about online economics resources and is described in another section of this article under the "Collection of Links."

REFERENCE RESOURCES

Economics Glossary
(http://bized.ac.uk/glossary/econglos.htm)

A basic economics glossary including over 1,200 entries is provided at the Biz/ed Web site. Biz/ed, a United Kingdom based resource, works to provide access to online business and economics information for students, teachers and lecturers. Two search options allow users to search only the glossary terms or both the terms and the definitions. A browse method for accessing entries is also provided via an alphabetical list of entries.

As well as providing basic definitions of terms, supplemental material is often supplied in the glossary. For example, referrals to related terms and diagrams are provided for many entries. Due to the U.K. origin of this resource, one important anomaly to bear in mind when using this glossary is the fact that discrepancies in spelling may occur, for example, labor may be spelled labour and organization may appear as organisation.

History of Economic Thought
(http://cepa.newschool.edu/het/home.htm)

According to the welcome message found at the History of Economic Thought (HET) site, the primary purpose of this resource is to serve "as a repository of collected links and information on the history of economic thought." HET serves up many major and minor works of historically important economists and also links to other archives containing similar full-text content.

An alphabetical list of economists with their birth and death dates links users to a bibliography of an author's major works and a set of links to outside online resources containing additional information about the person. The bibliography of works contains a link to any on-line full-text materials and also employs links to allow users to easily jump to entries for co-authors as well. In some cases, brief biographical information is provided.

Several other interesting resources are also included on the HET site. Brief essays providing descriptions or explanations of some of the important schools of thought and traditions in the field of economics from ancient times to the present are found in the "Essays and Surveys" section. One of the most important resources available is a collection of Web links allowing users to gain direct access to online archives of economics literature. Finally, links to organizations, journals, and many more online resources related to the history of economics are included on the HET site.

Index of Economic Freedom
(http://www.heritage.org/index/)

The Index of Economic Freedom, provided by the Heritage Group and the Wall Street Journal, provides an economic freedom ranking and an overview of the economic situation in various countries throughout the world. The site provides index data for numerous economics policies including banking, monetary or trade policy, and wages and prices for the most recent year. In addition to the current data and reports for each country, an overall index rating from previous years is provided from 1995 to the present. Rather than viewing data online, users can also download the data in a delimited format allowing easy importing options for various data software programs.

The Index allows users to access data and information utilizing several access tools. The "Simple Search" allows users to view all data sorted alphabetically or by rank. The "Advanced" search interface allows users to access data by selecting countries of interest with a simple click on the alphabetical list provided. Users interested in comparing all countries in a particular region can use the regional list instead of or in addition to the country list. The search results can be sorted alphabetically or numerically based on the index listing for a particular economic policy issue. Search results provide an overall index score and world rank, as well as index data for each policy issue. Clicking on the country name connects users with a brief report supporting the index data. Downloadable PDF versions of the reports allow for easy printing of the information. Besides the advanced search interface, a clickable map also allows users to produce a table of current index data for an individual country or a predefined region.

Nobel e-Museum
(http://www.nobel.se/economics/index.html)

The Nobel e-Museum provides information about the winners of the Bank of Sweden Prize in Economic Sciences in Memory of Alfred Nobel from 1969 to the present. Information on each Laureate might include a transcript or video file of their acceptance speech, photographs from the award ceremony, online videos of interviews, press releases relating to the award, and autobiographical information. The Web has provided a unique opportunity to share information about this historic event.

U.S. Department of State Bureau of Public Affairs Background Notes
(http://www.state.gov/r/pa/bgn/)

The State Department's *Background Notes* provide a wide array of brief information on various countries. The Notes typically contain government, political and economic information, as well as foreign and U.S. relations information for each country. Information is updated as it is received from the regional bureaus of the State Department. The currency of the content on this site varies with the oldest material dating from 1991. A majority of the notes, however, have been updated since 1999. Although the list of countries is extensive, *Background Notes* are not provided for every country in the world.

One of the keys here is the brief economic information for each locale. While some of the economic descriptions are noticeably brief, for example, only four paragraphs for Antigua and Barbuda, others provide more lengthy information related to numerous economic categories, including economic history, foreign investment, monetary, trade, employment and budget. The economic categories described vary depending on the country.

In addition to the textual description of a country's economic situation, don't miss the economic summary near the top of each Note. This section includes numeric information, covering gross domestic product (GDP), per capita income, and agriculture, industry and trade figures. Specific agricultural products and industry types are listed as well as export and import information.

COLLECTIONS OF LINKS

EconData.Net
(http://econdata.net/)

Econdata.Net, a site sponsored by the Economic Data Administration, provides a well-organized access point to 900 regional U.S. economic data resources. Despite the fact that EconData provides access to data freely available from many U.S. government sites, in addition to private and commercial resources, it provides several advantages over accessing the data directly. First, for the novice user, a list of resources covering ten important economics topics, for example, income, employment, and prices, can be found in one concise listing. Resources from various agencies, which cover the same subject area, are easily identified and accessed from one location. Descriptions of the types of data available via each link help searchers save time.

A second advantage provided by EconData is the opportunity to utilize several enhanced resources. Listings of key resources are provided for numerous government statistical gathering agencies. Rather than wading through all of the information available on a particular agency site, EconData provides a direct link to pertinent resources. Another enhanced item, the Ten Best Sites resources list, is based on usage and surveys of users and provides links to a wide selection of the most important and easily accessed data. Overall, Econdata.Net gets high marks for its organization of resources, concise descriptions, and simple navigation to valuable resources.

FreeLunch.com
(http://www.freelunch.com)

FreeLunch.com, part of the Economy.com network which includes an array of fee-based and free services or products, claims to be the Web's largest data library and provides access to over 1,000,000 free economic and financial data series. Several mechanisms are provided to access this large array of data including fourteen browseable categories from Industry (production, orders, inventories) to Real Estate (starts, completions and sales). A search interface allows users to access data by searching for keywords found within the data descriptions. A simple search interface is immediately available on the site and an advanced search screen is only a click away.

Despite the fact that the FreeLunch site has organized and reformatted data freely available from many different government sources, for example, the Bureau of Economic Administration and the Bureau of Labor Statistics, there are several obvious advantages to using this resource. The strength of FreeLunch resides in the various output formats readily available to users. Data can be viewed in either a chart or table format. The charts can be manipulated to focus on a specific time period with a variation in the data frequency as well. If the charts provided don't give the user what s/he needs, the data can also be downloaded in Excel format to be directly manipulated and analyzed. In order to utilize the strengths of this site, users must first register. Registering allows users to place a particular data series in "my basket" so that it can be easily downloaded.

Data and Program Library Service (DPLS)–
Internet Crossroads in the Social Sciences
(http://dpls.dacc.wisc.edu/internet.html)

DPLS' Internet Crossroads includes more than 650 annotated links to online data-related resources. Economics and Labor links are provided for four categories: U.S. Government links; U.S. Non-government links; International Government links; International Non-government links. Internet Crossroads not only links users to some of the most important online economic resources, but it also provides extensive annotations describing the information available from each site. One of the strengths of this resource is the information linking users to international economic data from both government and private resources.

Resources for Economists on the Internet (RFE)
(http://rfe.org/)

Sponsored by the American Economic Association, Resources for Economists is one of the most highly regarded sites on the subject of economics. RFE offers over 1,250 items separated into fifteen major sections, including "Data," "Other Internet Guides," and "Software." Each section is further broken down into numerous subsections in order to refine browsing strategies. Brief annotations describing each resource are also provided and help users determine the relevance or utility of each link. Finally, a search engine is provided allowing users to search headings, subheadings, resource titles, as well as the full text of each annotation. This highly selective resource is a great starting point for any researcher seeking economic information on the Web.

WebEc WWW Resources in Economics
(http://netec.wustl.edu/WebEc/WebEc.html)

If needed information is not found at the RFE site described previously, do not hesitate to stop at the more comprehensive resource found at WebEc. With over 1500 links, this resource is designed to connect academics with free economic information on the Internet. WebEc is divided into twenty-four categories and, as with RFE, each category also contains further divisions to assist browsing. A brief description of each site is provided to indicate the content and/or intended audience of each resource. WebEc is updated regularly with updates typically occurring in January, April and August. Although a search mechanism was provided at WebEc, it was not functioning when this site was reviewed. Despite this downfall, WebEc easily links users to content via the well-defined categories and sub-categories.

Best of the Web:
E-Commerce

Stephanie Jakle Movahedi-Lankarani

SUMMARY. E-commerce is one of the most popular current business topics. This chapter includes core resources of general news, how-to sites,
e-commerce technology sites, business-to-business sites, statistics, and academic research centers. *[Article copies available for a fee from The Haworth
Document Delivery Service: 1-800-HAWORTH. E-mail address: <docdelivery@
haworthpress.com> Website: <http://www.HaworthPress.com> © 2003 by The Haworth
Press, Inc. All rights reserved.]*

KEYWORDS. E-commerce, electronic commerce, Web sites

INTRODUCTION

E-commerce is the process of selling and buying goods and services on
the Internet. E-commerce can take many forms, depending on who is selling to whom: business-to-business (e.g., medical supply companies to hospitals), business-to-consumer (e.g., Amazon.com), consumer-to-business
(e.g., Priceline.com), consumer-to-consumer (e.g., eBay), government-
to-consumer (e.g., United States Postal Service), and business-to-em-
ployee (e.g., business services divisions within large organizations). Every
traditional business subject has an e-commerce equivalent, including mar-

Stephanie Jakle Movahedi-Lankarani is Library Assistant, Schreyer Business Library, The Pennsylvania State University (E-mail: sjm19@psulias.psu.edu).

[Haworth co-indexing entry note]: "Best of the Web: E-Commerce." Movahedi-Lankarani, Stephanie
Jakle. Co-published simultaneously in *Journal of Business & Finance Librarianship* (The Haworth Information Press, an imprint of The Haworth Press, Inc.) Vol. 8, No. 3/4, 2003, pp. 133-151; and: *The Core Business
Web: A Guide to Key Information Resources* (ed: Gary W. White) The Haworth Information Press, an imprint
of The Haworth Press, Inc., 2003, pp. 133-151. Single or multiple copies of this article are available for a fee
from The Haworth Document Delivery Service [1-800-HAWORTH, 9:00 a.m. - 5:00 p.m. (EST). E-mail address: docdelivery@haworthpress.com].

http://www.haworthpress.com/store/product.asp?sku=J109
© 2003 by The Haworth Press, Inc. All rights reserved.
10.1300/J109v08n03_02

keting, advertising, finance, banking, company research, industry research, business law, and business logistics.

Where do researchers who need current, up-to-the-minute information on the e-commerce economy go to find that information? Currently some of the best sources of e-commerce information are on the Internet itself. Traditional print sources of business information do not have the currency that the Internet can provide and, additionally, have been hindered by a lack of adequate industry codes under which to group e-commerce information sets. Many of the leading business news sites on the Internet have side-stepped this problem by creating their own e-commerce "stock exchange" listings which cover e-commerce specific companies, and by creating e-commerce industry groupings for their analyses. Additionally, as is the case specifically with reports generated by companies specializing in e-marketing or e-business analysis, Internet business news sites are able to gather news reports as they are released by companies, and are able to analyze the information and post relevant articles on their sites in very little time. The result is more up-to-the-minute and comprehensive business news coverage than even the most frequent print publication.

The very lack of defined information parameters, which allows Web sites the freedom to create their own information sets, does create some difficulty when searching for e-commerce information. Few Web sites use controlled vocabulary when indexing their articles, and this can make searching for information on these sites frustrating if researchers expect Web site search engines to act like commercial databases. Researchers must be prepared to conduct multiple searches with multiple subject terms in order to locate needed information. Moreover, not all sites provide their information for free, although almost all sites provide some useful information for free as an enticement to purchase more in-depth information from the site.

There are e-commerce Web sites that specialize in particular aspects of electronic commerce: how-to; e-business news; e-commerce technology; business-to-business e-commerce; and e-commerce statistics. There are also e-commerce Web sites that provide information as a part of their organizational mission: academic and research institutions; governments; organizations; and associations. Some Web sites are operated for profit and are heavily laden with advertising and product placements; other Web sites are non-profit and offer extensive collections of white papers and policy reviews. Researchers looking for specific subject information may want to first search a subject-specific site, but should not overlook the more general business news sites, as they provide a wealth of information in any area of e-commerce.

GENERAL E-COMMERCE NEWS AND INFORMATION SITES

Geared toward members of the e-commerce industry, these e-commerce news and information Web sites provide comprehensive and timely coverage of the latest e-business news, industry trends, and technology news. Some of these Web sites are e-commerce portals and contain a multitude of links to more focused, subject-specific areas of e-commerce interest. While all these sites cover the basic needs of the e-commerce information seeker, each site establishes its own presence in the e-business news and information market, with variations in site structure, presentation, and sub-genre focus.

allECommerce.com
(http://allec.com)

allECommerce.com is one of ten e-commerce sister sites on the *NewsFactor Network*. All the *NewsFactor* sites focus exclusively on e-business or e-technology and offer up-to-the-minute information and original, syndicated news stories. Included in the network are *NewsFactor. com, allEC.com, E-Commerce Times, Linux Insider, CRMDaily.com, TechNewsWorld.com, Wireless NewsFactor, OSOpinion, FreeNewsFeed. com, TechExtreme,*[1] and a variety of free newsletters.[2] The sites are updated every five minutes, 24-hours a day, seven days a week, with only the CRMDaily.com Web site and 'Market Watch' feature (found on most of the sister sites) updated every fifteen minutes during trading hours.

These sister sites are a good place to go for an overview of the industry, for e-commerce technology news, and for news and information on e-companies. The *NewsFactor Network* publishes hundreds of original articles every week, seventy to eighty percent of which are written by NewsFactor staff writers. The information is free for all users at these sites (including the special reports). Current and archived information on all sites is searchable at any one site, and searchers may limit their search to an individual site if they so desire. All the sites use similar presentation and layout, making navigation among the ten sites easy and straightforward.

Business 2.0
(http://business20.com)

The *Business 2.0* Web site covers general e-commerce industry and company news and information, contains a link to the online version of their magazine, *Business 2.0*, and features daily editorials and columns unique to the *Business 2.0* Web site. The best feature on this Web site is their "Web Guide," a continuously updated guide to e-commerce information, covering 13,000 topics and containing links to more than 50,000 carefully selected Web pages.[3] The guide was created, and is maintained, by professional research librarians and focuses on resources that follow current e-business news and support the editorial content of the magazine.[4]

The *Business 2.0* Web site also contains "e-Business," "Marketing," and "Technology" links that draw articles from the Web site's free newsletters,[5] and a link to an extensive glossary. The site also contains a "Web Files" link that connects to an issue by issue listing of selected *Business 2.0* magazine articles. Under each selected article is a further listing of related full-text articles (from *Business 2.0* and other magazines), a listing of related subject resource links in the *Business20.com* "Web Guide," and a list of links to people, companies, and technologies in the "Web Guide" related to the main article. The site is searchable using the search box provided.

BusinessWeek Online
(http://www.businessweek.com)

In addition to being the online counterpart to *BusinessWeek*, *BusinessWeek Online* offers free newsletters,[6] a "forums & chats arena,"[7] a "Today's Market" section by Standard and Poor's, and a "stock look up" search box which provides extensive company and industry snapshots from Standard and Poor's ("Internet" as an industry is covered). The outstanding feature of this Web site is its search engine, which provides for advanced searching and contains articles from both *BusinessWeek* and *BusinessWeek Online* back to January 1991. Both the paper and the online editions of *BusinessWeek* provide in-depth coverage of e-commerce, and the search engine gives researchers quick and comprehensive access to that information.

Computerworld.com
(http://computerworld.com)

Computerworld Inc. is an information services company focused on delivering information to professionals in information technology. The company publishes *Computerworld*, a weekly print publication, and *Computerworld.com*, a Web site that expands the focus of their print publication. In addition to providing current news analysis on the information technology sector of the economy, *Computerworld.com* offers focused IT information in their "Knowledge Centers."

A unique feature of this Web site is the "Communities" link. Each community on *Computerworld.com* is focused on a specific area of information technology, including e-commerce (http://computerworld.com/community/ecommerce). Many e-commerce news sites offer subject focused forums and online discussion groups, but the e-commerce community page on *Computerworld.com* is exceptionally well designed and informative. The page has clearly defined sections for discussions, feature stories, e-commerce news, and a side column containing quick links to other features, resources, services, and e-commerce related subject communities. The site includes a glossary and an event calendar.

E-Business Forum
(http://www.ebusinessforum.com)

E-Business Forum.com is produced by the Economist Intelligence Unit, a company which provides analysis and forecasts of the political, economic and business environment in more than 180 countries.[8] Clicking on the "doing e-business in . . . " tab at the top of their Web page takes you to a linked list of sixty countries for which up-to-date, detailed information on the e-commerce business environment is available. This site is global in scope and all information provided is free.

The "Best Practice" tab contains case studies on the use of the Internet in business (including e-commerce). The "Research" section contains assessments of the impact of e-business on specific industries, countries, and on how corporations function. This section also contains a ranking of the leading Internet resources focused on e-commerce. The "Global News Analysis" section profiles important developments in global e-commerce, and the "Thought Leadership" section contains interviews with and analysis by experts in e-commerce worldwide.

internet.com
(http://ecommerce.internet.com)

The *internet.com* network contains a vast amount of e-commerce and information technology news, information and resources. *internet.com*, together with its sister network *EarthWeb.com*, contains 160 Web sites (grouped into sixteen information technology related subject channels) and offers 225 e-mail newsletters.[9] The *internet.com* "ECommerce/

Marketing" channel contains more than seventeen groupings of pertinent e-commerce related information.

The *internet.com* network is noteworthy for ISDEX, an Internet stock index of fifty leading Internet companies, and "The Internet Stock Report" which tracks companies who derive most of their revenue from the Internet. Both of these tools are helpful to researchers tracking the e-commerce industry and are found on the main *internet.com* home page.

E-commerce and Internet-related headlines and news stories are also available at *internetnews.com* (http://www.internet.com/sections/news. html), another of the *internet.com* network sites. Two *internet.com* network sites of particular interest to e-commerce researchers are *ClickZ Network* (http://www.clikz.com) and *CyberAtlas* (http://cyberatlas. internet.com), located on the *internet.com* "Ecommerce/Marketing" channel. *ClickZ Network* specializes in commentary on Internet marketing and advertising from industry leaders and original case studies. *CyberAtlas* is especially useful for researchers looking for Web marketing information, as it focuses on Web marketing research, statistics, and resources. *CyberAtlas* gathers research from top research firms, such as Forrester, Jupiter, Media Matrix and AdKnowledge.[10] All *CyberAtlas* content is archived and the URLs of *CyberAtlas* articles do not change.[11]

searchEBusiness.com
(http://www.searchebusiness.com)

searchEBusiness.com offers e-business news and information gathered from more than 800 other e-commerce related Web sites. It advertises itself as "the Leading Network of Enterprise IT Web Sites." The Web site is focused more on e-commerce infrastructure (applications, core technologies, platforms, development) than other e-commerce Web sites in the general news and information sites category, but nonetheless offers a very lengthy listing of linked news headlines from a wide variety of Web sources. A look at the news headlines link on February 22, 2002 showed stories gathered from *NewsFactor Network*, *searchSecurity*, *InternetWeek*, *Knowledge@Wharton*, *c/net*, *CRMDaily*, *ASPstreet.com*, and *InfoWorld*, as well as original content from *searchEBusiness*.

The site contains a "Best EBusiness Web Links" section that offers the editors' choices for best-of-the-Web Web sites in fourteen subject areas, and includes categories for Case Studies–Management, Case Studies–Technology, and Wharton School of Business Publications. There is also an "EBusiness Career Center," which contains a searchable database of IT jobs (drawn from employer Web sites) and a searchable directory of technical professionals.

E-COMMERCE HOW-TO SITES

E-commerce how-to Web sites offer the researcher general overview articles on what constitutes e-commerce and information on how to set up and run an e-business. If you need an introduction to e-commerce, or are looking for instruction in e-business strategy or infrastructure set-up, these are good sites to search.

About–Electronic Commerce
(http://ecommerce.about.com)

About–Electronic Commerce offers quick-start categories such as "E-Commerce 101," "Start-Up Ideas," and "Research & Stats" to e-commerce searchers. One of several hundred Guide sites on the *About network*, *About–Electronic Commerce* covers the basic areas of e-business, and contains a "B2B Resources" link and a "Subject Library" link. In the "Essentials Box," you can locate a guide to e-commerce survival, e-commerce reports and statistics. Each *About* subject guide site is run by a subject professional who creates a comprehensive site around the subject, including timely information, relevant links, how-to's, and forums.[12]

Free Management Library
(http://www.mapnp.org/library)

The *Free Management Library*, designed and maintained by Carter McNamara, MBA, PhD of Authenticity Consulting, LLC, seeks to provide "20% of resources needed to address 80% of the challenges in business, management and organization."[13] This guide is divided into 675 topics, with seventy-two of the most popular topic categories listed on the main page.

The "E-Commerce" link provides a lengthy "Basic Guide to E-Commerce" that covers every possible aspect of e-commerce, from definitions and terminology and introductory over-views, to basic technical e-commerce needs, product development and market research, e-store basics, online marketing, and telecommunications laws. The guide also contains sections providing additional general resources, links to related "Free Management Library" subject guides, and relevant online discussion groups.

Northern Light Special Edition: Electronic Commerce
(http://special.northernlight.com/ecommerce/)

This special edition from Northern Light is a rich resource for e-commerce news links, links to organizations engaged in e-commerce, e-commerce research, government standards information, and infrastructure technology information. The site includes a "Special Collection Titles" section containing links to online e-commerce-focused journals.

webmonkey
(http://hotwired.lycos.com/webmonkey)

webmonkey is a hands-on, how-to guide that provides all the information and instruction necessary to build a Web site. The tutorials come in beginners, builders, and masters levels, and the site contains a comprehensive how-to library (including a how-to guide to e-business), and a quick reference library containing a glossary, style sheets, a HTML cheat sheet, JavaScript code library, and a Unix guide. The site is searchable and offers a daily newsletter on Web creation topics and newsletters from Wired News.[14]

WilsonWeb
(http://www.wilsonweb.com)

WilsonWeb, authored by Dr. Ralph F. Wilson, PhD, contains many general information and introductory materials on e-commerce and Web marketing. *WilsonWeb* focuses on "the doing" of e-commerce and Web marketing, and provides background information, news, product reviews, and research articles supportive of the small to mid-sized e-business.

The site contains an "E-Commerce Research Room," where you can search for articles in all sixty sub-sections of the room simultaneously, or limit your search to seven broad categories of e-commerce, including "Introduction to E-Commerce," "Industry Case Studies" (twenty-nine different e-commerce industries listed), "Legal and Governmental Issues of E-Commerce" (under the "Miscellaneous" heading), and "Pricing Strategies" (again, under the "Miscellaneous" heading).

The "Web Marketing Info Center" on the site contains information sections divided into six main subject areas, including "Introductory" materials and "Business Web Site Design." Articles specific to analyzing site traffic, Web demographics, and legal issues (copyright and trademark) are located under "Miscellaneous."

Also located on *WilsonWeb* is "Doctor Ebiz," a syndicated feature at over 300 Web sites, providing "Practical Answers to help your online business succeed."[15] A free email version of "Doctor Ebiz" is available after registering at the Web site.

workz.com
(http://www.workz.com)

workz.com provides detailed and comprehensive how-to information for small e-commerce businesses. Content is arranged into ten "How-To Guides," including "Build Your Site," "Make Money," "Attract Customers," "Save Money," "Web Site Design," "Web Site Operations," "Web E-Commerce," "Web Marketing," "Web Advertising," and "International." Each how-to guide contains articles from *workz.com* researchers that cover a range of complexity from the very introductory ("How Computers Link to the Internet" and "Application Service Providers Explained") to the detailed ("3 Microcommerce Business Models" and "Branding Implications of Domain Names").[16] This is a good site for researchers needing comprehensive background information on how business e-commerce is constructed and conducted, or for small business e-commerce entrepreneurs who need practical information.

E-COMMERCE TECHNOLOGY SITES

These Web sites focus on the technology and infrastructure that underlie e-commerce. Most sites contain e-commerce technology news headlines and articles, product reviews, and product, as well as technology provider directories.

BRINT.com
(http://www.brint.com)

BRINT.com is a knowledge portal focusing on business and technology information. It contains hundreds of resources in the areas of general business, technology, knowledge management, and e-business. The *BRINT.com* Web site is well laid out and easily navigated. Site content is divided into subject group channels, and resources and community pages. In addition to the channels, the main page has subject category links that take you directly to topic specific listings of resources. The e-business category contains links to information and resources on strategy, e-business, e-commerce, customer relations management (CRM), supply chains, advertising, and more. The information on *BRINT.com* is geared toward the mid- to large-sized business.

c/net.com
(http://www.news.com)

c/net.com is all about Internet technology and news. The site combines current business and technology news with trend analysis and comprehensive coverage of Internet technology products. E-Commerce tech news is well covered, and the site content includes analysis as well as commentary. The site is keyword searchable. There are links to the other c/net networks, including *mySimon* (product and price comparisons), *TechRepublic* (Internet technology community) and *ZDNet* (comprehensive technology news and information).

ZDNet (http://www.zdnet.com) has a link to "eBusiness Info" in its services bar at the bottom of the page and an e-commerce link in its "Business Products" column. *ZDNet* channels include "News" (with an e-commerce link), "Tech Update" (with an e-commerce link), and an advice column on the "AnchorDesk" link. There are also links to international *ZDNet* sites, which contain original content relevant to their country and region of the world. There is information on all the *ZDNet* sites that is useful for any sized e-business, from small to corporate.

eaijournal
(http://www.eaijournal.com)

eaijournal, advertising itself as the "Resource for e-Business and Application Integration," is a good source for information on how e-business technology impacts the "doing" of e-business. Each monthly issue of *eaijournal* looks at how the technological infrastructure of e-commerce impacts the running of e-businesses and what the long-term business implications are of technology options employed by e-businesses.

In addition to the monthly issue, the Web site features current Internet market news and a "Departments" tab containing links to various sections of the site, including *The Business Integrator Journal*, "e-Business," "m-Commerce," "B2B," "e-services," and "Collaborative Commerce." The site is searchable and searches return a tidy, straightforward listing of articles arranged by title.

IDG.net
(http://www.idg.net)

IDG (International Data Group) is a technology media conglomerate with more than 300 publications in eighty-five countries, and more than

12,000 employees worldwide.[17] Among its many publications are *PC World*, *ComputerWorld*, *The Industry Standard*, and *Info World*. The company estimates its readership worldwide, for all its publications, at 100 million each month.[18]

On the "IT Directory" (left hand column on main page) the "E-Business" subject link takes you to a well-designed page containing news, feature stories, and how-to and research articles. There are quick links to sub-topics on B2B, B2C, and e-commerce specific banking, investing, and technology. The site is searchable.

TechWeb
(http://www.techweb.com)

TechWeb is owned by CMP Media and its content is provided by three company publications: *InformationWeek*; *InternetWeek*; and *Network Computing*.[19] The site is focused on Internet information technologies and content includes news, reviews, analysis, opinion, and research.

The E-Business page (accessible by clicking on the "technologies" tab) contains sections devoted to e-commerce feature stories, in-depth articles on e-commerce technology, opinion articles, and product reviews.

BUSINESS-TO-BUSINESS E-COMMERCE

Business-to-business e-commerce is the largest sector of the e-commerce market. B2B e-commerce is expected to reach $4.8 trillion globally by 2004, with forty percent of all purchasing done by U.S. companies completed online.[20] Business-to-business e-commerce Web sites not only provide news and information on all aspects of e-commerce, but may also provide trade information and links, links to e-business financing sources, and e-business directories.

A2ZofB2B
(http://www.a2zofb2b.com)

A2ZofB2B is a business-to-business e-commerce portal that offers current information on public and private exchange sites, e-markets, and e-commerce infrastructure and Internet technologies. If you are looking for B2B businesses with a Web presence, this is the site to search. The main page contains directories for news, B2B financial information, a how-to guide for B2B (including a glossary), and resources (including a research link). The site maintains a "DotComFlops" channel and an "A2ZofBiZ" section containing over 210,000 links to B2B business and association Web sites. The directory is hierarchically arranged by subject, from broad to specific, and maintained by site editors who evaluate sites for inclusion in the directory.[21] Businesses and organizations may suggest their site for inclusion in the directory, but the directory is not fee-based. The directory is searchable by keyword or business name, and has quick links to popular categories, recently added categories, and recent searches conducted in the directory.

American Trading Network
(http://www.atnworld.com)

The *American Trading Network* offers an exhaustive list of B2B resource links for searchers of international e-commerce trade information. Under the "Business Economic Trade, Investment, Finance" link, *American Trading Network* provides general information links to sources such as the Organization of American States Foreign Trade Info System and more specific information links to sources such as guides to companies in Japan, India, and Hong Kong.

The "U.S. Government Info Offices & Resources" page includes listings for various government offices or programs engaged in trade, and exhaustive international lists of chambers of commerce, embassies, and universities. The "Trade Opportunities Open Exchange" gives lists for "Trade Leads Opportunities," various fact books, commercial trade offices of various countries, and links to top international newspapers. The "World Trade Resources" page includes an "International Trade Directory" and a list of "World Wide Web Servers," "Import and Export Trade Links," and international trade show listings. The site is still under construction, so expect some broken links and incomplete listings.

EcomWorld
(http://www.ecomworld.com)

Owned by EC Media Group, *ecomworld* is a business-to-business portal that specializes in business intelligence, e-technology and implementation, Web marketing and order fulfillment. The site's main sections are devoted to daily B2B news and industry analysis. A side column details the offerings of the remainder of the site: editorials, *EC World* magazine, industry portals, technology portals, and subject-focused pages (such as management, executive profiles, and legal issues). There is also a "Vendor Research" link that offers free white papers, and under a resources link, an industry events calendar, associations listing, Web links, recommended books and a glossary of e-business terms.

ACADEMIC AND RESEARCH E-COMMERCE SITES

As the e-commerce economy grows, an increasing number of universities are creating e-commerce research centers. These centers typically partner with large business enterprises and draw faculty from a wide variety of disciplines including computer science, engineering, business, and economics, and they study a wide variety of topics related to e-commerce.

Center for Research in Electronic Commerce
(http://crec.bus.utexas.edu)

At *The Center for Research in Electronic Commerce* (CREC) at the University of Texas at Austin, researchers study how changes made to e-commerce infrastructure (technologies, products, processes, policies) impact the efficiency and effectiveness of global e-commerce. Using economic analysis and market efficiency measurements, researchers in a wide array of disciplines are developing technologies and applications that increase e-business productivity, consumer satisfaction, and market efficiency. The center partners and collaborates with various enterprises, including The National Science Foundation, Cisco Systems, IBM, and Pitney Bowes.[22]

Current research projects include, among others, Economic Modeling of Network Management, Digital Product Companies, Financial Bundle Trading System (FBTS), Developing Real-Time Distributed Applications, and Modeling Intermediated Electronic Commerce. Working papers and articles by CREC researchers are available in full-text and are free at the center's Web site. Other resources linked to CREC can be reached via the resources bar at the top of the main Web page, and include a variety of informational pages on e-commerce topics and a linked list of e-commerce research centers and business Web sites.

HBS Working Knowledge
(http://hbsworkingknowledge.hbs.edu/)

The Harvard Business School's *HBS Working Knowledge* Web site provides information on thirteen management subject areas, including "E-Commerce & the Marketspace"; "Knowledge & the Information Economy"; and "Leadership, Strategy & Competition." Each subject section contains feature articles, a Web site review, a book review, and is updated weekly. Past articles are archived and available via the linked title list at the bottom of each section's Web page.

WeBi: Wharton e-Business Initiative
(http://webi.wharton.upenn.edu)

WeBi is a partnership of business leaders, Wharton faculty, and students engaged in interdisciplinary research in the workings of the e-commerce marketplace. Partners include a research alliance with the Gartner Group and corporate partners that include, among others, Bristol-Myers Squibb, Charles Schwab & Co., Inc., Enron Corp., and the Ford Motor Company.[23] The Web site contains feature articles on e-business subjects and, on the "Resources & Tools" tab, contains a link to Knowledge@Wharton, a free (registration required) online resource of business research, analysis, and information published by the Wharton Business School.

E-COMMERCE GOVERNMENT, ORGANIZATION, AND ASSOCIATION SITES

As e-commerce has grown in size and economic influence, organizations, government agencies, and associations have been formed to guide e-commerce policy, to provide business and consumer protection, to study best practices, and to promote cooperation and collaboration. The United States government established a national e-commerce plan and created, within the Department of Commerce, a Secretariat for Electronic Commerce. The following sites tend to be global in scope and are good sources for U.S. and international e-commerce policy information and e-commerce security issues.

CommerceNet
(http://www.commerce.net)

As announced on their main Web page, *CommerceNet* is a nonprofit consortium of business, government, technology and academic leaders bringing companies together to develop and implement new e-commerce technologies and e-business practices on a global basis. The *CommerceNet* agenda in 2001 included groups working in five key areas: evolving supply chains; next generation Internet applications; security and Internet payment; government, public policy, advocacy; and pervasive access and wireless technology. Ongoing projects include open buying on the Internet (OBI), e-checking, demonstrating the value of integrating three common component-based electronic commerce services (eCO), and a Social Security Administration pilot program dealing with online security and privacy.

There are many useful e-commerce technology and e-business practices documents and articles posted on *CommerceNet*. The site is searchable via a search box at the top right hand corner. Searching a term returns a set of citations sorted by relevancy and an options button that appears beside the search box. Clicking on the options button produces an advanced search form that allows researchers to substantially customize their search results, resulting in a much more relevant citation list.

Computer Security Resource Center (CSRC)
(http://csrc.nist.gov)

The Computer Security Resource Center works in five major areas: cryptographic standards and application; security testing; security research and emerging technologies; security management and guidance; and outreach and education. CSRC is within the NIST Information Technology Laboratory, itself a cooperative program. The NIST Information Technology Laboratory works to improve information system security by raising awareness of security risks, researching and devising solutions, and developing standards. NIST, the National Institute of Standards and Technology (http://www.nist.gov) is a non-regulatory federal agency within the U.S. Department of Commerce.

The Computer Security Resource Center Web site contains extensive links to other governmental bodies working in computer and information technology and posts bulletins and articles relevant to computer security from these groups on its Web site. The site also contains computer security news, governmental news stories, a cryptographic toolkit, a vulnerability index, a security bulletin links, links to policies, and a virus information link. The site also has an "Events" link and a listing of academic, government, and professional organizations.

Federal Trade Commission
(http://www.ftc.gov)

The Federal Trade Commission Web site contains extensive information of interest to the e-commerce consumer. The "Consumer Protection" link on the main pages sends searchers to a "Consumer Information Directory" arranged by subject. The "E-Commerce and the Internet" link produces a lengthy list of articles (available in text or PDF format) to searchers. In addition to advisory information on Internet security and privacy, there are consumer guides to e-payments, online investment opportunities, and online shopping tips. There is also an information section available for Internet businesses with information on various e-commerce rules, and a section devoted to Internet law cases. Both consumers and businesses may file a complaint online (a quick link is available).

International Web Police
(http://www.web-police.org)

The *International Web Police* investigate, track, and record Internet crime. They arbitrate complaints, prosecute Internet criminals, and shut down Internet enterprises engaged in illegal activities. Their services are free.

Web Police staff members are located in sixty-one countries and include agencies, governmental officials, police officers, and civilian volunteers who work closely and cooperatively with law enforcement agencies and government officials around the world. The *International Web Police* database contains records of criminal activity since 1986; and the site maintains links to their latest crime reports, latest scam reports, and latest Internet statistics pages. There are quick links for reporting a crime, reporting a scam, or reporting terrorist activities. The main page also contains a "Child Safety Center" and "Women's Task Forces."

OECD Online
(http://www.oecd.org)

The *OECD Online*, the Web site of the Organization for Economic Cooperation and Development, contains an enormous amount of information relevant to electronic commerce. There is an Electronic Commerce directorate (directorates are listed in the left hand column) which contains general information on e-commerce as well as a "What's New" column featuring e-commerce related OECD events worldwide, conference and workshops, and newly published OECD studies. There is a listing of all OECD activity groups working in e-commerce and information technologies, a list of OECD e-commerce relevant documents (including case studies, country surveys, manuals, policy briefs, statistics, and working papers). There is a "My OECD" option, which allows users to customize the site to their subject areas of interest and become their personal OECD home page.

E-COMMERCE STATISTICS SITES

The following Web sites specialize in e-commerce statistics and are connected to commercial entities. These sites tend to cover marketing, demographic, and trend information, but researchers may be able to obtain quality statistical information on other e-commerce subjects.

InternetStats
(http://www.internetstats.com)

Internetstats.com provides lists of business Web sites that contain research and statistical information on e-business marketing and trends. *InternetStat*'s main page is cluttered with product advertisements but does feature weekly "Ecommerce Stat," "International Stat," and "Internet Stat" sections, each with a feature article. There is also a "Business Channels" listing at the left of the Web page, which contains links to Internet, advertising, business, financial, trade, and trends subject statistics pages.

Each "Business Channels" statistics page on *InternetStats* is further broken down by type of statistic (such as "Industry Numbers & News" under financial statistics or "Businesses On-line" under business statistics). The business Web sites listed on these pages are hot-linked, and a brief description of the highlighted statistic is given, as well as whether the information is free and if the referred to Web site generally contains American- or Canadian-oriented content. On the business stats channel, statistics and information for seventy-five industries are available. Businesses may submit their Web site for inclusion on *InternetStats*, subject to review and approval by *InternetStats*.

Nua.com
(http://www.nua.ie/surveys)

The *Nua.com* database contains Internet demographic and trend information back to 1996. The site includes a weekly editorial, Internet statistics and trends articles, a "Graphs & Charts" tab, and a tab for "Nua Analysis." The "Nua Analysis" tab lists Nua online publications and provides links to the following publications: *The Weekly Editorial* (1997-to current); *Bi-Monthly Report* (1997-1999); *Year in Review* (1996-2000); and *Graphs and Charts* (assorted dates). The left hand column lists Nua Internet Surveys by category: sector (eighteen industries); society (security, privacy, community); tools (Internet technologies); and demographics (general, specific groups, usage patterns). Business and organizations may submit a site for inclusion, subject to review, via the "submit a survey" link. The site is searchable.

CONCLUSION

The Internet is fast becoming the research tool of choice, not only for those who study e-commerce, but also for those who study more traditional areas of business and economics. Information on all aspects of business and e-business are easily accessible on the Internet, with the Internet excelling particularly in the provision of up-to-the-minute business news. Researchers may need to search more widely and expend more effort in locating more targeted pieces of information, but the Web sites included in this survey provide a gateway to that world of information.

NOTES

1. Web sites of the NewsFactor Network sites include: NewsFactor (http://www. newsfactor.com), allEC.com (http://www.allec.com), E-Commerce Times (http://www. ecommercetimes.com), Linux Insider (http://www.linuxinsider.com), CRMDaily.com (http://www.crmdaily.com), TechNewsWorld.com (http://www.technewsworld.com), Wire less NewsFactor (http://www.wirelessnewsfactor.com), OsOpinion (http://www.osopinion.com), FreeNewsFeed.com (http://www.freenewsfeed.com), TechExtreme (http://www.techextreme. com).

2. Newsletters offered by NewsFactor Network include: E-Commerce Minute (daily), E-Commerce Times (weekly), Wireless Industry Alert (daily), CRM Industry Alert (daily), CyberCrime & Security Daily Report, and Top Tech News (daily). These newsletters are free. Subscribers can go to http://newsletters.newsfactor.com to sign up to receive any or all of the newsletters using the "Newsletter Management Wizard."

3. Sherman, C. A "Hidden Guide" to the Business Web, *Search Day #194*. [Online]. Available at: http://searchenginewatch.com/searchday/ January 31, 2002.

4. Ibid.

5. Newsletters offered by *Business20.com* include: Daily Insight, Brazen Careerist (Mondays), Marketing Focus (Mondays), Tech Investor, eBusiness Dispatch (Tuesdays), Barely Managing (bi-weekly), Talent Monger (bi-weekly), Wireless Report (Wednesdays), The Defogger (bi-weekly), The Conference Spy (Thursdays), and Future Boy (Fridays). These newsletters are free. Subscribers can go to http://www. business20.com/articles/web/newslettersub/ to sign up to receive any, or all, of the newsletters.

6. Newsletters offered by *BusinessWeek Online* include: BW Insider (weekly), European Insider (weekly), MBA/B-School Insider (bi-weekly), Careers, Frontier/Small Business (weekly), Market Week Ahead (late Fridays). These newsletters are free, but subscribers must sign-up (no fee) with *BusinessWeek Online* prior to signing up for the newsletters. Click on the 'Newsletters' link from the *BusinessWeek Online* main page (http://www.businessweek.com).

7. *BusinessWeek Online* forums & chats arena covers b-schools, investing, topics in the current issue of *BusinessWeek Online*, technology, careers, and small business.

8. *About Us* (n.d.). [Online]. Available at: http://www.ebusinessforum.com/ index.asp?layout+about_us February 21, 2002.

9. To sign up for newsletters: http://e-newsletters.internet.com.

10. *About INT MediaGroup.* (n.d.). [Online]. Available at: http://www.internet.com/corporate/about.html February 22, 2002.

11. *About CyberAtlas.* (n.d.). [Online]. Available at: http://cyberatlas.internet.com/resources/about/article February 25, 2002.

12. *AboutUs.* (n.d.). [Online]. Available at: http://ourstory.about.com/index.htm February 21, 2002.

13. *About the Free Management Library.* (n.d.). [Online]. Available at: http://www.mapnp.org/library/aboutnml.htm February 22, 2002.

14. *SIGNUP to our newsletters!* (n.d.). [Online]. Available at: http://hotwired.lycos.com/email/signup/webmonkey.html February 27, 2002.

15. *Doctor EBiz.* (n.d.). [Online]. Available at: http://doctorebiz.com February 25, 2002.

16. *About Us.* (n.d.). [Online]. Available at: http://www.workz.com/content/9.asp February 22, 2002.

17. *About IDG.* (n.d.). [Online]. Available at: http://www.idg.com/home February 21, 2002.

18. Ibid.

19. *AboutUs.* (n.d.). [Online]. Available at http://www.techweb.com/media/aboutus February 22, 2002.

20. Cyberatlas Staff. (January 30, 2002). *Online Purchasing Increases in Q4 2001.* [Online]. Available at: http://cyberatas.internet.com February 7, 2002.

21. *About the Open Directory Project.* (n.d.). [Online]. Available at: http://www.a2zofb2b.com/a2zofbiz/a2zofbiz.htm February 27, 2002.

22. *About CREC.* (n.d.). [Online]. Available at: http://crec.bus.utexas.edu/ February 27, 2002.

23. *Partners.* (n.d.). [Online]. Available at: http://webi.wharton.upenn.edu/St/partnersList.asp February 27, 2002.

Finance and Investments

Hal P. Kirkwood, Jr.

SUMMARY. Web sites for finance and investing are among the most pervasive. This chapter outlines key examples in the categories of market analysis and commentary, market news, initial public offerings, historical data, stock screeners, brokers, mutual funds, bonds, international investing, professional associations, and several other categories. *[Article copies available for a fee from The Haworth Document Delivery Service: 1-800-HAWORTH. E-mail address: <docdelivery@haworthpress.com> Website: <http://www.HaworthPress.com> © 2003 by The Haworth Press, Inc. All rights reserved.]*

KEYWORDS. Investing, investments, finance, Web sites

INTRODUCTION

The advent and impressive growth of the Internet has led to significant changes in the way people go about their daily lives. Access to an ever-increasing array of resources and services is made available daily over the World Wide Web. Online auctions, worldwide chat and e-mail, and music file transfer are just some of the areas that have had tremendous growth due directly to the development of the Web. Company research and online investing are another topic that has seen significant growth. The average person can now access information and resources that were once completely out of their reach.

Hal P. Kirkwood, Jr. is Assistant Professor of Library Science, Purdue University (E-mail: kirkwood@purdue.edu).

[Haworth co-indexing entry note]: "Finance and Investments." Kirkwood, Hal P., Jr. Co-published simultaneously in *Journal of Business & Finance Librarianship* (The Haworth Information Press, an imprint of The Haworth Press, Inc.) Vol. 8, No. 3/4, 2003, pp. 153-166; and: *The Core Business Web: A Guide to Key Information Resources* (ed: Gary W. White) The Haworth Information Press, an imprint of The Haworth Press, Inc., 2003, pp. 153-166. Single or multiple copies of this article are available for a fee from The Haworth Document Delivery Service [1-800-HAWORTH, 9:00 a.m. - 5:00 p.m. (EST). E-mail address: docdelivery@haworthpress.com].

http://www.haworthpress.com/store/product.asp?sku=J109
© 2003 by The Haworth Press, Inc. All rights reserved.
10.1300/J109v08n03_03

An area that has had significant development online is access to information and resource on finance and investments. The resources available vary from the Securities and Exchange Commission's EDGAR database of company financial filings to the "backroom" information at Earnings Whispers to the contrarian investing at Tulips and Bears. Hundreds of sites sprouted up as investment portals. The coverage of the information spans free investment analysis to fee-based financial research. Tools such as bulletin boards for discussion, forms for requesting more information, stock screeners and portfolio trackers for online investing are widespread. Individual investing has created an ever-growing demand for financial data, news and analysis.

The access to an abundance of investment-related information has dramatically affected the equities markets. The "average" investor now has an incredible and overwhelming amount of information to peruse. The variety of sites is now almost as large as the number of sites themselves: market news; technical analysis; fundamental analysis; historic data; bonds; mutual funds; "bearish" sites; "bullish" sites; commodity trading; company resources and annual reports; venture capital; initial public offerings; online brokers; associations; tools; calculators; and screeners. The list goes on and on.

The list that follows is not comprehensive. It is a sampling of especially useful sites. Most categories are represented by at least two sites. The annotations highlight the useful information and tools that can be found at each site. There are many similar sites. Many of the investment sites share tools and outsource information to each other. Portfolio trackers, for example, are the must-have feature for many sites. Selecting the choicest sites was an extremely difficult task. It is my hope that besides seeing some sites that you are familiar with you will find some hidden gems you were unaware of previously.

META-SITES

Investor Links
(http://www.investorlinks.com)

Boasting a collection of over 12,000 links, Investor Links is arguably the most comprehensive directory for investment sites and resources. The site is organized into sixteen main categories with numerous subcategories available. A majority of the sites are briefly annotated. Features on this site include "WallBoards" discussion bulletin boards, a portfolio tracker, and a free newsletter of market activity and investment news.

MARKET ANALYSIS AND COMMENTARY

CBS Marketwatch
(http://cbs.marketwatch.com)

MarketWatch is a complete analysis site with "News & Commentary," "Personal Finance," "My Portfolios," "Research & Tools" and "MarketWatch TV & Radio." In addition to the standard dose of market news, the site provides a solid amount of analysis and commentary for potential investors. A concise stock screener, interactive charting, and several other investing and personal finance tools make this an informative and functional site. Of particular note is the "TV & Radio" section with an abundance of investment commentary and interviews including a section of executive interviews. Free registration is necessary for some content. Features on this site include a portfolio tracker, an intraday screening tool, and an alerting service for price/volume changes and breaking news announcements. A wireless option is also available.

Quicken
(http://www.quicken.com)

Quicken provides access to a wide array of financial and investing resources. Categories available include "Bills & Banking," "Taxes," "Small Business," "Home Loans," "Insurance Quotes," and "Retirement." It is not necessary to own the Quicken software to enjoy the benefits of the site. The "Investing" section is particularly strong with a portfolio tracker, stock screener, and excellent quote and charting information. "Intraday and Analyst" commentary is clearly provided within the navigation. The "Evaluator" feature provides a clear breakdown of growth trends, financial health, management performance, market multiples, and intrinsic value. Research reports and clear presentation of recent insider trading is also available. Additional features of this site include a mutual fund finder and evaluator, capital gains calculator, and information on DRIPs, 401(k)'s and other long-term investment options.

CorporateInformation
(http://www.corporateinformation.com)

CorporateInformation has been and remains one of the most information-rich free sites on the Web for public company information. It requires a free registration as this site which is in the midst of a significant redesign. The content remains extremely solid with over 20,000 unique company profiles from Wright Investors' Service as well as a search engine to thousands of other company profiles and corporate snapshots across the Web.

Additional features include full-text research reports on companies, companies organized by country, industry reports by country, an exchange rate calculator, and current news headlines.

Clearstation
(http://clearstation.etrade.com)

Clearstation, a subsidiary of E*trade, provides a combination of investment analysis and education to offer an excellent investment Web site. Information is provided on all three primary types of investing: technical; fundamental; and community. Clearstation provides very specific commentary on the actions of stocks (i.e., whether it is trending up, a community favorite, or has recently been up or downgraded by an analyst). Free registration is available for customization features but not necessary for general content. Additional features include a portfolio management tool, the "Tag & Bag" section of screened stocks for potential investment, and the extensive "Education" section.

MARKET NEWS

Bloomberg
(http://www.bloomberg.com)

Bloomberg provides several fee-based services for financial, investment, and market news. They also provide an excellent amount of information on their Web site for free. In addition to the solid financial reporting on a wide variety of topics (i.e., earnings news, profit warnings, stocks on the move), there is full-text access to articles from Bloomberg columnists on specific issues such as executive pay, bonds, European companies, small cap stocks, and mutual funds.

Notable sections include the "Earnings News" calendar of scheduled earnings announcements, "Stocks on the Move" with brief summaries of potentially volatile stocks, and a "Tech Stocks" section with news and investment data on the different technology sectors.

Financial Times
(http://www.ft.com)

The *Financial Times* site is an excellent source for news on markets and investments. Five years of archived articles from the *Financial Times* are available as well as numerous other international business newspapers and publications. A substantial amount of full-text information is available. FT provides deep reporting of international markets and investments. A

"Global Investing" section contains numerous stories and special reports on companies and industries. The "FT Investor" section contains tools for exploring fund prices and interactive charting of funds and equities. Free registration is necessary for some features and tools. Other features include a United Kingdom share price search, an interactive charting tool for international markets, and a United Kingdom broker comparison tool.

CNN/Money
(http://money.cnn.com)

Formerly known as Cnnfn, the new site is a joint venture between CNN and *Money* magazine. A wealth of national and international financial news, investment analysis, and personal finance information is available. The "Industry Watch" under "News" contains recent headlines on several dozen industries with a handy "Executive Summary." Other sections of note are the "International" section under "News" and the "Commentary" section with numerous columns on the investment world. Features include the "Calculators" section with handy tools for screening mutual funds, calculating rate of returns, employee stock options, stock screener and portfolio tracker.

S&P's Index Services
(http://www.spglobal.com/)

S&P's Index Services is a focused site on market index activities. Descriptive information, methodology, constituents, and recent data are all provided here by S&P for U.S. and international indexes. A calendar is often available for upcoming corporate actions related to each index.

Features include the "Global Industry Classification Standard" (GICS) and related S&P index tickers, exchange links, and a "Special Data" section with information on items such as total return, market attributes, earnings, turnover and several others. The "Sector Scorecard" is a useful tool for reviewing sector and sub-sector performance over a variety of time periods.

IPOs

IPO.com
(http://www.ipo.com)

In addition to breaking news on the initial public offerings market, a database of IPO filings is available. Search options include underwriters, law firms, accountants, executives, and venture investors. IPO information is available for companies back to 1998. Features include VC Funding research reports for a fee and an extensive secondary market breakdown.

IPO Central
(http://www.ipocentral.com)

Hoover's Online provides information on the IPO market at their IPO Central site. In addition to IPO news and filing dates there is the "IPO Scorecard" feature that serves up information on the total values of recent IPOs as well as statistics by industry, best and worst returns, biggest first days, and several other lists. Also available is an "IPO Beginner's Guide." Features include "Aftermarket Performance Data" and "Postponements."

Alert-IPO
(http://www.alertipo.com)

Alert-IPO is part of the Internet.com family. While Alert-IPO contains similar information to IPO.com and IPO Central, it does have several unique features. Specifically it allows for the searching of IPOs by state, country, and by competitor. Alert-IPO has a free IPO newsletter available as well as several fee-based services, e-mailed alert services, and nightly news feed summaries. Additional features include a "Bull/Bear Ranking" tool and an "IPO Dictionary."

HISTORIC DATA

BigCharts
(http://www.bigcharts.com)

Supported by sponsors and advertising, BigCharts is an excellent resource for charting and historic data. Pricing information is available for more than ten years for most companies. The "Interactive Charting" feature provides over a dozen chart options including averages, indicators, comparisons, as well as nine different chart formats and numerous customizable presentation options.

Features include three-month performance data for Dow Jones U.S. Industry Sectors and the "BigReports" section with information on securities within each market and the state of the markets.

Yahoo! Finance: Historical Prices
(http://table.finance.yahoo.com/k?)

The historical prices feature of Yahoo! Finance provides tabular numeric data on daily, weekly, and monthly stock price information. Dividends can also be displayed. The information is presented in an HTML table, but can be downloaded in spreadsheet format.

STOCK SCREENERS

Multex MarketGuide Screener
(http://www.multexinvestor.com)

A somewhat non-intuitive entry page leads to an extremely powerful stock-screening tool at Multex Investor. Twelve different categories including "Earnings Estimates," "Growth Rates," "Financial Strength," and "User Defined Variables" with numerous sub-options make this a tool for the informed investor. A "Simple Screening" tool is available. Full descriptions of each variable are available. At the time of this writing, 9,331 active companies were in the database.

MSN Moneycentral
(http://moneycentral.msn.com/investor/finder/predefstocks.asp)

The "Custom Search" provides access to eleven criteria-types menus for a novice-friendly screening tool. A "Deluxe Stock Screener" is available as a free download with many more criteria filtering options. The "Pre-Defined Search" area has six carefully set screens for different types of investing strategies including high momentum, cheap stocks, high yield, and "dogs of the Dow."

Business Week
(http://prosearch.businessweek.com/businessweek/general_free_search.html?)

Business Week provides a "Quick Stock Search" tool and an "Advanced Stock Search" tool with many variables and options. The "Advanced" version contains approximately eighty criteria. Especially useful are the linked definitions for each variable with information on scale and how to use it effectively for investing strategies. Filters are available for exchange, industry, and type of stock. There is also a specialized screening tool that uses the Business Week 50 and S&P 500 to create even more focused lists of potential investment targets.

BEAR ANALYSIS

Bearmarketcentral
(http://Bearmarketcentral.com)

Investing consists of two opposing "sides," the "bulls" and the "bears." The "bears" are historically more pessimistic regarding the stock market and its general future success. Bearmarketcentral, while heavy with advertising and self-promotion of products, serves as a valuable source for "bearish" or contrarian investing. Information and guidance is provided on short selling, "bearish" investing, and "bearish" market news.

Fall Street
(http://Fallstreet.com)

Fall Street is a rich source for "bear" investing information. Current news articles, a recurring "Spotlight" column, and an extensive directory of links are available. A discussion board is also provided for "bear" investors.

BROKERS

Gomez: Broker Scorecard
(http://www.gomez.com/)

Gomez, Inc. is a provider of e-commerce measurement and benchmarking services. As a service to the investing community, they provide a regularly updated evaluation of online discount and full-service brokers. Brokers can be sorted by criteria (ease of use, customer confidence, on-site resources, relationship services, overall cost, and overall score) as well as by user type (hyper-active trader, serious investor, life-goal planner, and one-stop shopper). Each broker is scored and briefly reviewed by Gomez.

CNN/Money: Best Online Brokers 2001
(http://money.cnn.com/best/brokers/)

This excellent article ranks and reviews online brokerage services. Detailed information on their methodology is provided while the brokers are organized by user type (mainstream investors, frequent traders, wealthy investors, and beginners). While the article is beginning to be somewhat dated, it still contains useful information and analysis to assist investors under current conditions.

MUTUAL FUNDS

Morningstar
(http://www.morningstar.com)

Morningstar is the premier name in mutual fund information. Its Web site contains an abundance of information and resources. The mutual fund section contains a "Fund Quickrank," "Fund Selector," "Investment Radar" interactive map of the top 500 funds, and a fund comparison tool. Some features are available with a free membership, while enhanced features are available with a premium fee-based membership. Fund lists, news articles, and analyst opinions round out this excellent site.

Brill's Mutual Funds Interactive
(http://www.brill.com)

The "FundLink" section contains URLs to a large number of mutual fund companies. The site also provides full-text articles from investment "experts," mutual fund primers, profiles of fund managers, and an extensive Q&A forum.

BONDS

Bureau of the Public Debt
(http://www.publicdebt.treas.gov/)

In addition to being the primary site for U.S. public debt information, the Bureau of Public Debt is the main source for U.S. Savings Bonds, T-Bills, and Treasury Notes. Information available includes rates, payback dates, cancellations, and purchase details.

Investing in Bonds
(http://www.investinginbonds.com)

This excellent site contains information on municipal, corporate, and treasury bonds. The municipal and corporate sections have a searchable, browsable, and sortable report of daily transactions. A bond glossary and an investor's checklist support the bond information. There is substantial introductory and explanatory information on this site for the novice investor.

Bonds Online
(http://www.bondsonline.com)

Overflowing with bond information, Bonds Online provides a greater level of granularity in navigating the information than other sites in this section. A solid section of general bond information, "the Bond Professor," and yield curve tables are just a few of the available resources.

COMMODITIES, OPTIONS AND FUTURES

CommodityVille
(http://www.commodityville.com/)

CommodityVille consists of two primary sections, "Commodity Central" and "Commodity Café." The "Café" is a moderated discussion forum for commodity traders. "Commodity Central" is an extensive portal to all types of commodity sites and resources. Separated into approximately twenty-five categories including "Commodity Charts," "Educational Resources," "Online Paper Trading," and "Trading Systems & Methods," the site is filled with a valuable collection of links. Updated regularly, this is an excellent starting place for anyone seeking commodity and futures related information.

Futures Guide
(http://www.futuresguide.com)

Futures Guide is a useful source of recent news and opinions on the futures and options markets. Of particular note in this site are the "Market Forecast" report on currency and commodity futures and the "Historical Data" section with daily settlement prices back to March 1999.

Future Source
(http://www.futuresource.com)

Future Source is a commodity portal with regularly updated news articles, market announcements, contract specs, charting tools, quotes, and a discussion forum. Registration is free and necessary to access portions of the information. More enhanced services are available for a fee.

INTERNATIONAL

World Federation of Exchanges
(http://www.world-exchanges.org)

The International Federation of Stock Exchanges is the global trade association for the exchange industry. Membership consists of fifty-five regulated members from around the world. Information available includes specifics on each of the member exchanges, recent news articles and announcements, and other publications including an annual report, market information, studies and workshop reports, and other association related documentation. Several of the publications are available only to members.

Numa Web: Directory of Futures and Options Exchanges
(http://www.numa.com/ref/exchange.htm)

This is a massive directory of over 100 countries and their exchanges. Contact information is available including address, telephone numbers, e-mail address, and URL. Numa Financial Systems provides this directory as part of their derivatives information site.

JPMorgan ADR
(http://www.adr.com)

JP Morgan provides a central source of American Depository Receipts and international equities information and data. Introductory and expert information can be found on ADRs. Current information is available on top performing ADRs, world markets, and industry overviews. Searchable by country, region, industry, and ticker symbol company information is available on financials, earnings estimates, and institutional ownership along with a concise tear sheet. Free registration is available for the customizable portfolio tool.

Oanda 164 Currency Converter
(http://www.oanda.com/convert/classic)

The FXConverter provides current and historic exchange rates between 164 currencies. Options include "Interbank," "Typical Credit," and "Typical Cash" rates. The "Converter" is available in English, German, French, Italian, Portuguese, Spanish, and Swedish.

ASSOCIATIONS/ORGANIZATIONS

Securities & Exchange Commission
(http://www.sec.gov)

The United States Securities & Exchange Commission provides a wealth of investment information. Specifically the site contains information on SEC rules and regulatory information, the EDGAR database of public company financial filings, news and press releases, speeches and public statements, and litigation releases. For the individual investor there is a collection of tools; i.e., "Mutual Fund Cost Calculator," "Investor Quizzes," and several others. The site offers over fifty online publications including "Tips for Online Investing," "Investment Clubs and the SEC," and "Stock Market Fraud 'Survivor' Kit." Also available is a complaint center and information on evaluating and selecting brokers and advisors.

American Association of Individual Investors
(http://www.aaii.com)

The AAII's purpose is to represent and instruct individual investors. Instructional resources include reports from financial gurus, publications on investing strategies, tax relief, and broker guides. A fee-based membership provides access to additional resources including financial planning tools, tax resources, portfolio management, stock investing and analysis, and a community bulletin board.

National Association of Securities Dealers
(http://www.nasd.com)

The NASD is the regulatory organization for the securities industry. The site contains news and press releases, regulatory documents, a streaming investor university, tips and criteria for evaluating brokers, investment guidance documents, complaint submission, and more information for brokers, securities firms, and regulators.

GLOSSARIES

Yahoo! Finance-Financial Glossary
(http://biz.yahoo.com/f/g/g.html)

Yahoo! provides access to an extensive collection of investing terms with clear and short definitions. This glossary is especially strong in acronyms.

Motley Fool Glossary
(http://www.fool.com/school/Glossary/glossary.htm)

The Motley Fool's Glossary is not as extensive or as heavily cross-referenced as some other glossaries. The definitions are written with a novice user in mind and are clear and jargon free.

Global Investor Glossary
(http://www.finance-glossary.com/pages/home.htm)

This glossary consists of 2,000 investing terms with extensive definitions and cross-references.

Investor Words
(http://www.investorwords.com)

A massive glossary of 6,000 terms and 20,000 cross-references makes this one of the most extensive investment/financial glossaries on the Web. It is searchable and browsable.

Campbell R. Harvey's Hypertextual Finance Glossary
(http://www.duke.edu/~charvey/Classes/wpg/glossary.htm)

Competing with Investor Words as the largest finance glossary is the Harvey's Finance Glossary. Boasting 7,200 terms and over 18,000 cross-references, this is an excellent resource for finance and investment definitions and acronyms. Browsing is by alphabet only.

UNIQUE TOOLS

ValuePro: Baseline Valuation Calulator
(http://www.valuepro.net/index.shtml)

While primarily a site advertising the ValuPro 2002 valuation software for purchase, ValuePro does provide an extremely interesting tool to sample what the full version can do. The "Baseline Valuation" tool takes a submitted ticker symbol and calculates an "Intrinsic Stock Value." It accomplishes this by calculating twenty financial variables to provide this value amount. Especially useful is the ability to alter the evaluated criteria based on user input and then to recalculate the stock's value. Thus the visitor can create a valuation on currently available information or on specific numbers and parameters. A clear explanation of what the online valuation is doing is available. A "Value Screening" tool and "Portfolio Valuation" tool are planned for the future.

Prophet Finance: Java Charts
(http://www.prophetfinance.com/charts/pc.asp)

The investment portal Prophet Finance provides access to the most powerful charting tool on the Web. Entering a ticker symbol provides the standard stock price chart and volume data. However, there are many additional features available. The interactive Java chart allows for zooming in to the stock price information, chart display options, adding indexes and companies to the chart for comparison, and viewing lists of selectable gainers and losers from the major exchanges. The "Technical Analysis" features include dozens of clickable options on moving averages, upper studies, lower studies, market studies, trend studies, volatility, and more. An enhanced version with historical data is available for a monthly fee.

Motley Fool: Pegulator
(http://www.fool.com/Pegulator/pegulator.htm)

The Motley Fool is an excellent, rather irreverent site that encourages and instructs on investing. A key tool for analyzing a company for possible investing is the "Price to Earnings Growth Ratio" (PEG). The Fool provides a handy tool and explanation for how to calculate and use the PEG ratio.

S&P/SmartMoney Map of the Market
(http://www.smartmoney.com/maps/)

Standard & Poor's, in collaboration with *SmartMoney* magazine, have created a very interesting visual tool of market activity. Companies are grouped into sectors and then color coded by their activity and recent price direction. You can view the recent performance of industry sectors and of competitors. The "Map Control Panel" allows for the viewing of gainers and losers and the change from a selection of dates. Maps are available for the S&P 500, mutual funds, IPO market, sector maps, and a customizable map for your own portfolio.

Quicken's One-Click Scorecard
(http://www.quicken.com/investments/ strategies/)

Quicken has created a unique analyst tool with its "One-Click Scorecard." The "Scorecard" allows for the review and analysis of companies by one of four prominent investment strategies. After selecting a company and an investment strategy a recommendation is given as to whether it is of "interest" or not to further research the company. Details are provided on a variety of criteria for each strategy and why it passes or fails that strategy. An excellent source for gaining insight into how certain investment strategies work and what their reaction would be to a given stock.

The Best of the Web:
Hospitality and Tourism Web Sites

Diane Zabel

SUMMARY. This chapter on hospitality and tourism Web sites includes key sites for the lodging and gaming industries, restaurants and foodservice, and the tourism industry. *[Article copies available for a fee from The Haworth Document Delivery Service: 1-800-HAWORTH. E-mail address: <docdelivery@ haworthpress.com> Website: <http://www.HaworthPress.com> © 2003 by The Haworth Press, Inc. All rights reserved.]*

KEYWORDS. Hospitality, tourism, travel, Web sites

INTRODUCTION

Hospitality is an umbrella term that encompasses a wide range of diverse industries. The hospitality industry consists of fragmented services: foodservice in restaurants; foodservice on planes and cruise ships; foodservice in clubs; foodservice in college dormitories, school cafeterias, hospitals, nursing homes, and jails; lodging; and recreational facilities ranging from casinos to resorts. The tourism industry also involves a spectrum of commercial activities. Tourism is an industry con-

Diane Zabel is Endowed Librarian for Business, Schreyer Business Library, The Pennsylvania State University (E-mail: dmz@psulias.psu.edu).

[Haworth co-indexing entry note]: "The Best of the Web: Hospitality and Tourism Web Sites." Zabel, Diane. Co-published simultaneously in *Journal of Business & Finance Librarianship* (The Haworth Information Press, an imprint of The Haworth Press, Inc.) Vol. 8, No. 3/4, 2003, pp. 167-179; and: *The Core Business Web: A Guide to Key Information Resources* (ed: Gary W. White) The Haworth Information Press, an imprint of The Haworth Press, Inc., 2003, pp. 167-179. Single or multiple copies of this article are available for a fee from The Haworth Document Delivery Service [1-800-HAWORTH, 9:00 a.m. - 5:00 p.m. (EST). E-mail address: docdelivery@haworthpress.com].

sisting of an amalgamation of services that support a traveler's need for transportation, food, lodging, amusement, and entertainment. The tourism industry involves industries as wide ranging as tour operators, rental cars, hotels, bars, gasoline stations, theme parks, and attractions. Although the terms hospitality and tourism are often used interchangeably, they are not quite synonymous. The tourism industry serves travelers, people away from home. In contrast, the hospitality industry also includes businesses (such as restaurants) that serve people in their local town. Olson and Blank provide an example that helps explain this difference: "A restaurant illustrates this distinction–it is always a part of the hospitality industry, but only that part of sales to people away from their usual residence or work area can be considered tourism."[1]

Together, hospitality and tourism represent a major industry. In 1999, travel expenditures within the United States by domestic and international travelers totaled $522.9 billion.[2] The industry is also a major source of employment. The travel and tourism industry is the third largest private employer in the United States; only the health services and business services sectors of the economy employ more workers.[3] It also generates new jobs faster than other sectors of the economy. In 1999, travel and tourism generated jobs in the United States totaled 7.7 million, a twenty-four percent increase from 1990.[4] Tourism is also a growth industry worldwide, especially in developing countries. Even the poorest of the poor nations have contributed scarce resources to tourism development.

The hospitality and tourism industries are important for more than economic reasons. Tourism has significant environmental, social, and cultural impacts. Although tourism can bring economic prosperity, it can also bring over-development, strip-development, and loss of an area's uniqueness. Although tourism generates money, it also requires major capital investment on the part of host countries. For example, visitors increase the demand for garbage collection, police protection, and other municipal services. The flow of tourists into a region can significantly alter the environment. It can result in traffic congestion, pollution, a depletion of natural resources, and a shift in the ecosystem. As a result of these negative environmental consequences, ecotourism (tourism sensitive to the environment) has emerged as one of the hottest topics in hospitality and tourism studies.

Hospitality and tourism studies is still in its infancy as an academic study. The academic discipline of hospitality involves numerous areas of study, including cookery, nutrition, finance, accounting, marketing, management, law, and information technology. Tourism studies in particular has drawn from the scholarly expertise of other fields such as geography, sociology, psychology, political science, economics, and anthropology. The development of tourism as a separate field of study did not occur until the 1960s and 1970s, the same period when specialized research journals emerged in the discipline. In the past two decades, hospitality and tourism education has grown dramatically. In the United States alone, there are almost 300 institutions awarding degrees (ranging from associate degrees to doctorates) in the culinary arts, restaurant and foodservice management, hotel/lodging management, and travel and tourism management.[5]

Librarianship in hospitality and tourism studies is both challenging and specialized. Reference questions can range from queries about the history of a specific cuisine to inquiries about the socio-demographic characteristics of consumers who have taken a cruise in the past year. Hospitality and tourism students and researchers make heavy use of business-oriented materials, especially those of a statistical nature. A unique body of literature has emerged in hospitality and tourism studies. Professional trade associations, like the National Restaurant Association, and specialized publishers, such as consulting firms, produce much of the relevant literature. It is not surprising that these types of data producers have also produced the "best" Web resources. The following Webliography excludes consumer travel Web sites. The focus is on authoritative and substantive sites representing all parameters of the hospitality industry, as well as sites treating tourism as an economic activity.

GENERAL HOSPITALITY SITES

Hospitality Net: All of Hospitality on the Web
(http://www.hospitalitynet.org)

This comprehensive, professionally designed site was established in March 1995. It provides current industry news, industry reports, job listings, a directory of industry vendors, an index to other hospitality Web sites, and more. Industry news is updated daily and the site's news archives go back to 1995. The "Industry News" file can be searched by category, date, or keyword. Some industry news is in a multimedia format (i.e., audio and video interviews delivered via streaming media). Users looking for recent financial information relating to a sector of the industry or specific company can select "Financial News" from the main menu. Selective reports from major industry consultants are available free of charge by clicking "Market Reports" from the sidebar.

Among the consulting firms providing reports are Andersen, Global Hospitality Resources, HVS International, Jones Lang La Salle, Hospitality eBusiness Strategies, Overlook Hospitality Management AB, PKF, PricewaterhouseCoopers, Smith Travel Research, and the Cornell Center for Hospitality Research. This feature is invaluable as the firms supplying these reports are the leading consultants for the industry. The "Associations Update" link on the main menu provides recent news from several key organizations, including the American Hotel & Lodging Association, the National Restaurant Association, the Travel Business Roundtable, the Travel Industry Association of America, the World Tourism Organization, the World Travel & Tourism Council, the Hospitality Financial and Technology Professionals, and the Hospitality Sales & Marketing Association International. The "Industry Links" section allows users to search for organizations by keyword, category, or in alphabetic order. The section is fairly extensive, including not only major industry associations but also more specialized organizations such as the Asian American Hotel Owners Association and the Gaming Manufacturers Association. For each association listed, users can find more information or opt to visit the organization's Web site. Additionally, the "Industry Links" section links to hotel chains and online industry publications. Although by no means comprehensive, the "Bookshelf" menu option allows users to browse industry related books, videos, and CD-ROMS. Titles can be searched by broad category or keyword. Ordering information is available. This exceptional site (both in terms of content and design) is one that all business librarians will want to bookmark.

LODGING AND GAMING INDUSTRY SITES

American Gaming Association
(http://www.americangaming.org/)

This site is useful for news and statistics relating to the casino industry, especially information on issues impacting the industry. The Association's members include casinos and other businesses that operate gambling games and machinery. The Association disseminates information on gaming, the casino industry, and responsible gambling. For example, by selecting "Casino Industry" from the main menu, users can access briefs on issues impacting the casino industry, an annual survey conducted by the Association, federal and state legislation impacting the industry, and other news about the industry. The "Publications" link from the main sidebar allows users to access selective articles from *Inside the AGA*, the Association's newsletter, free of charge. In addition to providing access to recent articles, an archive allows readers access to articles from the past five years. The "Publications" link also allows users free access to selected articles from two related newsletters: *Responsible Gaming Quarterly* and *AGA Ally*. Web site users can also sign up to receive free e-mail notification about changes to the Association's Web site as well as the bimonthly newsletter.

American Hotel and Lodging Association
(http://www.ahma.com/)

The Association, formerly known as the American Hotel and Motel Association, was established almost a century ago. It is the premier association for the U.S. lodging industry. The Association's Web site is a good source of news and data relating to the lodging industry. While there is a "Members Only" section, the site provides a wealth of information to non-members. By clicking "Information Center," users can retrieve a list of the top fifty hotel companies, an up-to-date profile of the lodging industry, a short chronological history of the lodging industry, and practical information for hoteliers such as energy conservation tips. There are also links to hospitality schools and hospitality related organizations. By clicking "Governmental Affairs," users get access to late breaking legislative news impacting the industry, briefs that the Association has prepared on issues ranging from compensatory time/flextime to ergonomics, and links to Congressional and other political Web sites.

American Resort Development Association
(http://www.arda.org/arda)

Consult this site for news and information about the resort, timeshare, and vacation home sectors of the lodging industry. This association's membership is comprised of developers of resorts and resort communities, timeshare properties, and second homes. Members also include suppliers to the resort development industry and other companies with an interest in vacation ownership. The Association conducts surveys and other research relating to the development of resorts and recreational properties. For example, by selecting "About the Industry" option from the "About ARDA" menu, users can retrieve fast facts about the vacation ownership and resort development industries. By choosing "Legislation" from the main menu, researchers can monitor new and proposed legislation relating to pertinent issues such as timesharing, real estate licensing, property management licensing, and taxes. Librarians selecting materials in this specialized area should note that the "Publications" link on the main menu leads to a listing of recent surveys relating to the timeshare industry, vacation ownership, resorts, and recreational property. Many of these reports are published or sponsored by the American Resort Development Association, with research conducted by leading consultants in this area.

Las Vegas Convention and Visitors Authority
(http://www.vegasfreedom.com/)

This site includes information and data relating to gaming and tourism in Las Vegas. It is the official site of the Las Vegas Convention and Visitors Authority. By clicking on "Facts" from the main menu, users can then choose "Las Vegas Facts," which includes a timeline that chronicles major developments in Las Vegas's history, population statistics, and information on the city's ethnic heritage. By choosing "Press" from the "Facts" menu, users can retrieve up to date news releases providing information on number of visitors, tourism trends, and initiatives to promote tourism in Las Vegas. The "Related Links" option under "Facts" provides useful links to governmental agencies and other travel and tourism industry organizations. Researchers needing detailed and historical data on the gaming industry in Las Vegas will find extensive data by clicking "Visitor Stats" under the "Facts" menu. There are detailed statistics relating to Las Vegas tourism from 1970 to the present. The answers to many reference questions about Las Vegas tourism can be found by clicking "Frequently Asked Research Questions" under the "Visitor Stats" link. This site should be the first stop for anyone researching the Las Vegas gaming industry. Unfortunately, the research value of this site is not readily apparent since most of the site's links relate to helping tourists plan their Las Vegas vacation.

New Jersey Casino Control Commission
(http://www.state.nj.us/casinos/)

This regulatory agency oversees gaming in the state of New Jersey. Their site provides a wealth of data on New Jersey casino revenues. By selecting "Casino Revenue" from the menu, users can retrieve monthly casino revenue data for the past five years. Data are broken down by individual casino. Aggregate casino industry data are also presented for New Jersey. By choosing "Publications," searchers can download Commission publications, reports, and brochures. Some publications are available only by subscription while others are free. One particularly useful free publication is the substantive report on casino gambling in New Jersey that was submitted to the National Gambling Impact Study Commission. The New Jersey Casino Control Commission also makes their annual report available free of charge on their site. This document is useful because it includes a wealth of data on New Jersey casinos.

Since the gaming sector of the hospitality and tourism industry can be difficult to research, this site provides a valuable service by making substantive data on New Jersey casinos available free of charge. The site also links to gaming regulatory agencies in other states as well as to other organizations related to gaming.

Smith Travel Research
(http://www.str-online.com/)

Smith Travel Research is a leading consultant to the lodging industry. Although this consulting firm's site has a "Clients Only Login" area, the site provides some current data on the lodging industry free of charge. For example, a visit to their site in February 2002 retrieved useful data such as preliminary figures on the 2001 performance of the U.S. lodging industry and global lodging statistics for September 2001. A notice on this site indicated that the company is in the process of enhancing and improving their Web site. This site will be useful to those libraries that can not afford to purchase Smith Travel Research publications, such as their weekly report, monthly newsletter, or detailed annual study of the hotel industry.

US Business Reporter: Lodging & Gaming Industry
(http://activemedia-guide.com/lodging_gaming_industry.htm)

US Business Reporter provides profiles of more than fifty industries free of charge. Most overviews average four to eight pages in length. All follow a similar format, covering the industry environment, current issues, emerging trends, and characteristics of a particular industry. These profiles are also a good source of composite industry data and market share data. The analysis on the lodging and gaming industry dated February 2, 2002 discussed many critical issues, including the impact of terrorist attacks, the impact of the recession, and threats to the industry (ranging from rising labor costs to Internet gambling). These clearly written essays will be especially useful to students needing background information on an industry, basic data, and a quick analysis of industry issues and trends. Additionally, this site includes profiles of major companies in this industry. US Business Reporter has a companion report on the restaurant industry. Users can access that report and other industry reports from the Lodging & Gaming Industry page.

RESTAURANT AND FOODSERVICE SITES

Foodsafety.Gov
(http://www.foodsafety.gov)

This site is a gateway to government food safety information. Since food safety is a critical issue for foodservice professionals, this is a core resource. This well designed site has several components: news and safety alerts; food safety advice for consumers; food safety resources for educators (including those teaching food safety to children and teenagers); resources for the general foodservice industry as well as segments of the industry (nursing homes, hospitals, schools, cruise lines, etc.); contact information for reporting food borne pathogens; information on governmental food safety programs; and links to state, federal, and international agencies concerned with food safety issues. This comprehensive site includes a search and site index.

National Restaurant Association
(http://www.restaurant.org/)

The National Restaurant Association (NRA) is the premier association for the restaurant and foodservice industry. Members represent all segments of the industry: restaurants; cafeterias; clubs; contract foodservice management; and institutional foodservice providers. The NRA plays an important role in the dissemination of information. The Association has a long list of publications ranging from industry annual reports to consumer research/marketing reports. The NRA home page is an indispensable source of information. By selecting "Magazine" from the menu, users can read excerpts from *Restaurants USA*, the NRA trade journal that publishes in-depth articles on foodservice trends, operations, and political issues impacting the industry. Because governmental affairs are so critical to the restaurant and foodservice industry, the site offers a "Governmental & Legal" file. This section provides the latest news on pertinent legal issues, background information on issues of interest to the industry, a guide to laws and regulations, and links to federal, state, and local governmental officials. The site also highlights recent research conducted by the NRA. This "Industry Research" file provides a wealth of information including extensive statistical data, operating ratios, and industry forecasts. Hospitality educators and career counselors will find the "Careers & Education" file useful. This section of the site links to a range of career resources, including a directory of culinary and hospitality schools, information on the job outlook for the industry, and other career advice.

Nation's Restaurant News
(http://www.nrn.com)

This site has been created by *Nation's Restaurant News*, one of the leading industry trade journals. The site is an excellent source of marketing, financial, legislative, and headline news for the foodservice industry. "Daily Specials" leads to headline news relevant to the industry. The well-designed interface allows users to easily e-mail or print these stories. The "NRN News" menu option categorizes important news stories by broad categories, such as "Financial News," "Marketing Mix," "Legislative Loop," "People on the Move," "E-Business News," "Quick Service News," "Fine Dining News," and more. The "Operations" menu option links to stories focusing on issues relating to operating restaurants and other foodservice facilities. The "Resources" file links to ranking and market share data from several NRA special reports. These special reports include the "NRA Top 100" and "Second 100," lists of leading public and private restaurants and foodservice operators.

Restaurant Report
(http://www.restaurantreport.com/)

This site claims to contain more than 700 pages of information "for hospitality professionals and food connoisseurs." It links to top food sites, online yellow pages for the hospitality industry, hospitality jobs and more. One of the most interesting features is the section listing "Top 100 Hospitality Sites." This directory includes sites relating to food, wine, cooking, restaurant operations, and more. Sites are given a rating for content, design, navigation, and overall experience. Web site users can also opt to subscribe to a free weekly e-mail newsletter containing feature articles, restaurant industry news, and reader feedback.

TOURISM INDUSTRY SITES

American Society of Travel Agents
(http://www.astanet.com)

The American Society of Travel Agents (ASTA), the leading association for professional travel agents, disseminates information on the travel industry. ASTA's Web site is an excellent source of up to the minute news impacting the travel and tourism industries. For example, a search on this site in February 2002 resulted in stories relating to terrorism alerts issued by the Federal Bureau of Investigation, changes in U.S. airport security screening, an increase in car rental prices, and new luggage designs to better accommodate new airline security procedures. These travel news stories were extracted from the *Wall Street Journal*, *USA Today*, the *New York Times*, the *Washington Post*, the *Las Angeles Times*, *Travel Management Daily*, and other sources (including Reuters, PRNewswire, MSNBC, ABC News, CNN, Fox News, Bloomberg, the Associate Press, and governmental agencies). The site also includes consumer travel information ranging from tips to ensure a healthy trip to advice on overseas travel.

Cruise Lines International Association
(http://cruising.org)

This site, sponsored by the official trade organization of the cruise industry, is a good source of information on the cruise lines industry. By selecting "Press & Media" from the menu, users can click on the "Consumer Press Release" area of the site to find profiles of cruise lines and ships, information about cruise destinations, and recent cruise news. By selecting "Cruise Travel Update," users can find special articles on current issues in the industry, such as cruise line security. Since the cruise industry is one segment of the tourism industry that is more difficult to research in standard sources (e.g., reference works, monographs, and periodicals), this site is a particularly useful resource.

International Ecotourism Society
(http://www.ecotourism.org)

The goal of this non-profit organization is to promote environmentally responsible tourism. This visually attractive, professionally designed site offers information to a range of audiences: travelers; students; conservation professionals; tour operators; and government officials. Travelers can use the site to find eco-friendly tour operators and accommodations. Professionals and students have access to statistical data and fact sheets on ecotourism. The Society also posts (usually as PDF documents) the text of recent scholarly papers on ecotourism. These published and unpublished papers were judged to be among the best in the world by Society staff. There is also a core reading list on ecotourism. Individuals interested in studying ecotourism can link to an ecotourism education fact sheet, which includes a directory of colleges and universities offering courses and programs on ecotourism. Librarians purchasing materials on ecotourism will want to explore the "Bookstore" in order to purchase Society publications. The Society is a major publisher in the area of ecotourism and their publications range from practical guides for ecotourism planners and managers to recent case studies. Members of the Society have access to a range of benefits, depending on membership levels. The "Members Only" part of the site provides access to special pricing of books and materials, a directory of ecotourism professionals, a quarterly newsletter, and an online resource center.

ITA Tourism Industries
(http://tinet.ita.doc.gov/)

Tourism Industries was created in 1996 within the Trade Department Area of the U.S. Department of Commerce's International Trade Administration. Their Web site provides information about the statistical reports available from Tourism Industries. Tourism Industries is a prolific publisher; their current publications catalog indicated that they have more than 900 products available. Many of these can be reviewed free of charge or purchased for a nominal amount. Many of these publications provide detailed data on visitors to the United States as well as data on U.S. travel abroad. In addition, the site provides other substantive data free of charge. For example, users can subscribe to "TI News," a good source of recent data on travel to and from the United States. A new section of the site, "Tourism Industries Outreach," links to current statistics, analysis, and reports on inbound and outbound tourism. These pages provide access to current international tourism research and specific agency announcements regarding a specific region or country.

Meeting Professionals International
(http://www.mpiweb.org/)

This is the Web site for the world's largest meeting professionals group. There are more than 19,000 members in more than sixty countries. This site is a good source of information on the meeting industry. By selecting "News & Publications" from the sidebar, users can read issues of several trade periodicals for meeting and event planning professionals free of charge, including "The Meeting Professional," "Meeting Europe Newsletter," "Canadian Communique," and the "Chapter Leader Newsletter." By selecting "Weekly Newsbytes" under the "News & Publications" option, users can retrieve timely news impacting the meeting planners industry. For example, the February 26, 2002 Newsbytes link retrieved stories relating to the recovery of the cruise industry, tourism decline in Tacoma (Washington), and other stories. By selecting "Research Tools" from the "Professional Resources" option, users can retrieve statistics about the meeting industry, a profile of the meeting and travel industry, and significant legislative trends affecting the industry. Sections of the site are restricted to members only. For example, MPI membership is required for users who want to post a resume to this site. However, resume listings could be viewed free of charge as well as job postings as of late February 2002.

Travel Industry Association of America
(http://www.tia.org)

The Travel Industry Association of America is the leading trade association for the U.S. tourism industry. The Association represents all components of the industry and its goal is to promote travel to and within the United States. It conducts market surveys and economic impact studies relating to tourism as an economic activity. The Association is the major source of tourism data in the United States. It publishes several key annual publications including the *Domestic Outlook for Travel and Tourism, Tourism Works for America, The Impact of Travel on State Economies*, and *The International Outlook for Travel and Tourism*. Additionally, it publishes reports on segments of the industry. For example, recent reports have been published on the shopping traveler, e-travel consumers, travelers who gamble, middle-aged travelers, and minority travelers. Data from these publications are the basis for the free "Fast Facts" link on the Association's Web site. The "Fast Facts" link is also a good source of trend information relating to the industry. The "Press Releases" link provides news about the industry free of charge. Users needing information about legislative trends can select the "Government Affairs" link to learn about proposed legislation and regulations impacting the tourism industry. The Association's Web site also provides links to other sources of legislative news, travel statistics, demographic/economic statistics, technology trends, travel organizations, and more. Additionally, Association members have access to an online membership directory, executive summaries of several reports, and detailed statistical data.

World Tourism Organization
(http://www.world-tourism.org)

The World Tourism Organization (WTO), based in Madrid, promotes tourism and serves as a clearinghouse for tourism information. It collects tourism data and conducts research. Research findings are disseminated through its publication series. The organization also sponsors workshops and forums on tourism development and tourism policy issues. The WTO's Web site is an excellent source of global tourism data. By clicking "Facts and Figures," users can retrieve detailed data on international tourism, including short-term and long-term forecasts. By selecting "Newsroom," users can access the full text of recent news releases issued by the WTO. These press releases (which are sometimes in the form of speeches) are significant because many report major research findings or summarize data from recent surveys. Librarians with collection development responsibilities in this area will want to choose "Infoshop" from the menu in order to access WTO's catalog of publications as well as listing of new publications.

NOTES

1. Olson, R., and U. Blank. (1994). "Research Needs of the Restaurant Industry," In J.R. Brent Ritchie and Charles R. Goeldner (Eds.), *Travel, Tourism, and Hospitality Research: A Handbook for Managers and Researchers*, 2d ed., 306. New York: Wiley, 1994.
2. *The Economic Review of Travel in America*, 2000 ed., 10. Washington, DC: Travel Industry Association of America, 2000.
3. Ibid., i.
4. Ibid., 5.
5. *A Guide to College Programs in Culinary Arts, Hospitality, and Tourism*, 6th ed., 357-359. New York: Wiley, 1999.

Web Sites
for Human Resource Development
and Organizational Behavior

Kaiping Zhang

SUMMARY. This chapter covers high-quality Web sites in the areas of human resource development and organizational behavior, including professional organizations and associations. *[Article copies available for a fee from The Haworth Document Delivery Service: 1-800-HAWORTH. E-mail address: <docdelivery@haworthpress.com> Website: <http://www.HaworthPress.com> © 2003 by The Haworth Press, Inc. All rights reserved.]*

KEYWORDS. Human resources, organizational behavior, Web sites

INTRODUCTION

The selection of human resource development and organizational behavior Web sites is based on the following criteria: relevance; quality; authority; currency; and quantity.

The Web sites selected in human resource development cover topics such as benefits, compensation, discrimination, diversity, labor law and legal issues, recruitment, safety, training, and technology. The sites for organizational behavior include topics on benchmarking, communication, decision-making, organizational ethics and theory, and training and development. Sites selected are relevant to the above areas. Most of the

---

Kaiping Zhang is Business/Economics Reference Librarian, University of Oregon (E-mail: kzhang@oregon.uoregon.edu).

[Haworth co-indexing entry note]: "Web Sites for Human Resource Development and Organizational Behavior." Zhang, Kaiping. Co-published simultaneously in *Journal of Business & Finance Librarianship* (The Haworth Information Press, an imprint of The Haworth Press, Inc.) Vol. 8, No. 3/4, 2003, pp. 181-186; and: *The Core Business Web: A Guide to Key Information Resources* (ed: Gary W. White) The Haworth Information Press, an imprint of The Haworth Press, Inc., 2003, pp. 181-186. Single or multiple copies of this article are available for a fee from The Haworth Document Delivery Service [1-800-HAWORTH. 9:00 a.m. - 5:00 p.m. (EST). E-mail address: docdelivery@haworthpress.com].

10.1300/J109v08n03_05

sites selected are also intended to target faculty, students, HR professionals, but also general public users who have interest in these fields.

Quality is a major concern for selection. A good site must provide reliable information. For example, The HRzone site includes research-based
articles with reference of sources. The organization behavior resources
site links to professional journal Web sites. The OB WEB site links to
teaching materials that faculty are willing to share over the Internet.

Web pages of professional associations, organizations, and societies
are selected because they represent members and professionals in the
related fields. Their Web pages include authoritative works from these
professionals.

Currency is another criteria in the selection. Most of the sites selected
are updated and monitored on a regular basis. Although the date on
some of the index pages has not been changed, the information covered
might be current.

Most of the sites include expansive information. Some sites include
Web search engines; news sites in addition to human resources sites.
This addition provides users other ways of access to information. Based
on the above criteria, the following sites have been chosen.

HUMAN RESOURCE DEVELOPMENT WEB SITES

Dr. Ed's Human Resource Cocktail
(http://www.hrmgt.com/welcome2.html)

This is the Web site of Dr. Edward H. Hernandez, Assistant Professor of
Management & Human Resource Management, School of Business Administration at California State University, Stanislaus. It is an extensive
and valuable collection of Internet sites devoted to human resources. The
"HR Law Mega-Links" page (http://www.hrmgt.com/hrlaw.htm) contains
links to hundreds of HR-related Web sites. Special areas of focus include
independent contractor law, wrongful discharge, employment-at-will, sexual harassment, age discrimination and religious accommodation in the
work place. The "Good HR Links" page includes the Human Resource
Management Resources on the Internet Site (http://www.nbs.ntu.ac.
uk/depts/hrm/hrm_link.htm). There are twenty categories of topics covering HR resource publications, development and training, and organization
and management theory. Dr. Ed's site also includes a chart of search engines and directories, a section of "Business Mega Links," and a section of
news from Interest!ALERT! (http://interestalert.com/). This Web site is
comprehensive and informative; however, the dark royal blue background

with the black-color cocktail wine glasses makes the page busy and difficult to read for some users and can be distracting.

HRGopher
(http://www.hrgopher.com/)

HRGopher is a comprehensive directory of links to over 20,000 human resource Web sites. The "HR Topic Index" on the left of the page lists subject areas ranging from absenteeism to workplace violence. There is a "Current HR News" section with selected articles from *Future*, *Entreworld*, and *Edinburgh Evening News*. The subject categories of this site are specific and inclusive covering subjects such as "Expatriate, Working–Living Abroad" which includes information on global employment and relocation, the embassies of Washington D.C., etc. Click on a subject of your interest and it takes you to a page of subcategories where you can further select a more specific area for your search. Many of the sites included are commercial. HR Gopher is a useful site for HR professionals.

HR-Guide.com
(http://www.hr-guide.com/)

HR-Guide.com contains an extensive list of well-organized links to Internet based resources for HR professionals and students. Topics covered include: "Benefits"; "Compensation"; "Education Programs"; "Equal Employment Opportunity (EEO)"; "Human Resources"; "HR Information Solution (HRIS)"; "Industrial and Organizational Psychology"; "Job Analysis"; "Labor, Law and Legal issues"; "On-line Documents and Forms"; "Safety"; "Selection and Staffing"; "Test Information"; and "Training and Development." Pages can be translated into French, German, Italian, and Spanish.

HRZone
(http://www.hrzone.com/index.html)

HRZone provides human resources information in the areas of benefit, compensation, diversity, discrimination, employment law, human resources administration, labor law, organizational effectiveness and psychology, personnel administration, selection and job analysis, training and psychology, and team building. Articles included are based on research findings and references are provided. The "Labor Law and Legislation" section (http://www.hrzone.com/webguide/labor_law.html) includes useful links to help users to understand employment law and labor law trends and the links are well annotated. This is a useful site for HR professionals as well as general public users who are looking for information in areas of human resources.

Human Resources Learning Center
(http://www.hrzone.com/webguide/labor_law.html)

The Human Resources Learning Center provides comprehensive information on human resource management and development. Topics covered include associations, benchmarking, conferences and events, employment law, new tools and technology, reengineering, and much more. The "HR Library" page includes a comprehensive resource center with links to over 400 free online articles, studies, and data relating to human resources. Articles are organized in the subject areas of benchmarking, benefits, compensation, diversity, employee relations, law and policy, management, recruitment, strategy, technology, training and other related topics.

International Personnel Management Association (IPMA)
(http://www.ipma-hr.org/)

The International Personnel Management Association (IPMA) is a non-profit organization representing the interests of agencies and HR professionals in the public sector human resources field. The navigation bar on the left of the screen lists the sections on the IPMA site. The "HR (Research) Center" is a good place to look for information on human resource trends, best practices, benchmarking, organization structures, job description, and a HR glossary and terms. The "Student Center" link is helpful for students who are interested in pursuing a human resources career. The "Financial Aid Resources" section includes sites where students can find financial assistance.

The "International HR" page covers "International News" from 1998 through 2002 updated monthly or bimonthly. Sources of articles published are listed in the news. At the bottom of this page is the section of "Resources." The "Global Resources" link in this section takes the users to the IPMA Global Human Resources page. This page provides a list of Public Personnel Management article abstracts as well as Web sites from Australia and New Zealand, Canada, Europe, Philippines, Singapore, and Sweden. This "Resources" section is useful and informative. It should be placed in a more prominent and easy-to-find place.

Society for Human Resources Management (SHRM)
(http://www.shrm.org/)

The Society for Human Resources Management (SHRM), the world's largest human resource management association, is "the leading voice" of the human resource and personnel profession. It represents the interests of more than 165,000 professional and student members from around the world. Its Web sites provide comprehensive information related to Human Resources, from online publications to HR job openings around the country to an information center and library of white papers, model surveys, questionnaires, and job descriptions. The "HR Links" page, in the section of "Publications Resources," includes well organized Web sites covering topics in areas of benefits, compensation, diversity, education and training, flexible work arrangements, international HR, labor and employee relations, management, recruitment and career, safety and work and life issues. Government legal resources are also included. HR professionals, teaching faculty and students who are interested in issues relating to human resource development will find the SHRM site informative and resourceful.

Workindex.com
(http://www.workindex.com/)

Produced and maintained by the publishers of *Human Resource Executive* magazine, in cooperation with Cornell University's School of Industrial Labor Relations, Workindex is a comprehensive index of workplace-related Web sites as well as human resource tools and information providers. There are two major sections: "Feature" and "Workindex: HR Links." The "Feature" section includes topics on "Stories from Human Resource Executives," "Expert Views," "Topics and Tactics," "Supplier News," "Jobnet Works," "Perspectives," "Monthly Survey," and "Legal Clinic." The "Workindex: HR Links" section contains a dynamic list of over 4,000 Web sites for HR professionals.

Workindex.com is also a searchable Web site. Users can go to the top left-hand corner of the page. In the "HR Category Search" box area, click on the arrow to reveal the drop-down menu of choices. Select the one related to your needs, for example: "Recruitment." You will automatically be taken to the list of categories on this topic and you may then select a narrower topic for your research.

You can also do a keyword search by typing a word or words in the keyword search box located just under the drop down menu and click "Find." The next screen displays a listing of references on your topic.

Scroll down the screen to select one to read the annotation or go to a specific site.

Workindex.com includes well-researched sites. Annotations of each link are also well done. By clicking on the "More Info" button, users can read the details of a specific site. This is a unique feature of this site.

ORGANIZATIONAL BEHAVIOR WEB SITES

Organizational Behavior Resource
(http://www.cps.usfca.edu/ob/resources/)

The Organizational Behavior Resources Web site is produced by the College of Professional Studies of University of San Francisco. It includes Web resources related to organizational behavior research and practice. There are twenty-seven subject categories covering benchmarking, communication, decision making, human resource development, organizational ethics and theory, training and development and more. In each category, there is a definition on the subject followed by links related to that topic. The links are from a variety of resources including journal articles, Web sites, and presentations. These resources serve as research and learning tools to support students' coursework, research activities, teaching, and lifelong learning interests.

OB WEB
(http://www.obweb.org/)

OB WEB is the official Web site of the Organizational Behavior Division of the Academy of Management (http://www.aom.pace.edu/). This site includes links to member pages, other related sites and more information about programs, research resources, syllabi, etc. The "Publications" link on the left index takes you to a page of Web sites links for journals of the Academy of Management as well as other professional journals related to organizational behavior. All journals sites listed require paid registration; however, users can review article abstracts, table of contents, sample articles or full text articles from previous issues. For example, *Journal of Organizational Behavior* provides free access to full text articles in issues in the previous years. The tabs across the top take you to specific areas of "Research," "Teaching," and "International." These sections are interactive. You can send e-mail messages to participate in online discussions. The OB WEB site is a good resource for teaching faculty and graduate students who are researching issues relating to organizational behavior.

Best of the Industry Information on the Web

Jen Venable

SUMMARY. Industry resources are another important area of business research. This chapter provides in-depth coverage of primary Web sources for industry research. *[Article copies available for a fee from The Haworth Document Delivery Service: 1-800-HAWORTH. E-mail address: <docdelivery@haworthpress.com> Website: <http://www.HaworthPress.com> © 2003 by The Haworth Press, Inc. All rights reserved.]*

KEYWORDS. Industry information, Web sites

INTRODUCTION

A researcher may seek industry information for a variety of reasons. Sales, marketing and human resources professionals search companies organized into industry groups for leads. Other users include entrepreneurs who gather facts on potential business ventures or investors who analyze markets by industry. Manufacturers may purchase a desired piece of merchandise on the Web if they know how to find relevant industry portals.

The free industry-related information available on the Web is so diverse and voluminous that it is most logically organized by purpose. I have grouped the "best of the industry Web sites" as they relate to the following categories:

Jen Venable is Assistant Management & Economics Librarian, Purdue University (E-mail: jenv@purdue.edu).

[Haworth co-indexing entry note]: "Best of the Industry Information on the Web." Venable, Jen. Co-published simultaneously in *Journal of Business & Finance Librarianship* (The Haworth Information Press, an imprint of The Haworth Press, Inc.) Vol. 8, No. 3/4, 2003, pp. 187-204; and: *The Core Business Web: A Guide to Key Information Resources* (ed: Gary W. White) The Haworth Information Press, an imprint of The Haworth Press, Inc., 2003, pp. 187-204. Single or multiple copies of this article are available for a fee from The Haworth Document Delivery Service [1-800-HAWORTH, 9:00 a.m. - 5:00 p.m. (EST). E-mail address: docdelivery@haworthpress.com].

10.1300/J109v08n03_06

- General Profiles, Overviews and Descriptions
- Portals and Directories
- News and Investing
- Product Sale and Purchase

Free, stable, Web-based industry resources are difficult to find. They are elusive in that the companies that publish the quality content are often preparing to move that information "behind the wall" or to a log-on based charge section of their Web site. For this reason, I have included a review category called "cost status change possibility." If the company plans to eventually charge for the industry information, I have mentioned it here, and tried to get a general idea of when this free-to-fee transition will take place.

Inconsistencies are common when dealing with the methodology and classifying systems used by each Web site to name and categorize the many industry sectors and sub sectors. Some sites use the industry names available from the stock exchanges; others use SIC code categories and others create their own.

Some of the Web sites chosen are dedicated entirely to providing industry information, and some provide industry information along with other services. My focus is on the quality of information, regardless of whether the site is completely dedicated to industry information, or if the industry portion has only a minor presence.

CATEGORIES

- General Profiles, Overviews and Descriptions

    These are Web sites that provide a current, comprehensive synopsis of a particular industry's situation, including financial background, consumer spending, history, and top players.

- Portals and Directories

    These are Web sites that point the researcher to other Web sites about specific industries.

- News and Investing

    These are Web sites containing financial data, market share information, outlook, and analyst predictions for specific industries. These include the "latest and greatest" news that is available free online. This information is used by business researchers for the purpose of investing.

- Product Sale and Purchase

    These are Web sites geared toward the businessperson seeking to buy, sell or trade products. These Web sites usually have a primary directory organized by industry.

Fee or Free?

The bulk of the Web sites I have selected for each category do not cost money to use, as I believe the "best of the Web" are resources that are both high in quality and free of charge.

Selection Criteria

- Content quality (writing or data quality/accuracy/volume/sources/relevance)
- Site organization (location of industry info/navigation/layout)
- Authority (organization/company sponsoring site)
- Search Relevance
- Endurance Factor (will this site be around next year?)
- Cost status change possibility (will this site change from free to fee?)
- Value-Add

Exclusions

Barred are the Web sites focused on a single industry. An industry-specific organization or enthusiast usually sponsors such sites. These will often have questionable ownership and maintenance. My reviews are focused on portals and services backed by "deeper roots" and are therefore more likely to be in existence and retain their quality for a longer duration. I have included portals that point to market-dedicated Web sites for researchers who seek this information.

Format

The top rated Web site in each category is listed first in full detail. "Runner-up"/"Runners-up" sites follow in a more abbreviated review format.

GENERAL PROFILES, OVERVIEWS AND DESCRIPTIONS

Hoover's Online
(http://www.hoovers.com)

Description of Service

Hoover's has been utilized by Web roving business information seekers as a principal destination for company information since the Web site launched eight years ago. Aside from presenting financials and skillfully written descriptions of over 18,000 public and private companies, the resource now offers useful industry information available from the *Companies & Industries* tab off the site's main navigation bar.

Goal/Aim/Purpose of Site

"To be the lowest-cost business information tool on the Web for professionals."

Historical Highlights

Hoover's began in 1990 as a book company called *The Reference Press*, which published business reference books containing profiles of companies. The content of these books were company profiles containing descriptions of "big player" companies. The descriptions were unique. They contained financial information and intelligently written historical synopses of the "big corporate players."

After a few years of dabbling in electronic delivery, the company lobbied for capital from Time Warner Books in 1994 and launched Hoover's Online. The service grew and Hoover's went public in 1999, expanding its Web features. The site now offers profiles/capsules of over 18,000 companies and a new section of industry "lowdowns" and descriptions.

Content Quality

Writing Quality: Hoover's has their own team of journalists who write the company and industry profiles. This group of roughly fifty-five writers and editors are organized into industry-based teams (e.g., "Finance & Healthcare" and "Entertainment & Information"). So this means a particular writer/editor consistently covers a group of companies in a particular industry. Why is this important? It means that the creators of the industry profiles are experts. The industry synopses are insightful, well written, and entertaining.

Hoover's, unlike other business Web sites, does not regurgitate previously existing information on the Web. What you find in these profiles are free, original overviews of the goings-on of an industry.

Accuracy: Hoover's has quality control experts responsible for finding errors in content. A "Feedback Form" is located on the site where users may report inaccuracies.

Volume: Hoover's offers descriptions of over 300 industries that are organized into twenty-eight industry "sectors." Researchers should focus on the sectors because their descriptions are each roughly one page long. The remaining 270+ "sub" industry areas are described in a sentence or two and followed with a list of relevant companies. The amount of information offered will be ideal when all of these industries are treated with full "Lowdown"-type descriptions.

Sources: Hoover's reveals the "types" of sources used for researching companies, but is unclear on where the journalists search to find overall industry information. As stated in an FAQ section of the Web site, Hoover's journalists use sources such as annual reports and 10-Ks, article searches, other reference material, and even interviews with company representatives.

Site Organization

Location of Industry Information: This meaty information is not advertised with bells and whistles on the home page. However, the tab called "Companies & Industries," located on the home page main navigation bar, gives the novice Hoover's researcher a hint.

Navigation: To arrive at the information, the user chooses the "Companies & Industries" page and chooses the third tab on the left navigation bar. The user is then lead to highlighted tabs presenting an A to Z list of over 300 industries/sectors and a list of the twenty-eight sectors with links to the descriptions, called "Industry Snapshots." Aside from "The Lowdown" feature and the twenty-eight snapshots, other elements include a "who's who" collection of relevant companies that link to the Hoover's capsules and less useful lists of links to news and associations and links to journals and conferences.

Layout: Hoover's has been known for carrying a more cluttered design than other business Web sites. Recent streamlining has skimmed some of the fat, allowing for easier navigation.

Authority

The Web site has been operating for eight years, and is known as one of the more senior members of the "good 'ol boys" online business information club. Hoover's has an expert staff writing the content.

Search Relevance

The A to Z hot linked directory list eliminates the need to use a search engine.

Endurance Factor

The company is eight years old and the stock looks good compared to the financials of rival companies. This URL will be functioning for a while.

Cost Status Change Possibility

Industry profiles will not always be available for free. Users may access free profiles for at least the next six months.

Value-Add

Hoover's contains well-written, authoritative information that is witty and understandable by the "layman" business researcher. Hoover's "List of Lists" located under the "Companies" tab off the "Companies & Industries" page is also a valuable tool and free to the public.

RUNNERS-UP

US Business Reporter
(http://www.usbrn.com)

Description of Service

This Web site offers free, comprehensive industry data for over fifty industries. The industry "composites" are written by market analysts originating from the company's parent company, Centium, Inc. These reports, sometimes up to eight pages long, cover a list of industry concerns including "Industry Environment," "Industry Background," "Industry Issues," "Industry Trends," "International Environment," "Environmental Issues," and "Industry Characteristics." The overviews are current and are updated regularly. Upon going through each report, I could tell (based on the revised date stamp) that the oldest reports were six months old, where most were written within the past two months. The interface is very simple (blue text on white background) and is free of advertising. The search engine/directory, which is presented in the form of a simple alphabetical industry drop box, is effective. The service has been in existence for about three years and is a "best kept secret" among academics and corporate researchers. It serves as a showplace for the research of its corporate analysts from Centium, Inc. and was initially used as a revenue builder to bring in market analysis business to its parent company.

Why I Consider This to Be a "Second-Best" Site

US Business Reporter plans on placing this valuable content "behind the wall" by March 2002. That means that the company will charge a $99 annual subscription to users. Compared to other business information sites, the charge is meager. However, after speaking to a company representative, I discovered that 100 percent of the information will become available by charge only, unlike the partial free arrangement Hoover's offers. My criteria for "best of the Web" prioritizes free sites.

Business Week Online Special Report Industry Outlook 2002
(http://www.businessweek.com/magazine/toc/02_02/B3765indout02.htm)

Description of Service

Each January, *BusinessWeek Online Magazine* publishes a special industry report issue describing the "state" of certain industries. In broad categories, the journal covers manufacturing, information, finance, life sciences, distribution and services. Descriptions are "newsy" and current. They are written in layman's style. The issue is geared toward informing investors of the economic outlook. *Businessweek* incorporates events influencing industries and provides commentary regarding what the public can expect for the coming year. Businessweek journalists effectively shine a "newsy light" on industries that cannot be found on the other Web sites. This special issue is a nice second-priority industry research source.

Why I Consider This to Be a "Second-Best" Site

In spite of the assurance from *BusinessWeek Online Magazine*'s Web master that the URL is unbreakable, I have my doubts. The URL to this issue just doesn't seem stable. In addition, once you break down the industry listings to the subcategory level, you realize that only twenty-one industries are covered.

CorporateInformation.com
(http://www.corporateinformation.com)

Description of Service

This site provides free overviews of thirty industries in sixty-five countries. Unlike the other Web sites, this particular source is focused on international business. Along with an average one-page overview of each industry, you may locate news, dealers, and related organizations, so it doubles as a portal. "Corporate Information" serves as an aggregator rather than a provider of original content. This service does not employ its own writing team like Hoover's or US Business Reporter to write the profiles, so the authority of the content is dependent upon the source from which it is obtained. Often the user is pointed to the link of another industry Web site instead of presented with the text of a profile. The length and quality of the overviews vary from one industry to another. The service claims that it provides direction to over 350,000 profiles, but sometimes these links are broken.

Why I Consider This to Be a "Second-Best" Site

The profiles are pulled from various trade journals instead of written by journalists employed at CorporateInformation.com, so the quality of the overviews are questionable and the existence of the profiles is unreliable. The profiles are often too short. Finally, the site now has a login requirement. It is possible that this site may be moving to a fee-based arrangement.

Current Industrial Reports (CIR)
(http://www.census.gov/cir/www/index.html)

Description of Service

The U.S. Census Bureau's Economics and Statistics Administration publishes annual quantitative reports of the Manufacturing, Mining and Construction industries. The data shows the shipping amounts of a particular product along with the value of the shipment. A one-page synopsis of the findings plus the data itself are available free. The consistently high quality of government information is another benefit.

Why I Consider This to Be a "Second-Best" Site

This information is only available for products (certain products related to manufacturing, mining and construction) and not services. SIC code-based statistics are useful as specific, supplemental type of industry research and not for general industry research.

PORTALS AND DIRECTORIES

Business.com
(http://www.business.com)

Description of Service

Business.com is a business-focused search engine. The company profits through the fees it charges organizations and companies that "get listed" in its directory. Business.com charges different fees based on where the company/organization prefers to appear in a results set. The "feature listing" charge floats a company to a box at the top of the results list, and serves as a kind of advertisement for the company. The search engine indexes over 400,000 listings within 25,000 industry, product and service categories. The "Yahoo!-style" interface allows the researcher to search all listed companies and organizations in the directory by industry. Business Week's *Frontier Magazine* calls it "a Yahoo! for the advanced entrepreneur."

Goal/Aim/Purpose of Site

"To help the business professional find exactly what [(s)he's] looking for."

Historical Highlights

Jake Winebaum and Sky Dayton of eCompanies launched the Web site in 2000. Business.com acquired the Work.com URL in 2001, which increased site traffic. The company is private. The company's heavy hitter partners include Cahners.com, BusinessWeek Online, Primedia, The McGraw-Hill Companies, CBS MarketWatch and Google.

Content Quality

Writing Quality: Brief, useful one-sentence descriptions of an organization or company are shown next to the hotlink of each result. Unlike the results sets displayed in Google and Yahoo!, the small descriptions are not written in a consistent style, and are not flashy, yet they are informative.

Accuracy: Company descriptions are written by those individuals who subscribed their organization to the service. At worst, these short write-ups may contain some bias, but inaccuracies are probably infrequent.

Volume: The list of companies and organizations offered when searching the directory by industry are relevant, yet too selective. In this case, quality is favored over quantity. The researcher wants the more limited, focused result set. The exclusive database of 400,000 listings is useful to a user whose goal is to weed out irrelevant and unofficial companies and organizations during an industry search. Business.com offers a solution to the "too many hits" problem one encounters when entering a search string like "advertising companies and consultant" into Google or Yahoo! But there are still too few listings to offer the researcher enough choices.

Sources: Business.com taps the Financial Times, Dow Jones, Reuters, Thomson, and McGraw-Hill for information used to compile company profiles.

Relevance: The directory listings are organized under relevant categories. The searches reveal listings of companies and organizations relevant to the industry searched.

Site Organization

Location of Industry Information: The directory of twenty-four general industries is clearly arranged on the home page. This list of industries is bolded, hot linked and occupies about eighty percent of the page.

Navigation: The user clicks on an industry and links to a page showing the alphabetical list of search results on the lower half and a collapsed directory of links for that industry's sub-sectors (called "categories") located on the upper portion of the page. There is a separate feature located in the middle of the page called "Resources," featuring links to "Associations," "Education & Training," "Employment," "Events," "News" and "Reference." It is helpful that these types of sites are separated from the main list of results.

Site Layout: Clear blue text on a white background with limited advertising makes this site surf-friendly. The layout mimics the Google and Yahoo! directories. Partnership logos are advertised on the home page; a limited amount of ads are shown on the results pages.

Authority

Two factors make this tool more reliable than many commercial e-commerce portals: the fact that it was developed by librarians and seasoned Internet gurus as opposed to e-commerce sales people; and the impressive corporate backers that put their money and their reputations on the theory that Business.com is a valuable tool.

Search Relevance

Using the A to Z hot linked directory list yields more accurate results than using the search engine, especially if the user is searching by industry.

Endurance Factor

We can trust that this Internet portal may be one of the survivors based on its strong partnerships.

Cost Status Change Possibility

Not likely as revenue generating plans do not appear to be user-targeted.

Value-Add

This tool also offers 25,000 company profiles of private, public and international companies.

RUNNER-UP

Stanford GSB Jackson Library Rosenberg Corporate Research Center Selected Business Websites
(http://wesley.stanford.edu/library/links/index.html)

Description of Service

This is a graduate-student run Web site listing topic areas that represent most industries. The Web site has a clean layout, and the links are well chosen.

Why I Consider This to Be a "Second-Best" Site

This Web site is not particularly rich in directory listings. However, this is a useful secondary research source, especially considering the overwhelming amounts of information available from other directories. The Web site was not created for industry research; the topics are more general.

NEWS AND INVESTING

CBS MarketWatch
(http://cbsmarketwatch.com)

Description of Service

CBS MarketWatch provides financial news and information like its competitor Yahoo! Finance. CBS MarketWatch stands out because of its great features that facilitate easy searching and sorting of financial information by industry.

Goal/Aim/Purpose of Site

To be the top-rated financial news and information source on the Internet. This source provides "the story behind the numbers."

Historical Highlights

MarketWatch.com is a public company owned by CBS and Pearson plc (Financial Times Group) and headquartered in San Francisco, California. Introduced in 1997, the company is a major financial communications player running enterprises including BigCharts.com, CBS MarketWatch Weekend and the MarketWatch.com Radio network. The company employs over seventy journalists in nine bureaus around the world.

Content Quality

Data Quality/Accuracy/Volume/Sources: This data is extracted from the major financial indexes and exchanges and is not original or qualitative content. The focus of this particular review is on organization and searchability of the data as opposed to review of the data itself.

Site Organization

Location of Industry Information: The "News Alerts" feature is easily found on the home page. However, links advertising the existence of the "Industry Analyzer/Industry Index" tools and the other eight industry-related tools are not evident from the home page. The user must intuitively know that the "good stuff" is located on the blue "Research and Tools" tab off the main navigation bar at the top of the page.

Navigation: After reaching the "Research & Tools" page there are nine different industry search features available. These links are located in multiple spots on the initial page and at deeper levels. The nine tools include "Industry Analyzer," "Industry Index," "Industry Analysis," the "Dow Jones U.S. Sector Directory," "Keyword/Symbol Industry Search Engine," "Stock Performance Search Engine," "Industry Chart," "News Alerts," and "News" (by company).

One disappointing navigation factor is that when clicking on an industry search tool, the result page is unnamed and there is not a viewable history tracker to allow the user to understand the path they took to arrive. For example, clicking on "Industry Analyzer" jumps to a default page showing "The Dow Jones US Sectors" directory, the "10 Best Performing Industries" and "10 Worst Performing Industries," a "Search For Industry" search engine and an additional search engine clumsily named "Compare a stock's performance to its industry: Enter Symbol or Keyword." Clearly, the idea is to use this page as a portal to most of those nine tools. These services, along with the free "News Alerts" which can be accessed from any of the "Create Alerts" icons located on several of the pages, allow the user to perform a range of research functions.

The logical place to start this industry tool "searching adventure" is on the central portion of the page where the "Industry Analyzer" and "Industry Index" links are visible. Don't get distracted by the repeated "Industry Analyzer" link under the "Research Tools Top 10 Features" on the left side of the page, as it leads you to the same result.

Look a bit lower and you see a "Stocks in a Box" feature listing an option that sounds similar to "Industry Analyzer" called "Industry Analysis." This tool does not exactly provide the same type of search. The user may justifiably ask: "Do these link to the same page or different pages?" The answer is different pages. The "Industry Analyzer" is actually another portal page to access the comparison charts and lists of industries and companies. The "Industry Analysis" tool prompts you to enter a stock ticker and then presents you with a chart identifying how your stock compares to its industry.

The tools are redundantly displayed and have confusing names. However, these are the benefits they provide for industry research:

- Quick shots at the best and worst performing industries
- A list of the best performing companies within an industry complete with chart
- Comparison stock charts of how a particular company is functioning compared to its industry
- An A to Z presentation of miniature stock charts for all companies in an industry

- A complete list of Dow Jones Industry indices
- Industry-specific news delivered directly to a researcher's e-mail address

Layout: Based on the description of the nine random industry information locations, it is easy to envision that the "Research & Tools" layout looks pretty disorganized. I am not a fan of placing multiple links that lead to the same page on a Web site. I also think that inconsistent naming of a tool is confusing. CBS MarketWatch should organize the ten industry tools under something called the "Industry Page" instead of displacing them everywhere.

Authority

This source is the child of established media moguls CBS Broadcasting Incorporated and Data Broadcasting Incorporated. It has expanded to a more international level with the launch of FTMarketWatch.com, proving the Financial Times has confidence in its success. Top-tier publications praising this Web site include *Forbes, Barron's, U.S. News & World Report, Esquire, Fortune, The Washington Post* and others.

Search Relevance

CBS MarketWatch offers various search engines. One is the "Industry Analyzer," which gives a directory list of industries to choose from. Another, the "Search For Industry" search box, prompts the user to provide a keyword of the desired industry. The other approach by which the user finds information is through entering a stock ticker into a search engine. The result will show how the company's stock compares with the industry as a whole. This variety allows for a greater chance to find relevant results.

Endurance Factor

The Web site's five-year status makes it a "grandfather" compared to its competitors. Its ties with CBS encourage its strong survival rate.

Cost Status Change Possibility

Information on CBS MarketWatch has a strong chance of remaining free. Revenue streams appear to be generated from advertising.

Value-Add

This site is valuable because of the ability to create news alerts by industry.

RUNNER-UP

Yahoo! Finance
(http://finance.yahoo.com)

Description of Service

Yahoo! Finance is stronger in industry news than in industry research. The tools relevant to news and investment by industry are accessible from the "News by Industry" under the "Financial News" link of the home page. "News By Industry" offers exactly what it advertises, without forcing the user to create a MarketWatch type of "News Alert."

The other facet of industry research is found in the "Stock Researcher Center" section. The new "Sector/Industry Analysis" link shows nine points of analyst data (one-day price change, market cap, P/E, etc.) for the twelve main industries in a spreadsheet format. Researchers may break down the financials of an industry area further. For example, one of the twelve main areas shown is "Energy." If the researcher wants a spreadsheet of financial data comparing the four sub-industries of "Energy," which are "Coal," "Oil and Gas-Integrated," "Oil and Gas-Operations," and "Oil Well Services and Equipment," it can be done by clicking on the "Energy" link. The next comparison level breaks down to a list of relevant companies. Clicking on "Coal" yields an A to Z list of analyst.

Why I Consider This to Be a "Second-Best" Site

This site has a cleaner, more organized design than the MarketWatch site. However, overall, MarketWatch offers more features like "compare a stock to its industry" and "The ten best and worst performing stocks." In addition, it goes one step beyond Yahoo! Finance by providing industry charts. MarketWatch has the advantage of owning the Internet financial company BigCharts.com. MarketWatch provides a great value-added service that Yahoo! Finance can't by using the charts created by BigCharts to illustrate industry and company financial information.

PRODUCT SALE AND PURCHASE

Tradeworlds
(http://www.tradeworlds.com)

Description of Service

Many of the industry Web sites focused on B-to-B commerce are not effective knowledge portals. My original idea to use these as primary sources of industry information did not develop as successfully as sites chosen for the other categories. Because these commercial sites are generally disorganized, difficult to navigate, and often point to other irrelevant Web sites, I prefer to prioritize those Web sites in the other three categories as they are backed by organizations with deeper roots.

Given this, some secondary industry knowledge may be gleaned from B-to-B, trade and e-commerce driven Web sites. The sites are useful to an industry researcher because the home pages are usually arranged by industry or product. One can find unusual information related to products, organizations and general news that may not be found on the other Web sites mentioned. This Web site serves as a directory for product buyers and sellers. It looks at the manufacturing presence on the Web and extracts relevant information, organizing it into a directory by industry. The level of organization of the markets is very specific, so a user will find information on products of all types. This site also provides locator services that point the user to freight costs and product quotes. Another feature, the "Invitational Auction," works as a "member's only" store in which sellers of specific products may ask certain buyers to purchase goods.

Goal/Aim/Purpose of Site

Creating and managing a virtual environment dedicated to specific market portals.

Historical Highlights

Tradeworlds.com is a privately owned Italian company launched in 1997. The company is backed by giants Sun Microsystems and Amazon.com among others. It also has investment capital backing.

Content Quality

Data Quality/Accuracy/Volume/Sources: The information presented is primarily gathered information created by other sources. Main links available from the home page include the "Vertical Portals Directory,"

"Product Finder," "Client Finder," "Transport Finder," "Shipper Finder" and the "Invitational Auction."

Site Organization

Location of Industry Information: The industry information relevant to a researcher is mainly located in the "Vertical Portal Directory." The "Vertical Portal Directory" occupies the majority of the home page.

Navigation: Examples of portal topics include "Electronics and Equipment," "Pharmaceuticals and Medical" and "Energy." Clicking on a portal leads the user to the next layer of information: an alphabetically arranged subdirectory of that topic. After the specific level of the industry is chosen, the user is prompted to choose the type of information desired from a final set of links, whether that is "Companies," "Institutes," "Organizations" or another choice. Then a set of Web links with one-sentence descriptions is presented.

The lower portion of search results page focuses on news related to the industry that is currently being viewed. The news pieces are organized from most recent to oldest. The information originates from company press releases and some newswires.

Other items standard to all pages include a "fast find" search engine, a weekly poll prompting the user to electronically respond to a question, various vendor pop-up boxes prompting the user to purchase products related to the industry being researched, free newsletter gimmicks and the other service features like "Product Finder," previously mentioned.

Layout: The layout is busy but well designed. The designer has effectively executed the creation of an industry b-to-b portal with a sophisticated look using blue tones, modular layout and muted colors and boxes surrounding diminutive advertising. Compared to competing b-to-b portals, it has a more professional presence.

Authority

The Web site's backers are strong, which lends credibility to the quality and effectiveness of the product.

Search Relevance

A user may find the alphabetical directory listing links to be sufficient for searching. The "fast find" search box is also an effective free text search method.

Endurance Factor

This site has existed for five years. This is an impressive accomplishment for a venture capital-backed Internet start-up.

Cost Status Change Possibility

This site is not likely to charge its users.

Value-Add

The company's international base makes it stand out.

RUNNER-UP

IndustrySearch.com
(http://www.IndustrySearch.com)

Description of Service

This is a megasite for business-to-business information. This portal is focused specifically toward the manufacturing industry. It works as an industry portal, like Tradeworlds.com, but it is focused on domestic buying and selling. A convenient state-to-state search engine is available. The site's goal is to "link industrial buyers with suppliers." The important portion of the content concerning an industry researcher is the "Other Product/Service Portals" directory. When a user clicks on "forklifts," for instance, he/she gets a page of broad reaching links ranging in subject area–from certification and training to used equipment and distribution. Other features include a "shopping cart" logo that leads to an Amazon.com-style product buying interface.

Why I Consider This to Be a "Second-Best" Site

There are fewer industry portals in this service than some of the other sites appraised. It is also difficult to find the ownership and history information, which makes it hard to legitimize the content. The design is busy with company logos monopolizing many of the pages. Some features are misleading. One misleading feature is "Power Search" which initially appears to be an advanced search tool, but is actually a straight list of companies that paid for a premium listing location.

Insurance

Joseph Straw

SUMMARY. The Web provides access to a vast amount of information related to insurance. This chapter covers portals, sites to obtain insurance ratings, and resources for statistics related to insurance. *[Article copies available for a fee from The Haworth Document Delivery Service: 1-800-HAWORTH. E-mail address: <docdelivery@haworthpress.com> Website: <http://www.HaworthPress.com> © 2003 by The Haworth Press, Inc. All rights reserved.]*

KEYWORDS. Insurance, Web sites

INTRODUCTION

Insurance is the business that sells and provides protection to people and businesses against the threat of sudden and accidental loss. The insurance industry is one of the largest sectors of the U.S. economy. The insurance market in the U.S. is the largest in the world with total earned premiums reaching $844 billion in 2000. Insurance products are generally divided into property/casualty, health, and life. Property/casualty, or personal lines, are those insurance products that provide protection for property and third party exposure; these include auto, homeowners, rental, business, and personal liability policies.[1] Health insurance products protect against the financial losses associated with illness and include hospitalization, group medical benefits, and personal health policies. Life insurance provides financial protection against the loss of life and includes things like personal, group, whole, and universal life policies.[2]

Joseph Straw is Associate Professor of Library Administration, The University of Illinois, Urbana-Champaign (E-mail: jstraw@uiuc.edu).

[Haworth co-indexing entry note]: "Insurance." Straw, Joseph. Co-published simultaneously in *Journal of Business & Finance Librarianship* (The Haworth Information Press, an imprint of The Haworth Press, Inc.) Vol. 8, No. 3/4, 2003, pp. 205-211; and: *The Core Business Web: A Guide to Key Information Resources* (ed: Gary W. White) The Haworth Information Press, an imprint of The Haworth Press, Inc., 2003, pp. 205-211. Single or multiple copies of this article are available for a fee from The Haworth Document Delivery Service [1-800-HAWORTH, 9:00 a.m. - 5:00 p.m. (EST). E-mail address: docdelivery@haworthpress.com].

http://www.haworthpress.com/store/product.asp?sku=J109
© 2003 by The Haworth Press, Inc. All rights reserved.
10.1300/J109v08n03_07

The insurance industry in the U.S. is very stable although the property/casualty sector has to plan for man-made and natural catastrophes that could happen at anytime. Insurance markets are highly competitive, although most of the written premiums are scooped up by larger companies. Both the property/casualty and life/health markets in the U.S. are highly developed, and premium growth is expected to be in the single digits for the near future. Real growth for U.S. insurers will come from penetrating markets abroad where opportunities are growing at fast rates. International movements towards more open markets will create a rich environment for growth for both premiums and investments. As insurance becomes more global, competitive pressures will increase and future consumers might be offered more specialized product choices, flexible pricing, and more innovative marketing techniques.

INSURANCE ON THE WEB

The information and reference problems posed by the insurance industry are vast. Librarians are faced with an immense array of print and electronic sources that cither deal directly with insurance or may be applicable in some way. In recent years, the Internet has become a popular medium for mounting and distributing information about insurance. Anything from rating insurance companies to quoting prices for auto insurance has become available over the Internet. The incredible size of the insurance industry itself is mirrored by an Internet presence that has grown to the point of saturation.

The emergence of the Internet as a major information source further complicates the problem of providing reference to patrons with an interest in insurance. The sheer volume of potential sites creates problems of selection and evaluation that are staggering. A basic list of core sites is likely to miss many worthy sites that may be of value for consumers or researchers. Time, Internet access, and knowledge will all conspire to limit the range of any listing of insurance links that can be compiled by one individual. The list that follows is a selection of potentially core sites that try to paint the industry with the broadest possible strokes. This list mainly concentrates on links that focus on the industry as a whole, and avoids sites that have a narrow, company, advocacy focus, or sell insurance services. None of these sites can truly provide one-stop shopping for the vast world of insurance. A detailed look at insurance will most likely demand that a researcher use these sites in combination with other print and electronic sources. Divided into categories for directories, rating sites, and research/statistical sites, the list will hopefully provide a good foundation for insurance research on the Internet.

CORE SITES

Directories

Claims Pages
(http://www.claimspages.com)

This site, designed by Michael Kay, is mainly for insurance claims adjustors and investigators. The large number of links makes it a good site for the insurance industry in general. Extensive links to news stories give good perspectives on issues of concern for insurance professionals. A series of topical folders link the user to a wide variety of valuable sites for both the consumer and the insurance professional. This site is a good starting point for a general look at the insurance field.

E-Insurance Directory
(http://www.e-insurancedirectory.com)

This is a substantial Internet directory for insurance in the United Kingdom. E-Insurance.com provides good access to insurance company Internet sites in the British Isles and Ireland. The site also has links to news and FAQ's about buying different lines of insurance. This site provides access to about 200 insurance sites across the Internet. E-Insurance.com is a good starting point for users that are interested in the insurance market in the United Kingdom.

Insurance.About
(http://insurance.about.com)

Some excellent links to the insurance world are provided in this broad informational site. Links at the top of the page allow users to access news stories and join insurance related forums and chat lines. General subject links connect users to a wide range of interesting sites from across the Internet. Some of the content on this site includes information about claims, research, statistics, company ratings, reinsurance, careers, and industry regulation. A spotlight section provides more focused topical information about issues of interest to both insurance practitioners and the general public. This site is one of the "about.com" series of directories that provide introductions to Internet resources for a number of subjects in the social sciences, business, and the humanities.

Insurance Company.com
(http://www.insurance-company.org)

The Insurance Company site provides some good general information about insurance. The site provides links to internet resources on the operational areas of insurance like actuarial science, underwriting, claims, systems, and agency. Information is also provided for different lines of insurance like life, health, homeowners, marine, and business. For both consumers and professionals this site can offer a credible starting point.

Insurance Industry Information Network
(http://www.iiin.com)

The Insurance Industry Internet Network is a very basic directory of useful links for the insurance industry. A series of directory icons takes the user to thousands of insurance related Web sites. The directories cover areas like insurance companies, law firms, corporate counsel, careers, news, agents, and brokers. The simple organization makes for fast and easy access for both the general public and insurance professionals.

Insurance Professional.Com
(http://www.einsuranceprofessional.com)

This site, created by Manoj Kumar, has a good listing of insurance related links. A simple subject arrangement provides access to sites about insurance companies, reinsurance companies, rating agencies, brokers and consultants, online insurance quotations, and insurance education. An impressive list of links to company information is one of the real highlights of the site. Kumar also provides a very extensive list of sites where consumers can get pricing information for all lines of insurance. For most types of users this site is a useful basic introduction to the insurance industry.

Insure.Com
(http://www.insure.com)

Insure.com is perhaps one of the most respected providers of insurance information on the Internet. This Web site provides some of the most extensive news coverage of the insurance industry from both industry sources and the mainstream media. Much of insure.com is a unique combination of news reporting and up-to-date educational and industry information. Insure.com is divided into consumer and professional files with each reflecting the perspective of its intended audience. Both files contain links for annuities, auto, business, health, home, life, ratings, insurance company guide, car crashes, lawsuit library, September 11, and reader forums. Users in the consumer file can click on the auto link and be taken to a page with news stories from a consumer perspective. They can also be directed to links that have features and advice on buying and using auto insurance. Insure.com also has excellent Standard & Poor's based company and rating information for over 2,500 companies that sell all lines of insurance. This site truly lives up to its reputation as one of the best insurance sites on the Internet.

Ultimate Insurance Links
(http://www.barryklein.com)

This site, maintained by Barry Klein, is perhaps the simplest yet most extensive insurance directory on the Internet. Little in the way of fancy icons or designs characterizes this site. A very simple subject arrangement connects users to information on property, casualty, life, vendors, organizations, and publishers. The actual links themselves are simply listed alphabetically and are quite large. Insurance organizations of every stripe that have some kind of Web presence seem to be covered. This site provides some excellent connections to some of the major organizational players in the insurance industry.

RATING SITES

A.M. Best
(http://www.ambest.com)

A.M. Best is the most recognized name in the area of insurance information and ratings. The respected print product has been a core feature in library collections for many years. A.M. Best is the oldest rating service for insurance companies in the United States. It is often seen as the standard rating tool for the industry as a whole. Insurance companies place great value on their Best rating and consider it very prestigious to get a high mark. The A.M. Best Web site is a subscription-based tool that allows users to access the Best reports for over 6,000 insurers. The site is fee based and users are billed for every report generated. Despite the costs that a user must face, this is still an essential site for anyone doing serious company or industry research in insurance.

Fitch Ratings
(http://www.fitchratings.com)

Fitch is another rating agency for insurance and financial services. Currently about 800 insurance companies in thirty countries are rated by the Fitch agency. The Fitch Web site provides access to the Fitch ratings, research reports, and international insurance news. Access to some of the ratings and research reports is free, but the bulk of the information content is subscription based. This site has particularly strong coverage of international insurers including some of the better coverage of European and Latin American insurance companies. The Fitch site also covers some of the larger insurance groups and international reinsurance syndicates that play a prominent role in the global insurance market. Despite the fees and subscriptions, the Fitch site can provide valuable information for professionals that are looking for insurance information from an international perspective.

Standard & Poor's Insurance Ratings
(http://www.standardpoor.com)

A growing competitor to A.M. Best for rating U.S. insurers, Standard & Poor's rates about 2,500 companies for life, property/casualty, and health insurance lines. Like other rating services, S & P rates for financial strength, solvency, credit, and claims paying ability. The S & P Web site provides free access to some of the rating files and insurer profiles. Unfortunately, most of the rating reports and sophisticated searching features can only be used by paid subscribers. In recent years, the S & P ratings have grown in their prestige across the industry, and companies place considerable importance on their S & P rating. The S & P Web site provides impressive ratings information that can supplement what a user might get from A.M. Best or other rating tools.

RESEARCH/STATISTICS

Insurance Information Institute
(http://www.iii.org)

The Insurance Information Institute Web site is a good place to get facts and statistics about the insurance industry. Topical links at the top of the page connect the user to consumer orientated information about auto, home, business, life, health, disabilities, and disasters. At the bottom of the page, more links take the user to facts and statistics, industry financials, hot topics, latest topics, media questions, audio/visual, and directory resources. In the "latest studies" link the Institute provides full-text access to studies that focus on issues of concern to the insurance industry. The Institute site is a good starting point for both consumers and professionals who want to get basic industry data.

Insurance Institute for Highway Safety
(http://www.hwysafety.org)

The Insurance Institute for Highway Safety is perhaps the most important insurance industry sponsored research organization. Studies and information generated by this organization often have national significance influencing both insurance industry decisions and public policy. The main charge of the IIHS is to study the problem of highway safety in the hopes of reducing accident fatalities, injuries, and damage to property. The IIHS Web site provides excellent access to research studies, news, facts, and other information about highway safety and its importance for the insurance industry. This site offers links to news releases and research bulletins that often summarize current IIHS research efforts. A link to "vehicle ratings" allows users to compare car makes and models to crash test standards, and a link to "safety facts" provides data on highway fatalities. For both researchers and the general public the IIHS site can provide useful information about the insurance industry's huge stake in highway safety.

Insurance Services Office
(http://www.iso.com)

The Insurance Services Office (ISO) is a major research organization for the property/casualty industry. ISO conducts research and distributes information to help insurance companies handle risk management and loss prevention. The ISO Web site allows users to connect to financial reports, standards, codes, and research studies. Users can get detailed reports of industry financial performance that go back to 1995, and access ISO sponsored studies that focus on everything from global markets to loss exposures. A good chunk of free information is available for the taking, but more still can be obtained by becoming a paid subscriber. The ISO site provides insurance professionals valuable insight into the complex workings of the property/casualty industry.

NOTES

1. Seifert, Catherine, A. (July, 19, 2001). Standard & Poor's Industry Surveys. Insurance: Property-Casualty. New York: McGraw-Hill.

2. Seifert, Catherine, A. (November 15, 2001). Standard & Poor's Industry Surveys. Insurance: Life & Health. New York: McGraw-Hill.

Knowledge Management on the Web

Meg Tulloch
Brent Mai

SUMMARY. Knowledge management is another valuable concept within the business world. The authors outline major Web resources for finding information on knowledge management as well as Web-based publications. *[Article copies available for a fee from The Haworth Document Delivery Service: 1-800-HAWORTH. E-mail address: <docdelivery@haworthpress.com> Website: <http://www.HaworthPress.com> © 2003 by The Haworth Press, Inc. All rights reserved.]*

KEYWORDS. Knowledge management, Web sites

INTRODUCTION

The origin of "knowledge management" (KM) can be traced to the early 1970s and the development of what, at that time, was called a "decision support system." Terms like "management information systems" (MIS), "expert system," and "artificial intelligence" (AI) soon joined the vernacular as advances in computer technology rapidly increased storage capacity, processing speed, and output options. Sprouting out of AI, the phrase "knowledge management" became the buzzword of the day in the mid-1990s. Despite KM initiative's eighty percent failure rate, applications of these concepts continue to be reincarnated.[1]

Meg Tulloch is Information Services Librarian, Walker Management Library, Vanderbilt University (E-mail: meg.tulloch-ray@owen.vanderbilt.edu).

Brent Mai is Director, Walker Management Library, Vanderbilt University (E-mail: brent.mai@owen.vanderbilt.edu).

[Haworth co-indexing entry note]: "Knowledge Management on the Web." Tulloch, Meg, and Brent Mai. Co-published simultaneously in *Journal of Business & Finance Librarianship* (The Haworth Information Press, an imprint of The Haworth Press, Inc.) Vol. 8, No. 3/4, 2003, pp. 213-221; and: *The Core Business Web: A Guide to Key Information Resources* (ed: Gary W. White) The Haworth Information Press, an imprint of The Haworth Press, Inc., 2003, pp. 213-221. Single or multiple copies of this article are available for a fee from The Haworth Document Delivery Service [1-800-HAWORTH, 9:00 a.m. - 5:00 p.m. (EST). E-mail address: docdelivery@haworthpress.com].

http://www.haworthpress.com/store/product.asp?sku=J109
10.1300/J109v08n03_08

Knowledge management is the systematic process of finding, selecting, organizing, distilling, and presenting information in a way that improves an employee's comprehension in a specific area of interest.[2] KM is an effort to identify what is known so that decisions can be made about the risks associated with what is truly unknown. Applications of this process can be made for the benefit of any organization whether corporate, non-profit, governmental, or academic. In many organizations, the most difficult part of this process is capturing the knowledge, skills, and competencies of what the business community would call human capital.

Until captured through some sort of knowledge management scheme, the knowledge, skills, and competencies of human capital are owned by individuals rather than the organization. A complete system of corporate knowledge management may also incorporate structural capital (i.e., the processes, structures, information systems, and patents that remain with a company when employees leave) and customer capital (i.e., relationships with customers and knowledge of their behavior relative to the organization's reputation, products/services, and prices). The trend is moving from using knowledge management as a stockpile organization theory to one of managing the flow of knowledge.

There are literally thousands of KM sites on the Web. Most seem to be associated eventually with some think-tank or consulting group. The three sites reviewed here are those that have been identified as the mega portals for the topic of KM: Brint.com; Knowledge Management Resource Center; and DM Review. There is original content to each one, but most of the topical information is found through links to other sites.

A statement to their stability is that each of these three sites has been around for several years and each appears to be up-to-date. When tested with a 100 Mbps Ethernet connection, the pages of each site load without hesitation. Very few, if any, dead links were found. These sites were last viewed on 15 February 2002.

Following the review of the three sites are direct links to organization and publication sites for KM. Most of these are included in the portal sites, but it is important to comment on them directly for a full understanding of the KM world on the Web.

Brint.com
(http://km.brint.com)

In addition to knowledge management, Brint.com serves as a portal to resources in general business, technology, and e-business. *Fast Company* notes, "If BRINT doesn't have it, then you probably don't need it."[3] BRINT's KM portal touts itself as "The Premier Knowledge Management Portal and Global Virtual Community of Practice for the New World of Business." That's a mouth full, but many sources give it credit for being one of the most comprehensive for coverage of KM and its related components.

Brint.com was established in 1996. Its stated mission is "Developing leading-edge thinking and practice on contemporary business, technology and knowledge management issues to facilitate organizational and individual performance, success and fulfillment." The site does not identify its intended audience directly but does imply that its linked resources are vital to KM executives. A cursory knowledge of KM jargon helps when using this site, which suggests that it is not intended for a complete novice to the field.

Brint.com aggregates content through arrangements with publishing houses, corporations, consulting firms, and experts on individual topics. BRINT's KM site identifies itself as the "virtual library on knowledge management." The KM Portal thoroughly explores many aspects of this specialty, including sections devoted to out-of-the-box thinking, a discussion list and archives, practitioner perspectives, an online magazine and forums, KM quotes, an event calendar, an executive's network, and executive job listings.

The discussion list is quite active with current additions on the day this review was written. Many of the discussions are driven by the postings to the "Out-of-Box Thinking" portion of the site. The archives of these discussions are extensive, going back to 1997, which is probably when they began. There is a box for keyword searching of the archived discussions.

The Knowledge Executive's Network (KEN) is an invitation-only group. Without admittance to this network, it is difficult to tell exactly what value it has, but the hype on the Brint.com site makes it sound critical to building and maintaining successful KM executives.

At first glance, this text-heavy site appears quite chaotic with heavy use of "bolding" and frequent font changes. A second and third glance may not change this perception, but there is a pattern of presentation. Some links go directly to content items while others go to further lists of links. BRINT may have it all, but it takes some effort to find it.

Recent articles grouped by topic are listed on the right bar. The left bar links to articles by BRINT authors and information about BRINT itself. At the top of that left bar is a search box that apparently searches the entire site. This box can be helpful when a unique word or phrase is sought. The center column of the screen is where the majority of the visual confusion lies. There is, however, near the top of this column a listing of the major headings as they appear further down the page. This listing provides a quick link to the information below.

The initial pages of the site make heavy use of acronyms (KM, CRM, XML, CIO, WAP, 3G, and B2B) so knowledge of KM and e-commerce related jargon is helpful for speedy navigation. Links to all four of the brint.com "channels" (general business, business technology, e-business, and knowledge management) are visible from many pages, and it is quite easy to jump from one area to another without realizing it.

The BRINT Institute is the entity behind this sponsor-financed site. Like many other KM sites, the consulting services offered by the BRINT Institute are at the heart of its existence. BRINT is a well-respected player in this field; so well-respected that a report by the Association to Advance Collegiate Schools of Business (AACSB) stated, "In ten years, we may read a *Business Week* or *U.S. News and World Report* ranking of the top learning portals. It remains to be seen whether the names on this ranking will still belong only to traditional business education providers or whether newcomers such as BRINT will be ranked between Harvard and Wharton."[4]

Knowledge Management Resource Center
(http://www.kmresource.com/)

The Knowledge Management Resource Center produced by the IKM Corporation provides background information about almost every area of knowledge management. It covers university KM sites, international KM sites, organizations, periodicals, news, community, and case studies links and is the first place to look for information about knowledge management.

IKM Corporation is a research, publishing, and consulting firm specializing in knowledge management for a general and an experienced KM audience. Its mission is "to support the implementation of intelligent knowledge management through research, training, publishing, and consulting"[5] with an emphasis on the use of KM in e-commerce, information technology management, and training.[6]

The Business 2.0 Web site (http://www.business2.com/webguide/0, 1660,8129,FF.html) recognizes IKM Corporation as a knowledge management service provider and mentions its Web site as an "extensive KM resource center."[7] The Knowledge Management Resource Center is a simple site. The home page is streamlined with only five content links to its main content areas: "What's New," "Explorer," "Bookstore," "Search," and "Feedback." "What's New" highlights recently added links to information, articles, case studies, conferences, and KM tools. The "Explorer" section covers a wide array of types of information about KM.

The "KM Explorer" section is divided into the following categories: "Introduction to KM"; "Case Studies in KM"; "Knowledge Links"–links to articles, essays, white papers, reports, reviews about KM; "In the News"; "Community"; "Lots of Links"–collections of links in KM disciplines; "KM Sites"; "Related sites"; "Products & Services"; "Conferences and Events"; "International KM"; "Knowledge Markets"; "Periodicals"; "Professional Organizations"; "Search Engines" and "Portals."

Under each of these categories are about fifteen to thirty sites with reviews of each site under the link to them. The reviewed sites are a mix of commercial, educational, and organizational hosted sites. For more information about the different areas of knowledge management, the KM bookstore section of the Web site has a bibliography of 216 titles with links to reviews on Amazon.com.

Under the site's "Search" section the search engine allows for Boolean searching. The "KM Resource Center" is also interested in feedback about the site and provides a form behind the "Feedback" link of the site.

It is very hard to tell how often the site is updated; it appears sporadically as new information is found. To check for the latest additions, go to the "What's New" section. When viewed in February 2002, the Web site had been updated with a copyright of 2002, and some sites have definitely been added in 2002.

Navigating through the different areas of the site is easy. The main navigational tool on all the pages except the Home page is a top right hand navigation bar. That top bar has links to the six main areas of the Web site that will help the user get back to any area of the Web page quickly. A brown box at the top of the screen identifies the path taken thus far with a "breadcrumb" trail and gives additional information about that page as well as making recommendations about other places in the site that could be helpful.

The Knowledge Management Resource Center produced by the IKM Corporation is well organized, easy to use and thorough.

DM Review
(http://www.dmreview.com/)

The DM Review Web site is based on the print *DM Review* and e-mail *DM Direct Newsletter* focusing on business intelligence, e-business, customer relationship management, and data warehousing. It is a hybrid of data management and knowledge management information and provides both technical and theoretical information about these subjects. *Business Objects* describes DM Review's readership as "corporate executives, IT professionals, consultants, integrators."[8] Its mission is to provide "both business and technology perspectives regarding issues, trends and solutions of interest to corporate executives and IT managers."[9]

The DM Review Web site is produced by the EC Media Group which is part of the Thomson Financial company. The material on the site is generated by the staff at EC Media Group and often comes from EC Media's publications.

DM Review offers white papers as well as articles, Web resources, and book reviews in each of its topic areas. While there are no stated criteria for inclusion of information, the coverage of the printed *DM Review*'s monthly publication would appear to apply to the Web site's philosophy: "*DM Review* taps the top industry experts to explore the important issues and bring informative and timely articles, data warehouse success stories, executive interviews, and third-party product reviews to its reader."[10]

Although the reader will most likely first notice the featured articles in the center of the home page, the sections outlined in the sidebar reveal the depth of information offered on the site. These sections are:

- "Stay Informed" has the articles from *DM Review* (the magazine) and *DM Direct Newsletter* that are available on the Web. This section also has a *Webcast Direct Newsletter*, industry news, special reports from DM, an archive of articles, online columnists, an industry events section, a content alert section, and a career center.
- "Resource Portal" takes different topics and provides a short description of each topic, articles about the topic as well as white papers and suggested books to read, associations having to do with the topic and additional Web sites that have more information about the topic.
- The "General Resources" section is a reference library with information about vendors in the field, articles that readers liked, articles that the editors deemed "classics," product reviews, software demos, a white paper library with all of DM Review's white papers, online posters, a bookstore with 250 books featured and reviewed, an author index, a glossary, and additional Internet resources.
- "Get in Touch" provides industry contacts to related associations and organizations as well as the opportunity to pose a question to the experts.

- "Corporate Information" is the last section in the sidebar. It provides the user with the normal array of contact information, customer service, subscription information to the *DM Review* magazine, DM awards, press release, and calendar information.

The DM Review Web site is constantly updated. On 12 February 2002 there was already a column from 11 February 2002 on the home page. Many stories are updated monthly when the print *DM Review* is published. Also, content is added from the weekly e-mail newsletter *DM Direct*. Other sections of the Website are updated constantly, such as the "Events" and the "Editorial Calendar."

The most common navigational tool throughout the DM Review site is the left-hand sidebar. The parent (or home page) level sidebar reveals the contents of the site. You can navigate to any major area from it. The disadvantage of such an extensive sidebar is that it is long. However, it does make navigating throughout the site easy.

In certain areas of the site, such as the portals, there are child level (or page level) sidebars that let the user easily reach more information on the page level subject. On every page the DM logo helps the user navigate back to the home page where the complete sidebar resides.

The DM Review Web site provides in-depth technical and theoretical information on the data management and knowledge management fields. It is an excellent and relatively easy to use Web site.

ORGANIZATIONS

American Productivity and Quality Center
(http://www.apqc.org)

The American Productivity and Quality Center is a member-based organization that offers education, training, benchmarking services, action research, and publications. It sponsors regular conferences on KM issues.

Knowledge Management Consortium International
(http://www.kmci.org)

The Knowledge Management Consortium International is a member-based organization that provides certification programs through the KMCI Institute. It publishes a quarterly journal and sponsors regular symposia around the world on KM concepts and practices.

The Knowledge Management Professional Society
(http://www.kmpro.org)

The Knowledge Management Professional Society is a member-based organization that conducts training and certification programs and networking opportunities.

Society of Competitive Intelligence Professionals
(http://www.scip.org)

The Society of Competitive Intelligence Professionals is a member-based organization that supports those involved in creating and managing business knowledge through education and networking opportunities.

PUBLICATIONS

There are many publications which cover the world of KM or its components. Several of those most often sited are briefly examined here.

CRM Magazine
(http://www.destinationCRM.com)

From the same publishers as *KMM*, *CRM* (Customer Relationship Management) focuses on issues and ideas that can help organizations better understand and leverage their customer knowledge. It is also available for free in several CRM focused areas via e-mail.

KM Metazine
(http://www.ktic.com)

This Web magazine is cited by many sources as a premier publication in the field of KM. It appears, however, to be defunct as of this review.

KM News
(http://www.kmnews.com/)

KM News is a free e-mail newsletter that has a Web site with back issues of the newsletter and supporting information about knowledge management. The technology chart with software categorization and linking Web sites is a unique feature.

KMWorld
(http://www.kmworld.com)

Formerly *ImagingWorld*, *KMWorld* appears in both print and electronic formats covering document, image, and workflow systems. Online issues are available back to its prototype debut. Of particular strength is its product information.

Knowledge Inc.
(http://www.knowledgeinc.com)

Originally a Web-based newsletter for executives who are engaged in or exploring opportunities in knowledge and intellectual capital management, it no longer appears to be subscription-based. The site still includes many worthwhile case studies and interviews with executives. The focus of the site, however, has moved toward provision of consulting services.

Knowledge Management Magazine
(http://www.destinationKM.com)

Line56 Media's *KMM* inaugurated its new digital-only version on December 12, 2001. It is available via e-mail free of charge. The publication has an enterprise-wide focus. Do not confuse this title with Bizmedia's *Knowledge Management Magazine*, which is primarily a print publication.

NOTES

1. Fluss, D. (2002, February) "Why Knowledge Management is a 'DIRTY' Word," *Customer Interface*, 15 (2), 40.
2. Knowledge Management Glossary. [Online]. Available at: http://www.bus.utexas.edu/kman/glossary.htm February 15, 2002.
3. *Nerds Need Apply.* [Online]. Fast Company.com. Available at: http://www.fastcompany.com/online/34/firstsite2.html February 15, 2002.
4. *Learning Portals: Reshaping Business and Corporate Education.* [Online]. At Issue. Available at: http://www.westerbeck.com/files/Issue.htm February 15, 2002.
5. IKM Corporation. [Online]. Available at: http://www.ikmcorp.com/mission.htm February 15, 2002.
6. IKM Corporation [Online]. Available at: http://www.ikmcorp.com/who.htm February 13, 2002.
7. Business 2.0 [Online]. Available at: http://www.business2.com/webguide/0,1660,8129,FF.html February 13, 2002.
8. Business Objects [Online]. Available at: http://www.businessobjects.com/news/press/press2000/dmreview_readership2000.htm February 15, 2002.
9. DM Review [Online]. Available at: http://www.dmreview.com/marketing/2002/?NavID=42 February 15, 2002.
10. EC Media Group. [Online]. Available at: http://www.ecmediagroup.com/Magazines/dmreview.cfm February 12, 2002.

Labor and Collective Bargaining Web Sites

James E. Nalen

SUMMARY. This chapter outlines key resources in the labor and collective bargaining fields. The author covers Web directories, Web sites of the U.S. government and international organizations, unions, academic institutions, professional organizations, and interest groups. *[Article copies available for a fee from The Haworth Document Delivery Service: 1-800-HAWORTH. E-mail address: <docdelivery@haworthpress.com> Website: <http://www.HaworthPress.com> © 2003 by The Haworth Press, Inc. All rights reserved.]*

KEYWORDS. Labor, collective bargaining, unions, Web sites

INTRODUCTION

Unionized labor represents a significant portion of the overall United States labor market. According to the U.S. Census Bureau, in 1999 13.9 percent of wage and salary workers belonged to unions; a further 1.4 percent of workers were covered by collective bargaining agreements without formally belonging to unions. At the same time, public sector workers were far more likely than private sector workers to belong to unions, with 37.3 percent of the former and 9.4 percent of the latter union members.[1] While percentages for unionized workers in both the pri-

James E. Nalen is Social Sciences Librarian, The University of Akron (E-mail: jnalen@uakron.edu).

[Haworth co-indexing entry note]: "Labor and Collective Bargaining Web Sites." Nalen, James E. Co-published simultaneously in *Journal of Business & Finance Librarianship* (The Haworth Information Press, an imprint of The Haworth Press, Inc.) Vol. 8, No. 3/4, 2003, pp. 223-235; and: *The Core Business Web: A Guide to Key Information Resources* (ed: Gary W. White) The Haworth Information Press, an imprint of The Haworth Press, Inc., 2003, pp. 223-235. Single or multiple copies of this article are available for a fee from The Haworth Document Delivery Service [1-800-HAWORTH, 9:00 a.m. - 5:00 p.m. (EST). E-mail address: docdelivery@haworthpress.com].

10.1300/J109v08n03_09

vate and public sectors have declined over time, recent reports suggest an upsurge in organizing activities among certain groups of service workers, most notably doctors (see, for example, Greenhouse, 2001).[2]

Information sources on labor and collective bargaining are useful to a number of audiences. Web sites typically provide a wide range of information, including policy positions, news items, guides, reports, laws and regulations. Several directories that provide excellent coverage of and access to this range are described below. The Web sites of several U.S. government agencies and international organizations offer objective, in-depth analysis of the labor market, and those that include a particular focus on labor relations and collective bargaining are included below. These Web sites are often the best place to look for comprehensive statistical, legal and regulatory information on organized labor. Finally, Web sites maintained by unions, institutions of higher education, professional associations, and interest groups offer further analysis of labor and collective bargaining issues from a wide variety of viewpoints. Some of the information provided by these organizations will appeal to practitioners–union officials and organizers–more so than to union members and human resource managers or policy makers. However, each of the selected sites contains enough of a variety of information to appeal to a wide audience of users.

Several other useful Web-based resources were excluded from the list of Web sites below, including the Council on Union-Free Environment (http://www.cueinc.com), the Society for Human Resource Management (http://www.shrm.org), and BNA, Inc. (http://www.bna.com), since these require either paid membership or some other commercial form of access. Other useful sites on labor history (e.g., http://www.kentlaw.edu/ilhs/) were also excluded from the list. Those interested in print resources on labor and collective bargaining would do well to consult Joseph and Sparanese (2000)[3] and Lee and Kuhn (1996).[4]

Web sites that focus on the issue of labor and collective bargaining are important resources for a number of reasons. Both unions and employers stand to benefit from a good understanding of the values and positions of the other side, as well as the regulatory and legal context that informs their relationship. Traditionally, mutual understanding has helped to mitigate the adversarial nature of the grievance process or contract negotiations; further understanding of other types of information, such as cost of living data, has helped the respective parties to negotiate from a position of strength.

Beginning in the 1980s and continuing to the present, however, many employers have sought to involve union members on labor-management committees formed to address issues of organizational change or strategic planning. These committees have invariably bumped up against working conditions and other mandatory subjects of collective bargaining. While the Dunlop Commission on the Future of Worker-Management Relations, created in 1993 by former Secretary of Labor Robert B. Reich and former Secretary of Commerce Ronald H. Brown, recommended that "employee participation and labor-management partnerships are good for workers, firms, and the national economy,"[5] some unions have sought to restrict members' involvement in such partnerships. A more innovative approach is that of "continuous bargaining," wherein every conversation between management and labor is treated like traditional bargaining.[6]

Many of the Web sites described below begin to explore this new issue in the field of organized labor and collective bargaining. Human resource managers, union officials, employers, union members, and, ultimately, policy makers, need to begin to understand the parameters of "labor-management partnerships"; the Web is a good place to begin developing such an understanding.

DIRECTORIES

SocioSite Project: Industrial Relations and Trade Unions
(http://www.pscw.uva.nl/sociosite/TOPICS/indrel.html)

SocioSite Project: Sociology of Labor
(http://www.pscw.uva.nl/sociosite/TOPICS/Labor.html)

The Sociology of Labor and Industrial Relations and Trade Unions Web sites are part of the SocioSite Project, a set of Web directories providing annotated sets of links on various topics in the social sciences. These two directories are international in focus, and include links to various labor and general employment issues.

Union Resource Network
(http://www.unions.org)

The most useful feature of the Union Resource Network (URN), a Web site developed by the Communications Workers of America, is the Union Search. Union Search allows searching by state or by union acronym. Links to international labor organizations are provided elsewhere on the site. URN also features news releases from a variety of labor organizations.

Workindex.com
(http://www.workindex.com)

Workindex.com, created by the publishers of *Human Resource Executive Magazine* and the School of Industrial Labor Relations at Cornell University, focuses on all aspects of human resources, including labor relations and labor unions. Its well-maintained and organized sets of links provide comprehensive access to United States and international Web sites. Each link is briefly annotated; however, links to more information are also provided.

World Trade Union Directory
(http://www.cf.ac.uk/socsi/union/links.htm)

Steve Davies, a senior research fellow at the Public Services International Research Unit, University of Greenwich, maintains the World Trade Union Directory. The Directory provides extensive access to union Web sites across the world. These Web sites are organized first by geographic region, then by country. Within each country listing, the sites are grouped by national, state, or local level.

XPDNC Labour Directory
(http://www.xpdnc.com)

The Labour Directory groups sites into four broad categories: "Employment"; "Rights at Work"; "Social Protection"; and "Social Dialogue." Under these general headings are more specific sub-headings, such as "Arbitration Services" and "Labour Libraries." Web sites collected under these sub-headings are sorted by country; it is this international scope of the directory that makes it a significant resource. A glossary of labor terms and an exhaustive list of labor acronyms supplement the directory.

TOPICAL WEB SITES:
U.S. GOVERNMENT
AND INTERNATIONAL ORGANIZATIONS

Bureau of Labor Statistics
(http://www.bls.gov/)

The U.S. Bureau of Labor Statistics provides the most comprehensive information on labor market conditions in the United States and abroad. Many of the data sets available through the site are customizable, although "most requested statistics" are also featured. Particularly relevant to issues of organized labor are the sections on "Collective Bargaining," "Union Membership," and "Contract Escalation." "Collective Bargaining" includes a clearinghouse of private and public sector collective bargaining agreements, which are available for ordering; the section also includes detailed statistics on work stoppages. "Union Membership" provides data on the earnings of union-affiliated and non-affiliated workers, disaggregated by industry and occupation. "Contract Escalation" includes a guide to using the Consumer Price Index (CPI) as the basis for wage increases specified by a collective bargaining agreement or through negotiation.

Commission for Labor Cooperation
(http://www.naalc.org/index.htm)

The Commission for Labor Cooperation was established in 1993 under the North American Agreement on Labor Cooperation (NAALC) between the United States, Canada and Mexico, and is charged with implementing that agreement. In addition to the text of and press releases on the NAALC, the site offers a set of online publications on labor issues in North America. One such study is "Labor Relations Law in North America," which describes general and country-specific laws and regulations. Other documents deal with plant closings, the employment of women, and productivity. A Library Referral Service provides links to legislation, statistics, NAFTA, and other topics.

Department of Labor
(http://www.dol.gov)

The U.S. Department of Labor is responsible for the welfare of job seekers, wage earners and retirees, and performs this mission by administering federal labor laws regarding working conditions, minimum hourly wages and overtime pay, employment discrimination and unemployment insurance. While many sections of the DOL Web site are useful for general labor and employment issues, the Office of Labor-Management Standards is perhaps most pertinent to collective bargaining issues. OLMS is responsible for administering the Labor-Management Reporting and Disclosure Act, which seeks to ensure democracy and fiscal responsibility within private sector labor unions. The OLMS Web site provides information on recent criminal and civil enforcement actions, as well as regulatory and compliance information. Union officials and members will find the "Conducting Local Union Officer Elections: A Guide for Election Officials" and the various "Compliance Tips" especially useful.

European Industrial Relations Observatory On-Line
(http://www.eiro.eurofound.ie/)

EIRO forms part of the European Union's European Foundation for the Improvement of Living and Working Conditions. The Web site provides annual comparative and national reviews of industrial relations, collective bargaining, and labor market conditions in EU member states, as well as in Japan and the United States. Comparative studies of topics such as gender pay equity and working time are also available. Articles on current industrial relations issues can be browsed by country, sector, or date. The EMIRE database is a glossary of industrial relations terminology employed by individual member states. Finally, EIRO maintains an extensive set of links to government agencies, employers' groups, and trade unions in EU member states and beyond.

Federal Mediation and Conciliation Service
(http://www.fmcs.gov)

The FMCS provides dispute mediation, preventive mediation, alternative dispute resolution, arbitration, and other services to employers and unions in the private and public sectors. These services are described in detail on the Web site. The key section of the FMCS Web site is its set of case studies involving FMCS intervention. These case studies are relatively short, but focus on a wide variety of labor-management issues. Two recent case studies, produced with the cooperation of Northeastern University, are much more detailed, and include not only a description of the problem but a set of best practices.

National Labor Relations Board
(http://www.nlrb.gov)

The NLRB is charged with administering the National Labor Relations Act, which governs relations between unions and employers in the private sector. The NLRB organizes secret-ballot elections and investigates and remedies unfair labor practices. The Web site features services and activities of the NLRB, including its Weekly Summary of NLRB Cases, forms, decisions and orders, and rules and regulations. Several online publications will be of interest to both human resource managers and union officials, including "A Guide to Basic Law and Procedures under the National Labor Relations Act" and "The National Labor Relations Board and You: Unfair Labor Practices."

The National Mediation Board (http://www.nmb.gov/) provides similar services to both the railroad and airline industries in its administration of the Railway Labor Act, while the Federal Labor Relations Authority (http://www.flra.gov/) administers the Federal Service Labor-Management Relations Statute. The Office of Personnel Management's Labor-Management Relations Division (http://www.opm.gov/cplmr/index.htm) provides further guidance on these decisions. Labor-management relations in the state and local public sector are typically governed by state labor relations laws, which are administered by state-level labor relations boards.

International Labour Organisation
(http://www.ilo.org)

The International Labour Organisation, a specialized agency of the United Nations, formulates international labor standards; provides technical assistance in a variety of areas; and promotes and provides training to employers' and workers' organizations. The Web site provides a considerable amount of information on the work of the organization, including a catalog of publications, databases of international labor standards (ILOLEX) and national laws (NATLEX), and collections of press releases and speeches. LABORSTA is perhaps the most significant aspect of the ILO Web site: this statistical database contains detailed historical labor market data for a large number of countries. This data is included in ILO's annual *Year Book of Labour Statistics*.

TOPICAL WEB SITES:
UNIONS, HIGHER EDUCATION,
PROFESSIONAL ASSOCIATIONS, AND INTEREST GROUPS

AFL-CIO
(http://www.aflcio.org)

The AFL-CIO Web site offers a wealth of information on the federation's policy positions, leadership, and activities. AFL-CIO maintains a set of links to unions (and union locals) affiliated with the AFL-CIO. Various research products, including economic policy papers, technical working papers, and policy handbooks, are available online. These are of very high quality, and include titles such as "The Dollar and the Trade Deficit: The Costs of Policy Neglect" and "The Role of Institutions and Policies in Creating Unemployment: The Cross-Country Empirical Evidence." Other notable features of the site are a section on culture and history, which includes artwork, video and audio clips, and cartoons; the Executive PayWatch database, which describes and allows for comparisons with the salary and benefits of top CEOs; and practical information on employment rights.

American Arbitration Association
(http://www.adr.org)

Many collective bargaining agreements stipulate that grievances are subject to binding arbitration when these fail to be resolved at other levels, or steps. The American Arbitration Association provides arbitration, mediation and other dispute resolution services to a wide variety of industries. The "Focus Area" section on labor presents AAA's "Labor Arbitration Rules" and other rules, as well as forms and guides, including one on "Drafting Dispute Resolution Clauses."

American Federation of State, County and Municipal Employees
(http://www.afscme.org)

AFSCME, one of the largest public sector unions, makes available a wealth of information through its well-organized Web site. One key feature of the Web site is AFSCME's extensive list of online publications, which will appeal to union local officials, union members, and human resource managers. For example, the "AFSCME Steward Handbook" includes a glossary of labor terms, grievance forms and procedures, and a list of tactics. Other notable publications include "Knowing the Numbers: A Guide to Public Budget Analysis" and "Preventing Workplace Violence." AFSCME maintains a set of links to topical Web sites that focus on human resource and labor issues. Legislative updates and policy analyses also feature prominently on the site.

Center for Labor Education & Research,
University of Hawaii at West Oahu
(http://homepages.uhwo.hawaii.edu/clear/)

The Center for Labor Education & Research (CLEAR) Web site makes available a glossary of collective bargaining terms; the CLEAR Newsletter, which reports on legal and regulatory developments; and descriptions of aspects of labor law, such as Weingarten rights. The site also presents a well-organized set of links to government agency, higher education, and labor organization Web sites.

Institute of Industrial Relations, University of California at Berkeley
(http://www.iir.berkeley.edu/)

UC-Berkeley's Institute of Industrial Relations makes available a number of working papers, reports, and issues of the "Labor Center Reporter." The "Working Papers" focus on areas such as "Employee Involvement and Pay at U.S. and Canadian Auto Suppliers" and "Changes in the Employment Contract?: Evidence from a Quasi-Experiment." These publications are on par with those produced by the School for Industrial and Labor Relations at Cornell University in terms of quality (see below); however, many of the papers present a more international focus. The Institute of Industrial Relations Library maintains a Labor Research Portal, which contains Web guides and labor guides focusing on a variety of topics, including labor education and temporary workers, respectively. The Library also maintains sets of links to international and U.S. labor unions and labor news sources.

Berkeley is also home to the Agricultural Personnel Management Program (http://are.berkeley.edu/APMP/). The APMP Web site provides full-text access to several newsletters, as well as links to government and other sources of information on agricultural labor.

Labor Education Program, University of Missouri at Columbia
(http://web.missouri.edu/~labored/)

The Labor Education Program Web site provides an extensive set of links to union Web sites in Missouri, in the United States and around the world, as well as to other labor education programs. The "Research" section makes available outlines on federal labor law and on collective bargaining. Each of these outlines presents in-depth analysis; for example, the outline on collective bargaining covers bargaining techniques and the "arithmetic of collective bargaining," including sections on reckoning the costs of wage increases and fringe benefits.

Labor Policy Association
(http://www.lpa.org/)

"LPA is a public policy advocacy organization representing corporate executives interested in human resource policy." Some information is available only to members. The "HR Issues" section provides press releases on federal court decisions, legislation and regulations that impact human resources, especially labor relations. "Issues" also provides for tracking of federal legislation with implications for labor relations and other human resources issues. The full-text of amicus curiae briefs filed by LPA are available, as are in-depth analyses of human resources issues. LPA is also responsible for a number of related Web sites. The "HR Market" (also accessible at http://www.hrmarket.com) is a directory of product and service providers and provides links to companies specializing in various aspects of human resources, including alternative dispute resolution and labor relations. NLRBWatch.com (http://www.nlrbwatch.com) summarizes and provides links to federal court decisions related to National Labor Relations Board regulations. CodesofConduct.org (http://www.codesofconduct.org/) brings together various codes of conduct, including several union-sponsored codes. Finally, LivingWageLaws.org (http://www.livingwagelaws.org/) tracks information about local labor legislation, specifically related to living wage ordinances.

Labor Research Association
(http://www.laborresearch.org/)

A "non-profit research and advocacy organization" affiliated with LRA Consulting, the Labor Research Association (LRA) provides news and analysis on labor law, collective bargaining, labor organizing and other topics, including workplace privacy and temporary workers. LRA's *Union Busting Watch* brings together labor organization press releases and news stories on organizing disputes. *Union Trends and Data* includes statistical tables and analysis of labor trends, as well as practical information, such as advice on using company e-mail for organizing purposes. *Economic Trends* presents analyses of labor market conditions, as well as statistical tables.

Labornet
(http://www.labornet.org)

Formerly supported by the Institute for Global Communications, Labornet is now an "independent network that seeks to build up labor communication for all working people." Labornet's most useful aspect lies in its role as a clearinghouse for news on union activities. It co-sponsors a strike-tracking site (http://www.thebird.org/strikes/), and maintains a set of links to various labor resources. Its "Union Directory" is notable in that it includes labor organizations at both the national and local levels. The site features commentary and news briefs, as well as quick links to international sites, such as the United Kingdom's LaboursStart (http://www.labourstart.org).

Legal Institute, Cornell Law School
(http://www.law.cornell.edu/topics/collective_bargaining.html)
(http://www.law.cornell.edu/topics/labor.html)

Cornell Law School's Legal Institute has prepared a number of guides to legal topics, including collective bargaining and labor law. Each of these guides provides links to legal and regulatory material at the federal level and New York State level. An overview describes significant federal acts that pertain to a particular topic; for example, the overview of collective bargaining discusses the National Labor Relations Act and the Uniform Arbitration Act. These comprehensive guides also list links to relevant organizations and federal agencies.

Martin P. Catherwood Library, School of Industrial and Labor Relations, Cornell University
(http://www.ilr.cornell.edu/library/)

The Martin P. Catherwood Library, together with the Kheel Center for Labor-Management Documentation & Archives, serves students and faculty in the School of Industrial and Labor Relations at Cornell University. In addition to well-maintained research and Internet guides, on topics such as international labor and organizing, the Library is also responsible for the "Electronic Archive," a repository for U.S. and New York State government and AFL-CIO reports on industrial relations. Full-text searching of the archive is available, as are listings of reports. Catherwood intends to make these reports available over the long-term, and is actively collecting reports produced by governmental and non-governmental organizations. U.S. government documents include the report of the Commission on Family and Medical Leave and of the Commission on the Future of Worker-Management Relations, among many others.

National Labor Management Association
(http://www.nlma.org/)

A membership organization "open to all persons interested in labor-management cooperation efforts," the National Labor Management Association (NLMA) Web site is notable for back issues of its newsletter *Forward Thinking*; links to news stories, articles, and manuals that focus on labor-management committees; a directory of state and local labor-management committees; and, extensive sets of links to federal and state departments of labor, labor relations research centers, employee ownership programs, and other labor relations-related organizations. NLMA, with financial assistance from the Federal Mediation & Conciliation Service, also makes available its *Manual for Area & Industrial Labor-Management Committees*, a comprehensive guide to setting up labor-management committees.

Restructuring Associates Inc.
(http://www.restructassoc.com)

Restructuring Associates Inc. (RAI) is a Washington-based consulting firm that works with employers and unions in organizations undergoing organizational change. Its case studies and articles are useful. RAI recently made news by criticizing both Yale University and its labor unions for their particularly acrimonious relationship.[7] RAI's Web site presents a set of case studies that depict RAI's analysis and resolution of a particular problem of organizational change within unionized environments. The "Articles" section of the site provides similar case studies, as well as pieces that express RAI's general philosophy towards labor-management relations.

United Electrical, Radio and Machine Workers of America
(http://www.ranknfile-ue.org/)

UE is an independent union (unaffiliated with the AFL-CIO), representing just over 35,000 workers in a variety of sectors and industries. In addition to information on organizing and affiliating with UE, links to labor resources, and news and legislative briefs, the site's "Information for Workers" section offers practical information on a number of issues, including arbitrating, negotiating, and health and safety. Notable among these online publications are "Workplace Bullying," "Using ADA in the Workplace," and "Mid Contract Bargaining Changes." The advice contained in these publications would be useful for union officials and members; human resource managers would also do well to understand the approaches outlined in these publications.

W.E. Upjohn Institute for Employment Research
(http://www.upjohninst.org/index.htm)

The W.E. Upjohn Institute is a non-profit institution that engages in research on a wide variety of employment issues; it also administers programs for and provides services to unemployed workers. The key feature of the Institute's Web site is the availability of online staff working papers, employment research reports, and other publications. These documents are accessible through a master publications list or through various "Research Hubs," such as "Economic Development and Local Labor Markets." The publications are of a uniformly high quality, and include titles such as "Thinking about Local Living Wage Requirements" and "Nonstandard Work and Child Care Choices of Married Mothers." Other publications, including books and technical reports, are available for ordering. The Institute is also home to the West Michigan Data Center and the Employment Research Data Center. The latter serves as a repository for the U.S. Department of Labor's research and evaluation efforts; these DOL data products are available for ordering on CD-ROM.

NOTES

1. U.S. Census Bureau. (2000). *Statistical abstract of the United States* (120th ed.), table 712. Washington, DC: U.S. Government Printing Office.

2. Greenhouse, S. (2001, March 27). St. Luke's doctors unionize. *The New York Times*, p. B9. Retrieved March 11, 2002, from Lexis-Nexis database.

3. Joseph, D., & Sparanese, Ann. (2000). Reference sources for Labor History Month. *Booklist*, 96, 1778-1779.

4. Lee, A. H., & Kuhn, J. (1996). Look out bosses! Union power's going to get your employees a raise! *RQ*, 36, 48-56.

5. U.S. Commission on the Future of Worker-Management Relations. (1994). *The Dunlop Commission on the Future of Worker-Management Relations: Final report*, p. 8. Retrieved February 19, 2002, from Cornell University, School of Industrial and Labor Relations, Catherwood Library Web site: http://www.ilr.cornell.edu/library/e_archive/gov_reports/dunlop/DunlopFinalReport.pdf.

6. University of Massachusetts Lowell, Labor Extension Program. (n.d.) *Treat It as Continuous Bargaining: Dealing with the Changing Workplace–New Technologies, New Forms of Work Organization and Employee Involvement/Quality Programs*. Retrieved March 14, 2002, http://www.uml.edu/laborextension/pdf/contbarg.pdf.

7. Greenhouse, S. (2002, January 15). Labor consultant criticizes Yale and its unions. *The New York Times*, p. B4. Retrieved February 8, 2002, from Lexis-Nexis database.

Best Management Web Sites

Bill Kinyon

SUMMARY. Management is one of the most fundamental business concepts. The author of this chapter provides overviews of the most important Web sites related to management information, including sites from academic institutions and professional organizations. *[Article copies available for a fee from The Haworth Document Delivery Service: 1-800-HAWORTH. E-mail address: <docdelivery@haworthpress.com> Website: <http://www.HaworthPress.com> © 2003 by The Haworth Press, Inc. All rights reserved.]*

KEYWORDS. Management, Web sites

INTRODUCTION

There are many ways to define "management." Agha Hasan Abedi, who was President of the Bank of Credit and Commerce International in Luxembourg, once said "The conventional definition of management is getting work done through people, but real management is developing people through work." Peter Drucker, the noted management guru, said "Management means, in the last analysis, the substitution of thought for brawn and muscle, of knowledge for folklore and superstition, and of cooperation for force . . ." Of course, Drucker also made a more cynical observation, "So much of what we call management consists in making it difficult for people to work." Even that cynical comment, though, in-

---

Bill Kinyon is Director of Library Services, Mars Hill College (E-mail: bkinyon@mhc.edu).

[Haworth co-indexing entry note]: "Best Management Web Sites." Kinyon, Bill. Co-published simultaneously in *Journal of Business & Finance Librarianship* (The Haworth Information Press, an imprint of The Haworth Press, Inc.) Vol. 8, No. 3/4, 2003, pp. 237-244; and: *The Core Business Web: A Guide to Key Information Resources* (ed: Gary W. White) The Haworth Information Press, an imprint of The Haworth Press, Inc., 2003, pp. 237-244. Single or multiple copies of this article are available for a fee from The Haworth Document Delivery Service [1-800-HAWORTH, 9:00 a.m. - 5:00 p.m. (EST). E-mail address: docdelivery@haworth press.com].

10.1300/J109v08n03_10

dicates the nature of management, in that he is pointing to the fact that management involves the interaction between managers and their company and its employees.

In another sense, the term "management" could include any of the topics included elsewhere in this publication. Any of the Web sites discussed in these bibliographies could well be of use to a person who needs help in managing an enterprise of almost any kind. Management of a business obviously involves human resources, marketing and advertising, accounting, knowledge of relevant laws, familiarity with customers, and financial responsibility. From a broader perspective, and taking into account the quotations above, the functions of management can be broken down into a few major responsibilities. According to Carter McNamara, who developed the Free Management Library (discussed later in this article) the four major functions traditionally considered to constitute management are planning, organizing, leading, and coordinating of resources.[1] These responsibilities are directed both internally (to one's own company and employees) and externally (to the firm's competitors and to the market). It is these major functions that will be emphasized in the Web sites that are included here.

To be included, a Web site must offer significant amounts of real content; that is, information, or a well-organized set of links to other useful Web sites. Sites which are primarily self-promoting or which provide little more than advertisements for publications, activities or services have been left out. Most of the Web sites listed here are either completely free of charge, or at least offer a considerable amount of information for free. However, there are a few for which the information was so valuable that they were included even though there is a charge. Some sites also require registration, which is sometimes free and sometimes requires a fee.

About.com Guide to Management
(http://management.about.com)

This site is sort of a primer for new managers, although much of the information will be useful for experienced managers as well. Much of the content is written for laymen. An "Essentials" section covers such items as management tips and advice for beginning managers. Also provided by the site are links to articles, Web sites, and information resources in nearly thirty management-related categories, from big-picture subjects such as mergers and acquisitions to more personal topics such as public speaking.

Bpubs
(http://www.bpubs.com)

Bpubs provides links to full-text online articles in many fields of business. These can be articles from online magazines, government sources, or companies willing to make their expertise available. Items are selected for inclusion based on the company's own collection development policy, and the process seems to be highly selective. The intended audience is business users of all kinds, from entrepreneurs to academics to CEOs. "Management Science" is the category perhaps most relevant to the topic here. Documents in such areas as "Change Management," "Competitive Intelligence," and "Total Quality Management" are included.

BUBL LINK
(http://link.bubl.ac.uk/management/)

BUBL LINK (Libraries of Networked Knowledge) is a catalog of Internet resources in virtually all academic subject areas. Resources are evaluated before being selected for inclusion in the catalog. Upon selection, the resources are cataloged according to the Dewey Decimal Classification System. Therefore, the relevant classification here is 658. The site can also be searched via an alphabetical list of subject terms. "Management practice" and "Management research" will lead the user to a wealth of sites providing management-related information. BUBL LINK currently contains over thirty links in these two categories.

Business Management Supersite
(http://www.ioma.com)

The Institute of Management and Administration (IOMA) Web site is one of the few on this list that is fee-based. Registration and searching can be done for free, but articles must be purchased. However, selected articles are occasionally available for free. IOMA publishes nearly sixty pay-per-view or subscription-based newsletters on management topics, plus nine free e-newsletters. The free e-newsletters include such titles as *Business Technology Update, Leadership Newswire*, and *Office Management*. The fee-based newsletters include such titles as *HRFocus, Managing Training and Development*, and *Report on Customer Relationship Management*.

Business Researcher's Interests
(http://brint.com)

Billing itself as "the premier business and technology portal and global community network for e-business, information, technology, and management," this continuously updated mega-site leads the user to a huge multitude of Web sites. The "Reference Section" is divided into three parts: "Business Disciplines and Business Research"; "Business Administration and Business Functions"; and "Information Technologies and Information Systems." Many of the links here will be relevant to management in the context of this bibliography. The "Business Administration and Business Functions" section alone has links in over twenty-five categories of management, including such categories as data management, innovation management and service management. In addition, three "phases" of "subject portals" cover the areas of new economy business enterprises, e-business and e-commerce enterprises, and knowledge driven organizations. Links to the latest articles are included for some categories.

The Business Search Engine
(http://www.business.com/directory/management)

This is a business-focused search engine and directory aimed at business professionals. Industry experts and librarians developed the Web site. It provides links to hundreds of Web sites with management information, divided into seventeen categories. One caution: the "Featured Listings" section allows companies to pay for better placement of their site. However, all sites that are included in this directory, and only those deemed worthy of inclusion, are eligible to pay for a featured listing.

CEO Express
(http://ceoexpress.com)

As is stated on the main page of this very useful site, it is "designed by a busy executive for busy executives." The idea of this Web site is to pull together links to all the information an executive might need in the course of a workday. A wide variety of types of information is represented–news, business magazines, financial market data, government agencies, company research, legislation, directories, travel information, ready-reference sources and many others. It is organized in a very simple and clear arrangement.

Continuous Quality Improvement Online
(http://deming.eng.Clemson.edu)

A Web site devoted to quality improvement and education in quality, Continuous Quality Improvement Online provides links to online documents and other Web sites. The Deming Electronic Network (DEN) focuses on the philosophy of W. Edwards Deming, and includes links to selected papers and article reprints, the W. Edwards Deming Institute, information about Deming Associations, and other Deming resources. The "Public Sector Continuous Improvement Site" focuses on online resources intended to foster improvement in public sector organizations.

European Case Clearing House
(http://www.ecch.cranfield.ac.uk/)

This is an excellent resource for those interested in the case study method of management education. The ECCH collects and distributes case studies from many of the top management education organizations. The studies are international in scope with holdings from such United States institutions as the Harvard Business School, the Richard Ivey School of Business, and the Darden School at the University of Virginia and from overseas institutions such as the London Business School and the Cranfield School of Management. The original office of ECCH is at Cranfield University in England, and the North American operations are located at Babson College in Massachusetts. The site can be searched for free, including reading the abstracts, but there is a fee for acquiring the case studies. As of this writing, the corporate fee for a case study is $6 and the academic fee is $3.15.

Fast Company
(http://fastcompany.com)

This is the online version of the print publication of the same name. Founded by two former editors of the *Harvard Business Review*, its goal is to help businesses and managers keep up with the changing business world. Emphasis is given to new business practices, how companies creatively meet their competition, and people and companies that are effectively facing the future. Informative articles, live events, and opportunities to network with other readers are available at the Web site. Some articles are available only on the Web version. A subscription to the print version is required to have free access to the Web site, but it is very inexpensive. Archives are available all the way back to the first issue (November 1995).

Free Management Library
(http://www.mapnp.org/library)

Produced by the Management Assistance Program for Nonprofits, this site has useful links for both nonprofit and for-profit organizations. All areas of traditional management functions are covered here, plus some topics that are not typically included in discussions of management responsibilities. For example, there are groups of links for personal productivity, social entrepreneurship, and written communication skills. There is a wealth of useful information at this site, all of it free. Each link either provides content for free, or links to another Web site that is free. The library was developed with the intention of providing managers, particularly those with limited resources, with basic and practical information that will help them in the performance of their jobs. The site is well organized and user-friendly.

HBS Working Knowledge
(http://www.hbsworkingknowledge.hbs.edu)

Produced by the Harvard Business School (HBS), HBS Working Knowledge requires free registration. Included are full-text of interviews with HBS scholars and industry leaders, as well as HBS publications, and reviews and recommendations for both books and Web sites. Content is divided into thirteen topic areas; those which will be most relevant to management as defined here are "Entrepreneurship"; "Innovation & Change"; "Leadership, Strategy & Competition"; and "Organizations & People." The "What Do You Think?" column provides the opportunity to have a dialogue with an HBS professor on specific business events or activities. Special Reports are included, often coming from conferences such as the *2001 Harvard Business School Entrepreneurship Conference, Build to Lead* and *Dynamic Women in Business 2002.*

Knowledge@Wharton
(http://knowledge.Wharton.upenn.edu)

This is a product of the Wharton School at the University of Pennsylvania. Management topics covered include "Leadership and Change," "Strategic Management," "Public Policy and Management," "Innovation and Entrepreneurship," "Operations Management," and "Managing Technology." Emphasis is placed on current research, information and analysis. For each category, research papers, articles, interviews, book reviews, and links to other Web sites are included. Information is organized in layers to accommodate each user's needs. The layers are: brief summaries; short, professionally written articles in journalistic style; academic papers; and links to related Web sites.

Management Best Practice
(http://www.dti.gov.uk/mbp)

Managed by the Department of Trade and Industry of the government of the United Kingdom, this site offers many "key sites" which are sets of links to documents pertaining to business. One of the most useful for management information is the "Best Practice Guides, Tools and Publications" site, which links to documents discussing best practices from organizations in the UK and in other countries. It is divided into 11 specific management topics such as "General Business Management," "Partnerships with People," and "Information." Some examples of relevant titles are "Best Practice Benchmarking," "Total Quality Management and Effective Leadership," and "Making Information Work for You."

Management Link
(http://www.ocula.managers.org.uk)

Management Link is produced by the Institute of Management (IM) in the UK. Two sections, "Management Skills" and "Management Sources," pull together links to management Web sites. These sites have been assessed and selected by IM staff according to IM's established guidelines and are intended as a guide to valuable management sites, although not an endorsement of any particular site. "Management Skills" focuses on management techniques relating to such areas as people, change and performance, while "Management Sources" focuses on information resources such as professional and government organizations and company information sources. Some sites linked here may require either a subscription fee or registration.

ManagerWise
(http://www.managerwise.com)

Subtitled "Advancing the Practice of Management," the most useful feature of this site is the "Knowledge Bank" which features the full-text of many essays, thought pieces, and other documents that have been submitted to ManagerWise. Most of the submissions are from previously published authors and/or management consultants. While virtually anyone can submit a document, there is a set of editorial guidelines that must be followed, and items are reviewed before being added to the "Knowledge Bank." The documents are arranged in over forty management-related categories, such as "Communication," "Innovation," "Leadership," and "Motivation."

MIT Sloan Management Review
(http://mitsloan.mit.edu/smr)

This is the online version of the business journal of the same name, a quarterly peer-reviewed publication by the MIT Sloan School of Management, one of the world's top business schools. This is a for-fee site, but the articles in *SMR* should be worth the price for managers, and particularly top executives. Full archives are available back to Fall 1995, while selected articles are available as far back as Fall 1977; reprints can be purchased for any of these articles. While primarily an academic publication, the editors seek to provide articles that will be useful to managers in the "real world." A sampling of recent article or essay titles includes: "Building Competitive Advantage Through People," "Weird Ideas That Spark Innovation," "How To Make Strategic Alliances Work," and "Turning Online Browsers Into Buyers."

U.S. Business Advisor
(http://www.business.gov/busadv/)

The U.S. Business Advisor, sponsored by the Small Business Administration, consists of a collection of links designed to give the small business owner easy access to federal government information. Useful information can be found for starting and managing a business; dealing with taxes, laws and regulations; and workplace issues such as wellness, benefits and safety. Links to agency home pages and business pages should be useful, as well as the group of links to one-stop gateways. Several FAQ sections are provided, covering a variety of topics.

Working Papers in Management
(http://www.olin.wustl.edu/library/workingpapers.htm#MAN)

Working Papers in Management is maintained by the The Kopolow Business Library of the John M. Olin School of Business at Washington University in St. Louis. This site provides links to working papers in several business disciplines, including management. The papers originate primarily from academic institutions, although not exclusively. Full-text online is available for some documents, although for many others only abstracts are available. Coverage is worldwide, with documents from such institutions as the University of Melbourne Department of Management, the Manchester School of Management, and the Erasmus Research Institute of Management at Erasmus University of Rotterdam.

NOTE

1. McNamara, Carter, *Free Management Library* (n.d.). Retrieved February 15, 2002 from http://www.mapnp.org/library/mng_thry/mng_thry.htm.

Marketing and Advertising

Blake Carver

SUMMARY. The Web is one of the best starting points for marketing and advertising information. The author covers Web sites for top publications as well as sites from academic institutions and professional associations. *[Article copies available for a fee from The Haworth Document Delivery Service: 1-800-HAWORTH. E-mail address: <docdelivery@haworthpress.com> Website: <http://www.HaworthPress.com> © 2003 by The Haworth Press, Inc. All rights reserved.]*

KEYWORDS. Marketing, advertising, Web sites

INTRODUCTION

The World Wide Web and the advertising industry is a well-suited pair. The Web is an ideal place to aggregate, disseminate, and collect statistics used in the field. Search engines and access to databases make the Web an ideal place for an industry that thrives on data. The visual nature of advertising, coupled with the timeliness of information presented on the Web, find a convergence in a way not seen in many other industries. Advertisers are able to use the Web to gather statistics, while at the same time reaching new audiences and promoting new products.

Although the number of marketing and advertising sites available today can be overwhelming, focusing on better quality sites can yield

Blake Carver is Web Librarian, The Ohio State University Libraries (E-mail: carver.50@osu.edu).

[Haworth co-indexing entry note]: "Marketing and Advertising." Carver, Blake. Co-published simultaneously in *Journal of Business & Finance Librarianship* (The Haworth Information Press, an imprint of The Haworth Press, Inc.) Vol. 8, No. 3/4, 2003, pp. 245-252; and: *The Core Business Web: A Guide to Key Information Resources* (ed: Gary W. White) The Haworth Information Press, an imprint of The Haworth Press, Inc., 2003, pp. 245-252. Single or multiple copies of this article are available for a fee from The Haworth Document Delivery Service [1-800-HAWORTH, 9:00 a.m. - 5:00 p.m. (EST). E-mail address: docdelivery@haworth press.com].

10.1300/J109v08n03_11

more than enough resources for librarians, serving academic and business communities in search of marketing know-how, numbers or design inspiration. The Web offers more than just numbers and "how-to" advice; it transports users from the practicalities of terms used in online marketing, to turn of the century advertising for laxatives and vitamins, to the world of painted bovine billboards. Sites for this "best of the Web" were chosen based on information provided, currency of information, navigation, and popularity.

UTexas Marketing World
(http://advertising.utexas.edu/world)

The University of Texas' Marketing World is a metasite that lists hundreds of sites broken down by category. A great starting place, this site is ideal for someone unsure of what the Web has to offer in marketing or advertising resources.

Marketing World specializes in providing resources to professionals, students, and faculty. According to Jef Richards, Department Chairman and Professor of Advertising at UT "The mission, from the beginning, was to give our Department a Web presence. We have no advertising budget, per se, and this was created in the hope that marketing communication professionals would use it and become aware of our program." The primary target for the site is the marketing industry and the students who aspire to enter that industry.

The Marketing World homepage is an index of ninety-one categories, ranging from "Account Planning" to "Word of Mouth." Each category, in turn, consists of a page with a list of links to relevant sites; there are cross-references that point to similar categories as well. Initially, the shear number of categories can be overwhelming, but it is easy to find what you need if you can narrow your idea to a single topic. With so many topics, the cross references are a necessity.

PaintedCows.com
(http://www.paintedcows.com)

Do not let the name throw you, Painted Cows is one of the more useful marketing resources sites and no doubt the most fun site on this list. Put together by Shelley Delayne and Scott J. Karlson, the site aims "to provide a comprehensive, efficient and entertaining advertising and marketing Web site dedicated to the success of industry professionals worldwide." PaintedCows is updated frequently, and contains an extensive range of links to useful marketing and advertising sites.

PaintedCows includes news articles that are updated twice per week; the articles are from sites like *AdAge* and *American Demographics*. The site also offers an extensive list of links to other marketing sites and international marketing publications. The links are broken down by categories such as advertising, media and publications.

As for the name, Karlson says, "It was Shelley's idea based on an experience of mine on an Amtrak train ride across the U.S. While in the middle of a trip, I was watching herd after herd of cows pass by my window overlooking the highway and the fields beyond. Suddenly it occurred to me, 'shouldn't those cows have Pepsi logos on them or something?' " To advertise the launching of their site, PaintedCows used a real-live painted cow–making them the first marketers to promote cows as "bovine billboards." Fun and flashy, PaintedCows.com is a useful resource to find news, sites, and most anything you need in the world of marketing.

The VNU Media Group
(http://www.vnuemedia.com/)

The VNU Media Groups publishes several leading trade publications in the marketing industry. The VNU Media, Media & Marketing Group is made up of five sites: adweek.com; brandweek.com; mediaweek.com; salesandmarketing.com; and technologymarketing.com. Each site is the electronic version of a print publication and focuses on a specific area in the advertising or marketing businesses.

Adweek.com
(http://www.adweek.com)

Adweek.com is a site aimed at "leading decision-makers" in the advertising and marketing field. While the site does contain free articles, complete access to the *Adweek* archives is a "premium service" available only to subscribers. Articles cover the entire advertising industry.

Brandweek.com
(http://www.brandweek.com)

Brandweek aims to provide "competitive information and insights" through articles covering different brands and personalities in the marketing industry. The editors place special emphasis on "breakthrough campaigns," campaigns that break new marketing ground.

MediaWeek.com
(http://www.mediaweek.com)

Mediaweek.com focuses on breaking news in different areas of the mass media industry: television; radio; magazines; and the Internet.

SALESandMARKETING.COM
(http://www.salesandmarketing.com)

SMM is a site for sales and marketing professionals. Articles cover best practices, continuing education, and career advancement.

TechnologyMarketing.com
(http://technologymarketing.com)

Technology Marketing is a focus area of *Adweek Magazine* and is specifically written for the "highest-ranking marketer at a given technology organization." The site covers marketing in all areas of the technology industry.

VNUs marketing and advertising oriented Web sites are an excellent source of current industry news. Each site offers daily industry specific news, along with featured stories, columns, and some premium pay content.

The Rare Book, Manuscript, and Special Collections Library at Duke University (http://scriptorium.lib.duke.edu/) has three projects dedicated to the history of advertising.

Emergence of Advertising in America
(http://scriptorium.lib.duke.edu/eaa/)

The Emergence of Advertising in America has over 9,000 advertisements originally published from 1850 to 1920. The advertisements are broken down into eleven categories such as Lux Flakes, Chesebrough-Pond's, collectible cards, and tobacco. Most images are available in JPEG format, in high or low resolution, and may be reproduced for use in research, teaching, and private study. The items chosen help to illustrate "the rise of consumer culture, especially after the American Civil War, and the birth of a professionalized advertising industry in the United States."

Medicine and Madison Avenue
(http://scriptorium.lib.duke.edu/mma/)

This project explores the "complex relationships between modern medicine and modern advertising, or 'Madison Avenue,' as the latter is colloquially termed." The project contains images from 600 advertisements printed in newspapers and magazines in the early part of the 1900s. The images cover products like cold remedies, cigarettes, soaps, laxatives and vitamins. The site also includes text-only documents that "put health-related advertising into a broader perspective."

The Ad*Access Project
(http://scriptorium.lib.duke.edu/adaccess/)

Funded by Duke University's "Library 2000" Endowment Fund, the Ad*Access project has made advertisements from the Duke Library's J. Walter Thompson Company Archives collection of ads available to researchers via the Web. The image library contains over 7,000 advertisements that were printed in newspapers and magazines between 1911 and 1955.

The advertisements chosen for digitalization were those that attract research interest and help to reflect developments in American society, culture, business, and technology. The advertisements are divided into five main categories: "Beauty and Hygiene"; "Transportation"; "Radio"; "Television"; and "World War II." This helps to show advertising during this time period, but focuses on a limited number of areas. Unfortunately, there are no current plans to add additional advertisements to the site, as funding was only available for the pilot project. To find similar sites with classical ads that are updating and adding to content try (http://www.old-time.com/commercials/) and (http://www.adflip.com/) while current ads can be found at (http://www.luerzersarchive.net/home.htm).

Commarts
(http://www.commarts.com)

With a visually appealing interface designed to appeal to designers, Commarts is a source of creative inspiration to many. Commarts.com is broken down into three separate areas; commarts.com, an extension of the print magazine; designinteract.com, which focuses exclusively on technology and multimedia; and creativehotlist.com, a career oriented site for those on the creative side of marketing and advertising.

Commarts is "information and inspiration" for people who design and create the advertisements used in any type of media. All three sites contain articles that cover graphic design as well as other creative areas of marketing and advertising. Content is updated every two weeks and features "the insights of an influential participant in interactive industry philosophizing about some aspect of technology that is important to them." With a "Site of the Week" feature, and news that is updated every business day, Commarts provides fresh content regularly. Two monthly features–a profile of an interactive media developer and a project overview–add nicely to the features.

Commarts should be a regular stop for anyone interested in graphic design as a career, or anyone looking for creative ideas for designing an advertisement, Web site, or any type of promotional material.

MarketingTerms.com
(http://www.marketingterms.com)

Marketingterms.com is an extensive collection of terms used in Internet marketing. Founded to help outsiders get up to speed on basic online marketing terminology, the site is essentially an annotated online dictionary. With terms broken down into categories, recently added and updated terms and "fan favorites," the site is easy to use and navigate. Each one of the many definitions comes complete with links to sites and news stories that contain more information, and is fully cross-referenced. The site is best navigated by letter, and each individual definition page contains a definition, followed by a more in-depth "information" section that works to put the term in context and provides synonyms, related terms, and pointers to other sites and articles around the Web for more information. Terms are put in context in a way not available to a print dictionary. Founder Sean O'Rourke goes for "maximum knowledge and minimum duplication" on each page. The site is clean, quick and easy to use and provides information critical to understanding the terms listed.

Larry Chase's Web Digest for Marketers
(http://www.wdfm.com/)

Larry Chase and a team of four editors, send out "mercifully short" reviews of marketing oriented Web sites, once a week, via e-mail. With the current week's featured sites freely available on the site, and the full archives available for $49.00, wdfm.com is a great tool to stay in touch with the newest Web sites available. Each weekly email is broken down by categories that include "Team Marketing," "Trade Publications," and "Customer Acquisitions."

This is a Web resource that comes to you. Each week it lists new sites of interest that may have been missed in your daily travels on the Web. The mail covers online and offline marketing in a no-nonsense, direct way that allows for a quick and easy read.

Larry says, "Sites are selected on effectiveness, trend-spotting, and examples other marketers can learn from." The sites chosen are from all sides of marketing; you can expect resources in sports, technology, and most everything in between. Not every site chosen is an essential resource in itself, but with weekly updates, you are sure to build a great list of interesting sites in only a few months. Although heavy on self-promotion, wdfm.com is a good resource for anyone who wants to stay abreast of new sources of information in the marketing world.

Wilson Web
(http://wilsonweb.com/)

Wilsonweb.com is the leading site devoted to Web marketing, and is widely cited as an example of excellent site design and content. The site focuses on Web marketing resources and includes some free articles on Web marketing, links to other useful sites, Internet design and marketing "Tutorials," as well as a large paid-access archive.

Wilson Web is aimed at small business owners looking to learn how to effectively market on the Web, but the resources can be of use to anyone interested in learning more on Web marketing. Dr. Wilson has assembled a good, but expensive collection of articles useful to those who need more information on how to market goods and services on the Web. The free areas of the site make it worth a regular visit.

Fedstats.gov
(http://www.fedstats.gov)

Billed as "The gateway to statistics from over 100 U.S. Federal agencies," FedStats.gov is the central location for statistics compiled by the U.S. government and covers most official statistical information available from the U.S. Federal Government. Fedstats provides an easy way to access a bewildering array of governmental statistics without any knowledge of which agency provides the numbers. The site is the best place to start a search for any kind of government statistics when one is unsure of what agency is providing the numbers.

Site navigation is a snap. Users can simply browse more than 400 topics that range from acute conditions (colds and influenza) to weekly earnings. Some of the most useful numbers in marketing are demographics numbers from the Bureau of Labor Statistics (BLS). The BLS provides numbers on topics like employment, layoffs, and wages by occupation. If you are looking for demographic information, statistics, or other information on the American public, Fedstats is great place to start looking for raw data and some analysis.

American Demographics
(http://americandemographics.com)

American Demographics magazine is widely known for research and stories on the American public. The monthly magazine and Web site focus on marketing and consumer trends in the United States. *American Demographics* provide analysis of trends, and events relating to American consumers in areas such as spending, growth, and projections on work force trends. The stories and features provide information and in-depth analysis to anyone interested in further understanding marketing in America.

The site is designed to appeal to those in working in the marketing field, and focuses on articles that can help readers find a market, or understand the changes that are affecting our population. Stories work to explain raw data so the numbers can be used to effectively market to a wider audience. An "Ad Source Book" lists suppliers in areas like direct marketing, lifestyles, and business services. Full access to current *American Demographics* articles is only available to subscribers.

Adage.com
(http://www.adage.com)

AdAge.com is the Web site of *Advertising Age*, the seventy-one year-old trade journal. The companion Web site contains weekly news and information that cover marketing, as well as advertising and mass media. The Ad Age Group, which owns Adage.com, publishes a number of marketing periodicals including, *Advertising Age International*, *Business Marketing and Creativity*, and Adreview.com.

Content on Adage.com includes domestic and international news, features, special reports, and critiques of advertising strategies. Specific industry news comes from sources such as the "Ad Industry Pulse," a quarterly poll of agency executives and advertisers. The site also includes breaking news, which is updated throughout each business day. Features on people in the advertising industry, viewpoints and the "Data Center" all add up to an impressive collection of information on the advertising industry. Special areas of the site include the "Data Center," which includes a list of 100 Leading National Advertisers, the largest U.S. media companies, an annual Agency Report, and Ad Age's annual survey of the salaries of more than 200 top agency executives. Ad Age is a great site to keep current on the latest happenings in the advertising world.

Operations Management/Operations Research Web Sites

Emily Missner

Leslie J. Reynolds

SUMMARY. This chapter covers the field of operations management/ operations research. The authors provide in-depth reviews of prominent sites, including those of professional organizations and academic institutions. *[Article copies available for a fee from The Haworth Document Delivery Service: 1-800-HAWORTH. E-mail address: <docdelivery@haworthpress.com> Website: <http://www.HaworthPress.com> © 2003 by The Haworth Press, Inc. All rights reserved.]*

KEYWORDS. Operations management, operations research, supply chain management, Web sites

INTRODUCTION

Operations management, operations research, and management science are terms commonly used interchangeably to describe employing analytical techniques to help make better decisions and to solve problems. Operations management professionals work to understand and structure complex systems, and then use this understanding to predict behavior and improve performance.

Emily Missner is Information Services Librarian–Business and Economics, Drexel University (E-mail: emissner@drexel.edu).

Leslie J. Reynolds is Associate Director for Public Services, Walker Management Library, Vanderbilt University (E-mail: Leslie.Reynolds@owen.vanderbilt.edu).

[Haworth co-indexing entry note]: "Operations Management/Operations Research Web Sites." Missner, Emily, and Leslie J. Reynolds. Co-published simultaneously in *Journal of Business & Finance Librarianship* (The Haworth Information Press, an imprint of The Haworth Press, Inc.) Vol. 8, No. 3/4. 2003, pp. 253-264; and: *The Core Business Web: A Guide to Key Information Resources* (ed: Gary W. White) The Haworth Information Press, an imprint of The Haworth Press, Inc., 2003, pp. 253-264. Single or multiple copies of this article are available for a fee from The Haworth Document Delivery Service [1-800-HAWORTH, 9:00 a.m. - 5:00 p.m. (EST). E-mail address: docdelivery@haworthpress.com].

Operations management stems from a variety of disciplines–including engineering, psychology, management, and mathematics–and is closely related to applied mathematics, industrial and systems engineering, computer sciences, and economics. These fields are considered the "decision sciences."[1]

People in this field use mathematical techniques and computer models, such as simulation, linear and nonlinear programming, dynamic programming, queuing, econometric methods, expert systems, decision analysis, and the analytic hierarchy process, to manipulate systems composed of people, machines and procedures, and to make better decisions.[2] Specialists in operations management are both theorists and practitioners of management science. Those working in operations management enjoy varied applications ranging from industry work, public services, and consulting. Some operations management professionals remain generalists, while others specialize in specific areas or problems.[3]

The way that organizations produce goods and services is the most simplistic description of operations management. This professional discipline deals with how products and services are developed, produced and distributed.[4] Activities include supply chain management, quality control, and logistics. It incorporates engineering principles, management fundamentals, as well as psychology, economics, mathematics, and computer science to improve an organization's efficiency and effectiveness.

Following are reviews of three operations management Web sites, as well as annotations of sites that were found to provide gems of information, or at least have the potential to grow and improve into vital resources.

INFORMS–Institute for Operations Research and the Management Sciences
(http://www.informs.org/)

The INFORMS Web site is the online information service of the Institute for Operations Research and the Management Sciences, a professional organization of operations management and the management sciences. INFORMS, a member of the International Federation of Operational Research Societies, has over 12,000 members worldwide. The Web site for this organization is an excellent resource for information on a variety of aspects of operations research and the management sciences. Along with offering news and information about INFORMS, the site also serves as a full-service, singular stop for information on operations management, offering resources ranging from conference and employment listings to several searchable databases of publications, member information, and conference publications. The majority of resources found on the site are available for both members and non-members of the institute.

INFORMS is the online presence of the Institute for Operations Research and Management Sciences, thus the audience is the institute's members. Remarkably, the information on the site is free and available for the public. According to the INFORM's mission statement, the society is "dedicated to advancing the development and dissemination of all aspects of Operations Research and the Management Sciences . . . "

INFORMS Online is a tremendous resource for operations management professionals, teachers, and students. The home page for the Web site is crowded with links to and information about resources for operations management and other management sciences. Highlighted on the page are listings of upcoming INFORMS conferences and new INFORMS resources.

For example, the site recently added the "INFORMS Online Resource Page" which provides links and information about Web-based operations management resources. This fantastic database, stemming from Carnegie Mellon University Professor Michael Trick's Operations Research Page (http://mat.gsia.cmu.edu/), allows users to search through over 1,000 OM resources by category, by the date it was entered into the database, or by keyword. All the sites have been reviewed by a content editor and are briefly annotated. Small icons note whether a resource is newly added to the database, is an INFORMS site, is a site that is very popular, and whether the editors of the database think the resources are really note-worthy.

Another new online resource is the INFORMS Job Placement Service created in conjunction with the INFORMS annual meeting. This is a fee-based service, and includes both online and printed copies of job placement listings and applicant files.

Also found on the home page are the "Top Ten Websites," which lists the most important resources on the site. "What's New at INFORMS" provides up-to-date information on the Web site. Users can read this update online, or they may choose to sign up for an e-mail alert.

"PubsOnLine" offers online access to some of INFORMS journals including *Decision Analysis, Information Systems Research, Journal on Computing,* and *Interfaces.* This is a fee-based section of the Web site. There are subscription rates for members, non-members, and institutions.

The "INFORMS Newsroom" is a collection of all the press releases issued by the institute, archived from 1997 to the present. Covering news, events, and people in the world of operations management, the press releases are interesting to read and well-written. The site also contains a list of experts for journalists to contact, an excellent explanation of operations research, articles featuring issues in operations management, and a list of the INFORMS board of directors.

The "Continuing Professional Education" site provides information on a variety of learning opportunities. Detailed information about each course includes a course description, instructor's biography, prerequisites, and registration and fees. The courses are taught at locations throughout the United States.

Most of the information found on INFORMS is directly related to the institute. There does not seem to be a formal process for reviewing possible inclusions for the site. The INFORMS OR/MS Resource Collection simply has a form for users to fill out if they want a Web site added to the database; however, there are content editors who review the material.

Information on the site is extremely current and stable. New information is added almost daily. Most pages on the site had been updated very recently, and there were no broken links anywhere on the Web site. Archived information goes back to 1997. The INFORMS site is also very easy to navigate. The most important and/or current information is linked from the front page; however, the site also has a very good site index. Along with these browseable forms of navigation, the site offers an excellent keyword search feature for finding specific information.

Thanks to minimal graphics, this information-rich site loads quite quickly. The site is text-heavy, and uses some graphics to guide users through the site. The home page contains the most graphics, and therefore, is the slowest page to load on the site.

For news and information about operations research and management sciences, the INFORMS Web site is by far the most important Web site. The information on the site is tremendously relevant and easy to find. Along with events and activities in the field, the site also provides information on other Web-based resources, some online articles, and other resources. Even though some sections require registration fees, the free information found on the site is unmatched by any other online operations management resources.

TOMI–Twiggs Operations Research Management Index
(www.twigg.info/tomi)

TOMI, or Twigg's Operations Management Index, is one of several starting points for operations management information found on the

Internet. The first incarnation of TOMI was in 1994. After a period of neglect, however, the site's creator, David Twigg, has begun the necessary maintenance work (as of January 2002) to make this site vital again. The site includes links to information on a variety of operations management related topics, such as product design, inventory control, distribution logistics, process improvement and supply management. One of the most interesting pages on this site is the introductory section that explains why operations management impacts daily life.

David Twigg designed this site specifically for doctoral students at the Warwick Business School in the United Kingdom. However, it also covers introductory information that would be useful for a student or practitioner new to the operations management field. Since the author is based in Europe, the site targets a worldwide audience, instead of focusing solely on the United States.

This review concentrates on the "Catalogue" section of the TOMI site. All the links described are accessible from TOMI's main home page; however, the catalogue page provides longer annotations for sections and sites.

The "Directory" section focuses on Internet resources arranged by operations management subject areas, with one exception–the sub-section for "Business Directories." The "Business Directories" provides brief annotations of other subject directories on other business related topics. One helpful characteristic of this directory is the "see references" feature. The links included in each section seem to be limited to one or two quality sites, although several sections have as many as seven annotated links.

The "Reading Room" section is divided into the "Library," "Coffee Table" and "News Rack." The "Library" contains the TOMI Collection of very brief bibliographies, almost all written by Twigg. They focus on specific operations management topics and direct the reader to related books, articles and other (mostly print) materials. The bibliographies are not annotated nor have they been updated in several years. The "Reading Room" also has a list of over sixty online operations management journals, as well as publishers who focus on operations management. There is also the standard link to Amazon.com.

The "Coffee Table" section points to online journal abstracts from *Harvard Business Review, Technology Review* and *Prism,* the Arthur D. Little Quarterly Journal. The "News Rack" points to a couple basic news links like the *PR Newswire* and the *Financial Times.* This is not the site to visit if the reader were looking for current news information.

The "Working Papers–Case Studies" section is described on the catalogue page. There is also a link to this section from within the "Reading Room." This section mainly contains sources for working papers and teaching case studies. It provides links to case study indexes and lists. However, there are a few that provide full-text papers and cases. This section also contains a link to virtual tours that include graphics, sound and video.

The next section in the catalogue is described as "Other Resources." This includes the following subsets which are briefly described.

"Academic Sites" links to universities around the world that are involved in operations management; this section is divided into European and North American institutions of higher education.

"Career Information" provides no position advertisements but gives general information on employment opportunities in academia and industry. The sources are mostly located in the United Kingdom and are not solely focused on operations management.

The "Conferences" section lists conferences with a "high operations management presence (mainly European)." This section provides information on upcoming conferences. It also provides links to conference gateways that should lead the searcher to additional information.

"Mail Lists, Bulletin Boards and On-line Conferences" provides a quick reference to listservs that deal with areas of operations management. It also provides a link to search for listservs that are related to any other topic that might be of interest. Twigg has included subscription information right on his page, so that the reader can quickly sign up for the list of interest.

"Professional Associations" provides links to home pages of several organizations that are related to operations management.

"Research Resources" provides links to a few online notable online catalogs. However, a few of the sites listed require logins and passwords.

The "Software" section contains links to software packages that may aid in either the learning or the delivery of operations management. The software is not tested for reliability or applicability to specific operations management problems. The sites are listed as places to find learning programs, business management games, project management software and simulation programs.

The selection criteria are stated clearly. Sites are reviewed prior to inclusion and are periodically reviewed to ensure relevance and benefit to users. The site considers operations management related information that can support teaching or research needs at the university level or might be found useful to a practitioner. There are two basic questions Twigg asks before sites are included:

- Does the site provide a good starting point for operations management related issues, or fill some useful gaps of other sites?
- Is there a learning content to the site that promotes operations management for both academic and practitioner?

David Twigg created and maintains the TOMI site. He received his Ph.D. from Warwick Business School (United Kingdom) in 1996. His research interests have focused on the adoption and implementation of integrated technologies, specifically Computer Aided Design and Computer Aided Manufacturing, and the management of product co-design relationships within automotive supply networks. Currently, he is researching project management of complex product systems in the defense and construction industries. His articles have appeared in the *International Journal of Operations and Production Management, Sloan Management Review* and several others. Currently, Twigg is a Research Fellow at the ESRC Complex Product Systems (CoPS) Innovation Center in Brighton, England.

TOMI began in 1994. At this writing, the site's latest update was listed as January 30, 2002, the site was last reviewed on February 18, 2002. There is a statement on the site: "After a long absence from this site, I am in the process of updating pages and verifying links. My apologies for the long wait. This may take weeks or months–work commitments take priority. Nevertheless, rest assured the site will be updated shortly." Since this is a one-man site, there is always the possibility that the site will become unstable. However, I believe he has recommitted to maintain this site so that it will continue to be useful.

TOMI is a valuable resource for operations management. Should David Twigg continue his commitment to this site in a relatively consistent manner, this site will continue to be a good entry point to operations management articles and working papers, organizations, case studies, and software.

Operations Management Center
(http://www.mhhe.com/business/opsci/pom/)

Created and maintained by Byron Finch, a member of the faculty at Miami University in Oxford, Ohio, this site is sponsored by Irwin/McGraw Hill, an educational publisher, and is intended to serve students and faculty of operations management. The site, conceived by Professor Finch in 1996, was originally hosted by Miami University; however, it was moved to its current location in 1998. Although the Operations Management Center benefits from strategic partnerships with both Irwin/McGraw-Hill and the journal *Business Week Online*, the author stresses that it is more than just an advertisement for Irwin/McGraw-Hill and *Business Week*. Professor Finch intends for the Operations Management Center to offer exceptional "educational value" to its intended audience.

The mission of the Operations Management Center is to be the "source for faculty looking for pedagogical support or references and for students seeking current OM information." Rather than serving as a clearinghouse for all Web sites with operations management resources, only Web sites with relevant and useful information are added to the site.

As stated in the Operation Management Center's background and history section, the site's mission is to "provide a focal point for finding operations management resources that are valuable for students and faculty . . . OM center is designed to be a fast-loading informational site, with minimal glitter and glitz that would slow it down. We want it to be THE source for faculty looking for pedagogical support or references and for students seeking current OM information."

The Operations Management Center primarily wants to identify the best operations management resources found online. However, large sections of the content are from the site's sponsor, Irwin/McGraw-Hill. Also included on the site is a collection of *Business Week Online* articles, all which contain some kind of reference to operations management.

The site has no search feature; however, the layout of the Web site is very straightforward. Each section is clearly linked from the home page. The Operations Management Center does, however, have a site map that helps users navigate the site. Each section within the site looks similar to the front page, with the content clearly organized, but with no search engine. Because of the layout of the site, it is still relatively easy to browse for information on a subtopic of operations management, but it is very difficult to look for specific information or a specific article. There is no way to conduct a word search on this Web site.

The Operations Management Center does not produce any of its own content; however, it is a good place to find a collection of information from a variety of sources. Lacking a search engine, the Operation Management Center's content is all linked from the home page. The site is laid out in a grid, a design that is repeated throughout the site. Operations Management Center is divided into four main sections.

"OM Resources" offers links to other operation management resources online, including Web sites, teaching guides, links pages, and articles. The resources are organized by topic and include inventory management, quality management, manufacturing, and operations research. The sites are linked complete with brief annotations.

The "Company Tours" section provides an excellent directory to companies that have created online tours of their facilities. The tours are organized in alphabetical order by company name, and are accompanied by overviews, an explanation of the relevancy of the tour to operations management, and a ranking of in-class use.

Users can access full-text *Business Week* articles from this site in the *Business Week* Online section. The articles are listed in chronological order. Article summaries and descriptions of the type of operations management are also provided. The collection of articles spans from 1996 to the present.

The "Text Support" section links to teaching tools for instructors that are provided on specific textbook's home pages. Almost all of the textbooks listed are published by McGraw-Hill publishing.

The Operations Management Center Web site is kept fairly current. Relevant articles from *Business Week* are linked to the site as they are published in the journal–at the rate of about one every month to every other month. The article titles are listed and linked on the left side of the screen, and an easy-to-understand grid explains the topics addressed in the article: quality management; service management; inventory management; location; supply chain and logistics; capacity management; manufacturing; productivity; and advanced technology. Articles span from 1996 to the present.

The information on the site is not particularly time-sensitive, nor does it become outdated. For this reason, the Operations Management Center does not need to be updated daily in order to be relevant to the study of operations management. Instead, the Web site points to OM news feeds, articles, and online periodicals that will keep users up-to-date.

Because of the affiliation and sponsorship of Irwin/McGraw-Hill and the partnership with *Business Week*, there is a good possibility of the long-term stability of the Web site. As long as Dr. Finch continues to have an interest in updating the information on the site, it will remain a good resource for the academic community.

Due to the almost complete lack of graphics and other large files, the Operations Management Center Web site loads extremely quickly. Since the Operations Management Center was created to download information as quickly as possible, Finch has decided to do away with any whistles and bells, so the site has a very stark appearance.

Geared for students and faculty of operations management, the Operations Management Center offers a great starting place for finding information on this topic. The Web site offers a great breadth of informational sources from a variety of places; however, it lacks any kind of original content.

OTHER SITES OF MERIT

International Organization for Standardization: ISO 9000 and ISO 14000
(http://www.iso.ch/iso/en/iso9000-14000/index.html)

If an organization seeks to establish a quality or environmental management system, then such a system has a number of essential features that are described in the ISO 9000 (quality management) or ISO 14000 (to minimize harmful effects an organization's activities may cause to the environment) standard families. These standards are voluntary, unless a business sector makes them a market requirement. International in scope, these standards can be applied to any size organization producing any product or providing any service, in any sector of business or government. Under the "Basics" link is a tour designed to demystify both ISO 9000 and 14000. This fabulous resource was designed to clear up common misunderstandings about what these standards are and, more importantly, are not.

International Federation of Operational Research Societies Online Encyclopedia
(http://www.ifors.org/ioe/)

The International Federation of Operational Research Societies plans to provide an extensive collection of OR/MS materials, organized as an online encyclopedia. This site is currently under construction and will be launched officially at the IFORS 2002 Conference (July 8-12, 2002) in Edinburgh. The stated objective of the encyclopedia is to make operations research/management science more accessible to non-operations research professionals and therefore some of the material will be developed and presented with the general public in mind. Most of the encyclopedia is empty at this time, but will include: "Topics Depository" of links and bibliographies; "Glossary" with layman-oriented descriptions of operations management terms; "Dissertation Abstracts"; and a "Who's Who" of experts and professional organizations. When this resource becomes fully realized, it will be a wealth of information for operations management students and practitioners.

Operations Management
(http://www.mapnp.org/library/ops_mgnt/ops_mgnt.htm)

This site was produced by the Management Assistance Center for Nonprofits. It provides links to sites that describe most functions of operations management, from a general overview (which links to TOMI's introductory section) to procurement, management control, quality management, facilities management, and distribution channels.

Supply Chain Management Resource Center
(http://www.cio.com/research/scm/)

This site was developed by *CIO* magazine. *CIO* claims that each of its topical "Resource Centers" includes "articles, white papers, metrics, events, case studies, books and more." The site provides basic overview articles that appeared in *CIO* magazine. It is laid out well, is simple to use and labels advertisements that appear on the page. One interesting feature on this site is their "metrics" section. It provides interesting tidbits of metrics from a variety of sources that are searchable using a drop-down menu of subject categories.

TutOR
(http://www.tutor.ms.unimelb.edu.au/)

This site was launched in July 1999. The site's creators are in the process of developing a comprehensive, Web-based, interactive tutorial system for operations research. The site is designed for undergraduate students of operations research and related disciplines, and their teachers. It includes introductory information, problems, and case studies, and is growing in size. TutOR describes its activities as development of tutorial modules for specific OR topics, development of generic Web tools to facilitate the construction of the OR modules, and research of the WWW technologies pertaining to this project. The site was developed by Moshe Sniedovich, a Reader in the Department of Mathematics and Statistics, University of Melbourne, who holds a Ph.D. in Industrial Engineering.

VTOURS: Virtual Tours of Organizations Using Remote Systems
(http://forecast.umkc.edu/vtours/)

VTOURS presents reviews of about 100 virtual, Internet tours of organizations. This site is not pretty, but the tours it links to and reviews of them are extraordinary resources for academics and professionals in business, economics, and engineering. The site is updated regularly with new tours. The first tour listed is of a Kansas City based high-tech machine job shop using state-of-the-art technology and human resource management. Select the "Other Vtours" icon in the left frame or "Other Plant Tours" link in the text on the right to find two tables of contents (TOC) for Virtual Tours. The first TOC links directly to each company's tour. The second TOC provides brief annotations of the tours that are divided into industry categories from apparel/knitting processing to steel manufacturing to services.

NOTES

1. What is OR/MS? [Online] Available at: http://www.informs.org/Join/Orms.html.
2. "Operations Research Analyst" Occupational Outlook Handbook 2002-2003 [Online]. Available at: http://www.bls.gov/oco/ocos044.htm.
3. What is OR/MS? [Online]. Available at: http://www.informs.org/Join/Orms.html.
4. An Introduction to Operations Management [Online]. Available at: http://members.lycos.co.uk/tomi/whatis.html.

Real Estate

Joseph Straw

SUMMARY. The Web is an important tool for those interested in real estate and is a key tool for locating properties or researching loans. The author includes coverage of government Web sites for housing and loan information, as well as to major real estate directories. *[Article copies available for a fee from The Haworth Document Delivery Service: 1-800-HAWORTH. E-mail address: <docdelivery@haworthpress.com> Website: <http://www.HaworthPress.com> © 2003 by The Haworth Press, Inc. All rights reserved.]*

KEYWORDS. Real estate, Web sites

INTRODUCTION

Land and shelter are essential needs for all living human beings. The places where we live and work are ultimately bought, sold, and owned by someone. Real estate is the business that sells, rents, and leases the places where we as people live and transact business. In a very real sense it can be said that real estate is the bedrock of any economy. In a free capitalist system, real estate can be seen as the primal economic activity or as the business that must happen before any other business can take place.

The importance of real estate for the U.S. economy can never be overstated or exaggerated. Real estate in the U.S. involves assets, sales, profits, and investments that are in the trillions of dollars. The problems of

Joseph Straw is Associate Professor of Library Administration, The University of Illinois, Urbana-Champaign (E-mail: jstraw@uiuc.edu).

[Haworth co-indexing entry note]: "Real Estate." Straw, Joseph. Co-published simultaneously in *Journal of Business & Finance Librarianship* (The Haworth Information Press, an imprint of The Haworth Press, Inc.) Vol. 8, No. 3/4, 2003, pp. 265-270; and: *The Core Business Web: A Guide to Key Information Resources* (ed: Gary W. White) The Haworth Information Press, an imprint of The Haworth Press, Inc., 2003, pp. 265-270. Single or multiple copies of this article are available for a fee from The Haworth Document Delivery Service [1-800-HAWORTH, 9:00 a.m. - 5:00 p.m. (EST). E-mail address: docdelivery@haworthpress.com].

10.1300/J109v08n03_13

defining the precise parameters of this business are difficult, if not impossible, because it affects almost everyone in a very real and personal way. Real estate comes into the lives of almost every American that buys a house, rents an apartment, purchases land, or starts a business.

Real estate markets in the U.S. are highly fragmented and decentralized. The American tradition of private land ownership opens up the business to millions of potential players. Everything from housewives selling homes on their block, to governments buying millions of acres for regional development, are all important cogs in the real estate engine. The complexity of real estate is immense with distinct and different markets on almost every street, thus forcing the real estate industry to organize itself at an intensely local level.

Real estate is one of the most market driven segments of the U.S. economy. Changes in other economic sectors can have rapid positive or negative influences on the stability of real estate markets at any given time. Traditionally, banks in their roles as suppliers of money and credit have had the greatest stabilizing or destabilizing effect on the fortunes of real estate markets. Clearly, market forces will always make real estate one of the most profitable, yet one of the most volatile, sectors of the U.S. economy.

REAL ESTATE ON THE WEB

The information problems posed by real estate are immense. Besides the vast number of print and electronic resources that are available to librarians, the growth of the Internet has also created a whole new set of numbers. It's not surprising to find that a massive amount of real estate information can be found on the Internet. The highly local and market driven dimension of real estate mirrors itself on the Internet with an inventory of sites that is almost limitless.

For a person not currently in the housing market, surfing the Internet for real estate information can be a frustrating experience. The vast majority of sites emphasize getting people to buyers and sellers as quickly as possible. Trying to list sites that look at the bigger picture is a considerable challenge. The listing of sites that follows steers clear of sites that exclusively offer property listings, classifieds, agent referrals, local real estate offices, and buying advice. What follows is a potentially core listing of sites that give the broadest overview of real estate as a whole. This includes sites that are directories of information about real estate services, consumers, trends, and analysis.

CORE REAL ESTATE SITES

Freddie Mac
(http://www.freddiemac.com)

This quasi-government corporation is an important referral and financing entity for low- to moderate-income consumers. The Freddie Mac Web site has excellent information about multi-family housing, mortgage securities, debt securities, leasing, and property ownership. This site also has some very good FAQ pages that talk about issues of concern for housing consumers. The emphasis of the site is clearly on mortgaging and financing information for a whole range of potential buyers. The Freddie Mac site provides a wide range of important real estate information from a consumer perspective.

Free-Real-Estate-Info.com
(http://www.Free-Real-Estate-Info.com)

This site contains a very simple and generic selection of real estate related links from across the Internet. Folders for both consumers and real estate professionals allow the user to connect to sites about loans, financing, relocating, home values, news, and professional real estate education. This site provides a good starting point for both consumers and real estate professionals.

Ginnie Mae
(http://www.ginniemae.gov)

Ginnie Mae is a government corporation owned by the Department of Housing and Urban Development (HUD). The purpose of this agency is to serve low to moderate income homebuyers in financing and mortgaging houses. The Ginnie Mae Web site has some good links to general buying, mortgage, insurance, and home owning issues. This site also has some good FAQ pages about issues of concern to consumers. Ginnie Mae can provide some good connections for consumers interested in home financing options.

HSN Associates
(http://www.hsh.com)

This site is an excellent source to find Internet information about real estate, home mortgages, and financing options. HSH.com can link users to mortgage rates for all geographic areas and for all types of potential buyers. It has some good statistical links that provide information about housing indexes, borrowing rates, relocation costs, and loan rates. For both consumers and professionals the HSN site offers some very valuable information about home buying and the real estate financing maze.

Housing and Urban Development
(http://www.hud.gov)

This is the Internet site for the Department of Housing and Urban Development (HUD), an excellent clearinghouse for all kinds of property and real estate information from a largely consumer point of view. It has a good array of links to a large number of agencies that deal with housing issues. The site also has a large collection of subject links that to go to places that may be helpful to minorities, lenders, small businesses, women, and the homeless. Overall, this a first class site for the general public.

Ired.com
(http://www.ired.com)

This is the Web site for the *International Real Estate Digest.* Ired.com is perhaps one of the largest real estate directories on the Internet. A series of links provides connections to real estate sites for all the fifty states and about 115 foreign countries. This site would clearly be most useful for the real estate professional.

Jack Brause Library
(http://www.nyu.edu/library/rei)

This interesting academic site is the library for the Real Estate Institute at New York University. The site has a number of simple subject links that include commercial properties, government properties, residential properties, finance and investments, and academic resources. Under each subject is a bibliography of works from the library collection, and a list of external Web sites. The Jack Brause library is one of the most comprehensive real estate focused collections in the world, and it can be used as an important research tool for professionals and the general public.

Monstermoving.Com
(http://www.monstermoving.com)

This is a monster.com Internet site that looks at resources for relocating. In an effort to provide resources for moving, monstermoving.com instead becomes a good site for real estate services in general. Links and FAQs provide practical information on mortgage quotes, credit issues, apartments, housing values, and much more. Monstermoving.com is a first class site to get fast Internet information about moving and real estate.

RealEstate.com
(http://www.realestate.com)

RealEstate.com provides useful links to real estate services for both professionals and consumers. A consumer real estate center connects users to a wide variety of information about property values, appraisals, agent selection, mortgages, and buying information. Both consumers and professionals can purchase tools that customize the whole process of real estate transactions. RealEstate.com is a good site for business professionals and the real estate savvy consumer.

RealEstateDirectory.com
(http://www.realestatedirectory.com)

This site claims to be "the most powerful online real estate network in the world." A series of geographic links take the user to pages that focus on the real estate market for the fifty states and all Canadian provinces. Other links provide information on real estate markets for U.S. local and metropolitan areas. This site also boasts some good relocation tools including links to free moving quotes from some of the biggest van lines in the country. This is one of the larger Internet directories for real estate, and clearly would be of use to anyone wanting to understand local real estate markets.

The Real Estate Library
(http://www.relibrary.com)

This site is a directory of categorical links to real estate information across the Internet. Electronic maps can call up sites for lenders, realtors, and homebuilders for all the fifty states. The site has recently added video chat for users to pose questions to a live real estate expert. The site also has an excellent list of real estate related use.nets and discussion lists that are geared toward a professional audience.

REALS.com
(http://www.reals.com/)

REALS.com is one of the most comprehensive real estate directories on the Internet. A Yahoo!-style categorical arrangement offers information on apartments, builders, home buying, foreclosures, commercial real estate, and many other subjects. By clicking on the categorical links, a user can be connected to thousands of links that are further divided into subcategories and by geography. For consumers and professionals looking for a vast number of real estate links, REALS.com would be a good starting point.

REALTOR.com
(http://www.realtor.com)

This is the official site of the National Association of Realtors. The site features subject files that provide all kinds of useful information about apartments, moving, neighborhoods, home improvement, appliances and mortgages. A buyer and sellers guide provides helpful hints to consumers that are currently in or considering going into the housing market. The site also has links to news items that are of interest for both consumers and realtors. REALTOR.com is a site sponsored by a professional association, and a good deal of the information is promoting the services of real estate agents. If this bias is taken into account, a great deal of good information can be mined from this site.

Vandema
(http://www.homebuyingrealestate.com)

Vandema is another large collection of real estate links that is similar to REALS.com. A Yahoo!-style subject arrangement connects users to information about buying, selling, news, mortgages, statistics, guides, listings, and discussion forums. The links provided in this site may not be as extensive as some of the other Internet real estate directories, but it certainly would be a credible starting point for either consumers or professionals.

Small Business and Entrepreneurship

Glenda S. Neely

SUMMARY. Small business and entrepreneurship information is another area of strength on the Web. The author covers sites for general and start-up information, sites geared toward women and minorities, sites for advise and counseling, and sites for sources of capital. *[Article copies available for a fee from The Haworth Document Delivery Service: 1-800-HAWORTH. E-mail address: <docdelivery@haworthpress.com> Website: <http://www.HaworthPress.com> © 2003 by The Haworth Press, Inc. All rights reserved.]*

KEYWORDS. Small business, entrepreneurship, new business enterprises, Web sites

INTRODUCTION

Small business is part innovation, skill, hard work, being your own boss, and running your own business. It is synonymous with the "American dream" and provides approximately seventy-five percent of the net new jobs added to the U.S. economy. More than half of the private work force is employed by twenty-five million small businesses, and seven of the ten industries that added the most new jobs in the 1990s were in sectors dominated by small business. They account for thirty-eight percent of the jobs in high technology and dominate many categories of business statistics.[1] Entrepreneurs who are willing to take risks to create, in-

Glenda S. Neely is Business Reference Librarian, University of Louisville (E-mail: glenda.neely@louisville.edu).

[Haworth co-indexing entry note]: "Small Business and Entrepreneurship." Neely, Glenda S. Co-published simultaneously in *Journal of Business & Finance Librarianship* (The Haworth Information Press, an imprint of The Haworth Press, Inc.) Vol. 8, No. 3/4, 2003, pp. 271-280; and: *The Core Business Web: A Guide to Key Information Resources* (ed: Gary W. White) The Haworth Information Press, an imprint of The Haworth Press, Inc., 2003, pp. 271-280. Single or multiple copies of this article are available for a fee from The Haworth Document Delivery Service [1-800-HAWORTH, 9:00 a.m. - 5:00 p.m. (EST). E-mail address: docdelivery@haworthpress.com].

10.1300/J109v08n03_14

vest in and grow a business from its inception are increasing in number, due in part to downsizing and reductions in work force by large corporations. Self-employment has always been encouraged and praised in American society, and small businesses are the growth engine of the national economy.

Web sites for small business enterprises are among the fastest growing on the Internet and are sponsored by commercial and nonprofit organizations, the federal government, and educational institutions. Small businesses are also making up a large part of the network economy. Many Web sites claim to educate, train, and counsel the entrepreneur from the seed of an idea and raising needed capital to the final products and services that are requirements in managing a growing enterprise. They often include news, articles and other literature for small business managers and entrepreneurs, marketing plans and tools, professional products, services, counseling, trade missions and funding sources. There is an abundance of assistance for small business from private and public sources. Typing "small business" into Yahoo's search engine on April 3, 2002 yielded 6,788 sites, and narrowing the search to "entrepreneur" resulted in 621–still too many destinations. The Web sites chosen for this review were culled from several types of sources for evaluation.

The starting point was the Small Business page from the "Best of the Best Web Sites," sponsored by the Education Committee of the Business Reference and Services Section (BRASS) of the Reference and User Services Association (RUSA) of the American Library Association (http://www.ala.org/rusa/brass/bestsmb.html). Library sites from three institutions were visited for recommendations. They were Rutgers University Libraries' "Small Business and Entrepreneurship" page of Internet sites (http://www.libraries.rutgers.edu/rul/rr_gateway/research_guides/busi/smallbus.shtml); Pennsylvania State University Schreyer Business Library's "Entrepreneurship Web Sites" (http://www.libraries.psu.edu/crsweb/business/Entrepreneur/websites.htm); and the 3rd edition of "The Entrepreneur's Reference Guide to Small Business Information" (http://lcweb.loc.gov/rr/business/guide2.html), compiled by Robert Jackson and the Business Reference Services, Science, Technology, and Business Division staff at the Library of Congress. The latter is a guide to the literature of small business and entrepreneurship. Vivisimo, "the document clustering company" (http://www.vivisimo.com), was also checked for small business site rankings which showed the Web site of the U.S. Small Business Administration posted first on AOL and sixth on Yahoo. A 2000 article by Awe was studied for Web site evaluation.[2]

Web sites for small business were checked for practical, useful information, as well as for research purposes, rather than for selling products. They had to be well organized, easy to navigate, and include strong "linking" sites to take users to other helpful information. They also had to show evidence of currency. The sites are arranged by types of information. The first section is on comprehensive Web sites that offer general and startup information for new ventures; the second section is tailored to business information for women and minorities; the third focuses on counseling and professional association Internet sources. The last section contains Web sites that feature funding and venture capital sources.

GENERAL AND STARTUP INFORMATION

U.S. Small Business Administration
(http://www.sba.gov)

The U.S. Small Business Administration is the official starting site for resources and programs offered by the Small Business Administration (SBA). It calls itself "America's Small Business Resource" and is arguably the most extensive Web site for starting and growing a business. The site made its debut in August 1994 and receives over six million hits per week.[3] There are seventeen button links to major content including "Starting Your Business," "Financing Your Business," "Business Opportunities" (formerly "Expanding Your Business"), "FAQs," informative articles, a startup kit, "PRO-Net" (Procurement Marketing and Access Network), the "SBA Classroom," and "Your Local SBA Offices" which links to offices throughout the U.S. It is the primary destination for seeking government financing. The "BusinessLINC" (Learning, Information, Networking, and Collaboration) site contains business plans and a mentor network. There are publications and online forms and documents, many now available in Spanish. The authority, design and stability of information is outstanding, although when opening frames to site links it is sometimes tricky to back up to previous pages without returning to the home page.

There are other federal agencies with useful information for small business researchers. Some of the more notable are the Department of Commerce (http://www.doc.gov) for business statistics, speeches by Secretary Donald Evans, economic analysis, economic development and electronic commerce; the International Trade Administration (http://www.ita.doc.gov) and ITA's key links for export assistance, trade data, market access and compliance, advice on how to sell overseas, and the Export Portal; the U.S. Patent and Trademark Office (http://www.uspto.gov); and FirstGov (http://www.firstgov.gov)–the government gateway to business information.

Entrepreneurial Edge Online
(http://www.lowe.org)

Entrepreneurial Edge Online is the home page of the Edward Lowe Foundation, devoted to championing the entrepreneurial spirit. Lowe, who was the inventor of Kitty Litter, established the foundation to promote his philosophy of fostering and nurturing the American entrepreneur. This treasure chest contains over 1,400 ideas for growing your company under the "Business Builders" section. There are articles, books, and links to specialized small business sites, "CEO Perspectives," "Conferences," and the "Digital Library." Major article categories include leadership, strategy, human resources and funding. There are daily feature articles and hot topics. The publication section includes *Entrepreneur's News Digest*, *The Edward Lowe Report*, and *Media Tip Sheet*. Its strength lies in focusing on a variety of subjects that all entrepreneurs will invariably deal with as their businesses grow. Graphics load slowly at midday.

Entrepreneur.com
(http://www.entrepreneurmag.com)

Entrepreneur.com is maintained by *Entrepreneur Magazine* to support new business ideas and growing companies. It contains articles from *Entrepreneur*, *Start-Ups*, *Home Office*, and *Entrepreneur International*, and is exceptionally strong in franchising and home-based business information. Entrepreneur.com offers four newsletters via e-mail–"Starting a Business," "Growing a Business," "Franchise News," and "Sales & Marketing." There are resources for business developers, ready-made business forms to download, links to categories of franchising opportunities, and the Franchise 500 list.

Entreworld
(http://www.cntreworld.com)

Entreworld is sponsored by the Kauffman Center for Entrepreneurial Leadership at the Ewing Marion Kauffman Foundation. It uses "The Entrepreneur's Search Engine" to find the most current information on the Web for entrepreneurs, and content is divided among four areas–"Starting your Business," "Growing your Business," "Supporting Entrepreneurship," and "Social Entrepreneurship." The April 2002 "Entrepreneur's Byline" featured lessons from a failed partnership. Regular sections include "From Top Advisors," "The Kauffman Business EKG," and "From the Entrepreneur's Search Engine." It is not only an informative and comprehensive site, but also easy to navigate. It links to e-mail at SCORE, a counseling organization of retired executives. An example of a site from an educational institution is the Arthur M. Blank Center for Entrepreneurship (http://www.babson.edu/entrep), part of Babson College, which was ranked number one in the 2002 *U.S. News & World Report* ranking for outstanding undergraduate programs in entrepreneurship. Students in the program have won numerous awards for business plans.

Idea Café
(http://www.businessownersideacafe.com)

Idea Café, known as the "Business Owners' Idea Café," has a fun approach to serious business. It has a "busy" look to the graphics and page designs. Developed by successful entrepreneurs and authors of published guides on forming and running a business, it includes resources, practical advice, business and marketing plans in both service and manufacturing sectors, and business news. Business site links are summarized and reviewed. There is a grant center, profiles of people in small business ventures, financing focus section, and links to free trade publications. An expanded site for business plan samples is Bplans.com (http://www.bplans.com) which helps locate types of plans (marketing or advertising) for specific business sectors with help of the "plan wizard."

WOMEN AND MINORITY-OWNED BUSINESS SITES

According to the Small Business Administration's FAQs the number of women and minority-owned businesses increased during the 1990s, while self-employment as a whole declined. In 1999, 4.6 million women (39.3 percent of the total), 0.6 million Asians (4.7 percent of the total), 0.8 million blacks (6.8 percent of the total), and 0.8 million Hispanics (7.1 percent of the total) were self-employed. More detailed data for these businesses is available from the Economic Census (U.S. Census Bureau).

Online Women's Business Center
(http://www.onlinewbc.gov)

Online Women's Business Center has recently changed its address from an "org" domain. This is the site of the SBA's Office of Women's Business Ownership (OWBO). The "About Us" page reports America's 9.1 million women-owned businesses employ 27.5 million people and contribute $3.6 trillion to the economy, yet women continue to face unique obstacles in the business world. The OWBO is striving to level the playing field for women entrepreneurs. They promote the growth of women-owned businesses through training programs, technical assistance, access to credit and capital, federal contracts, and international trade opportunities. The side bar menu on the left has buttons which include tables of contents. For example, "Hot Topics" includes information on government contracting, e-commerce, exporting, disaster assistance, women with disabilities, research and development and young entrepreneurs. The menu is multilingual and includes Spanish, Russian, Chinese, Japanese, and Icelandic. Special software may be required to read in Chinese and Japanese. There is a directory of Women's Business Centers throughout the U.S., where training in finance, management, marketing, procurement and the Internet is offered. Issues such as welfare-to-work, home-based businesses, and corporate downsizing are also addressed.

The National Foundation for Women Business Owners
(http://www.nfwbo.org)

The National Foundation for Women Business Owners provides information on women entrepreneurs and includes the Center for Women's Business Research. They provide original, groundbreaking research to document the economic and social contributions of women-owned firms. The Center also offers consulting and public relations services. The National Association of Women Business Owners (http://www.nawbo.org) has chapters located throughout the country. They sponsor national and regional conferences, provide corporate networking opportunities, guest speakers for chapters, and sponsor awards.

The Minority Business Development Agency
(http://www.mbda.gov)

The Minority Business Development Agency is an organization of the U.S. Department of Commerce. Known as the MBDA, it is the federal agency fostering the creation, growth and expansion of minority-owned businesses in America. Its vision, adopted September 22, 2001, is as follows: "The Minority Business Development Agency is dedicated to becoming an entrepreneurially-focused and innovative organization, committed to empowering minority business enterprises for the purpose of wealth creation in minority communities." MBDA provides access to working capital, startup business financing, assistance to home business, online courses, conferences, access to markets, technology tools and the publications *Capital Trends, Demographic Trends, Industry Trends* and *Export Trends.* The MBDA has regional and district offices around the country. The home page connects to a mission statement approved in June, 2001: "MBDA's mission is to actively promote the growth and competitiveness of minority-owned businesses by providing access to public/private debt and equity financing, market opportunities, and management and business information; coordinating and leveraging public and private resources; and, facilitating strategic alliances." Other MBDA development programs include Native American Business Development Centers, Minority Business Opportunity Centers, and Business Resource Centers. Although the Web site is free, registration is required for accessing the *Phoenix Database of Minority Businesses.* Although in the past there was a Spanish version of this site, it was not mentioned on the main pages.

Other minority organization Web sites of note include the American Association of Minority Businesses (http://www.website1.com/aamb) founded in 1992 and dedicated to management and technical education of minority business owners, African American Chambers of Commerce (http://www.minoritychamber.com), the National Center for American Indian Enterprise Development (http://ncaied.org), the Latin American Association (http://lbausa.com) and the United States Hispanic Chamber of Commerce (http://www.ushcc.com). The latter has a site map and was more current and easier to navigate. All are actively involved in training, networking, and funding minority businesses.

COUNSELING AND PROFESSIONAL SITES

SCORE
(http://www.score.org)

SCORE is the Service Corps of Retired Executives and is a resource partner with the U.S. Small Business Administration. "SCORE is dedicated to aiding in the formation, growth, and success of small business nationwide." Retired executives serve as small business counselors and are dedicated to helping entrepreneurs succeed. Over 900 serve as virtual volunteers by providing free and confidential e-mail counseling. There are 13,000 SCORE counselors providing startup help for new business ventures as well as helping seasoned business owners with their problems. They strive to match counselors to specific needs of the requestor and the industry. Use "Find SCORE" on the left menu to locate an interactive map and chapter contacts. These one-on-one corps counselors are invaluable to preventing business failure. SCORE also offers workshops and seminars as well as follow-up meetings.

The Executive Committee
(http://www.teconline.com)

The Executive Committee is composed of chief executives working together to help their fellow CEOs. Chapters are located in major cities and there are over 7,000 members globally. The TEC home page says they have been "increasing the effectiveness and enhancing the lives of chief executives since 1957." The "Best Practices" series available to TEC members range from sixty to eighty-five pages, but executive summaries of five to ten pages are located on the Web site and provide comprehensive overviews. The Women Presidents' Organization (http://www.womenpresidentsorg.com) has twenty-six chapters in U.S. cities. The WPO provides peer support, mentoring and networking for entrepreneurial women whose business revenues are more than $2 million (if product driven) or $1 million (if service driven).

There are other nonprofit small business organizations that assist entrepreneurs and some that offer professional consulting services. Others watch out for political interests of small business owners. Another assists family business owners with their unique set of problems and opportunities. These are representative and select, but not comprehensive sites.

The National Federation for Independent Business (http://www.nfib.org) calls itself "The Voice of Small Business," and is the largest small business lobbying organization. The National Commission on Entrepreneurship (http://www.ncoe.org) was created "to focus public policy on the role of entrepreneurship in the national economy and to articulate policies that will foster its continued growth." The International Council for Small Business (http://www.icsb.org) is an umbrella organization which integrates activities of organizations and professionals who deal with small business. The United States Association for Small Business and Entrepreneurship (http://www.usasbe.org) is a nonprofit organization devoted to continuing management education for entrepreneurs and small business. Fambiz.com (http://fambiz.com) is "The Web's Leading Resource for Family Business Executives & Owners," according to their home page. This site tailors its information to family-controlled companies. The "Family Business Search Engine" provides family business articles covering such topics as life disposition of the family business, small business health insurance, sibling rivalry, strategic planning and non-family managers and employees. It also links to other family business sites. It is affiliated with Northeastern University's Center for Family Business.

FUNDING AND VENTURE CAPITAL

It is not easy getting the green, but the Internet makes it easier to make contact with prospective sources. Many of the sources mentioned and reviewed above have links to funding, some also overlap. The study of locating money could be an article on its own since there are so many types of funding sources. Government-sponsored funding from the Small Business Administration (http://www.sba.gov) represents the mother lode of available money and opportunity. "Financing Your Business" is clearly labeled on the SBA home page and leads to links for loans, programs, studies, and sources. Be sure to visit the "Hotlist" page (http://www.sba.gov/hotlist/busfin.html). The SBA offers a variety of financing options for small businesses. Its assistance is usually in the form of loan guarantees–they guarantee loans made by banks and other private lenders to business clients. Contacts can be made to related federal agencies like the Small Business Development Centers (http://www.sba.gov/sbdc), Women's Online Business Center (http://www.onlinewbc.gov), and the Commerce Department's Economic Development Administration (http://www.doc.gov/eda/html/2e_stateandloc.htm) for state and local sources.

Equity and insider funding can come from venture capital and angels (individual investors) as well as wealthy family members and friends. Venture capital is a field that has traditionally been covered by printed directory sources, but Web sites have brought currency and speed to coverage. Business incubators are facilities that house business together, usually in university settings, and newly formed (incubator) firms share space, rent and services. Contact the National Business Incubation Association (http://www.NBIA.org) to reach members who are incubator developers and managers, economic development professionals, and venture capital investors. The National Venture Capital Association (http://nvca.org) represents the venture capital community. Their Web site provides helpful information on recent issues affecting the venture capital community. Some government sites, including the SBA, link to ACE-Net, the Angel Capital Electronic Network (https://ace-net.sr.unh.edu/pub). ACE-Net has raised approximately $700 million since 1997 with an average deal of $1.2 million according to the Web site. SCORE (http://www.score.org) and the Service Corps of Retired Executives have excellent connections to capital along with their proven consulting expertise. Also check Entreworld (http://www.entre world.com) and Minority Business Development Agency (http://www. mbda.gov) for funding in addition to the educational and training opportunities discussed in the previous section of this article.

Commercial Web sites offer a wealth of contacts for small business funding. Garage.com (http://www.garage.com) from Garage Technology Ventures serves as a venture capital investment bank. EarlyBirdCapital.com specializes in financing for early-stage companies looking to raise between three million and ten million dollars in fast-growing industry segments including information technology, e-commerce, medical technology, and telecommunications. Dalewood Associates manages its venture capital fund. Although listed sites have concentrated on the U.S., you can think global since there are investors matching companies and investors around the world. There are investment sites like OneCore.com (http://www.onecore. com) and Wells Fargo (http://www.wellsfargo.com/biz). The Web pages of the Commercial Finance Association (http://www.cfa.com) serve as a type of directory for commercial finance companies.

A few venture capital sites are reporting the need for refilling their coffers, possibly due to events of September 11, 2001 or to the general economic environment of the past year. The angel investors are going to be in high demand.

NOTES

1. United States Small Business Administration (2001), "Small Business Vital Statistics," available at: http://www.sba.gov/aboutsba/.

2. Awe, S.C. (2000). "Small Business Resources on the World Wide Web: an Evaluative Guide," *Reference Services Review*, 28 (1), 95-102.

3. Ren, W. (2000). "U.S. Small Business Administration," *Journal of Business & Finance Librarianship*, 6 (2), 37.

Taxation

Deborah L. Harrington

SUMMARY. Tax sites continue to grow in popularity as users download forms and search for tax help on the Web. The author of this chapter covers such areas as governmental/legal sites, e-commerce, state and local resources, and international resources. *[Article copies available for a fee from The Haworth Document Delivery Service: 1-800-HAWORTH. E-mail address: <docdelivery@haworthpress.com> Website: <http://www.HaworthPress.com> © 2003 by The Haworth Press, Inc. All rights reserved.]*

KEYWORDS. Taxation, Web sites

INTRODUCTION

Tax research is multi-faceted and requires timely, accurate, and reliable information for keeping abreast of the latest changes. Gary White and Diane Zabel, in a recent column for *Reference & User Services Quarterly (RUSQ)*, provide an excellent framework of tax research by explaining the history, terminology, types of taxes, and outlining core source titles.[1] Tax documents and publications, mentioned in the column, were not readily available on the Web for either tax professionals

---

Deborah L. Harrington is Instruction Coordinator Librarian, Auburn University at Montgomery, Montgomery, IL (E-mail: dharringtona1@hotmail.com).

[Haworth co-indexing entry note]: "Taxation." Harrington, Deborah L. Co-published simultaneously in *Journal of Business & Finance Librarianship* (The Haworth Information Press, an imprint of The Haworth Press, Inc.) Vol. 8, No. 3/4, 2003, pp. 281-290; and: *The Core Business Web: A Guide to Key Information Resources* (ed: Gary W. White) The Haworth Information Press, an imprint of The Haworth Press, Inc., 2003, pp. 281-290. Single or multiple copies of this article are available for a fee from The Haworth Document Delivery Service [1-800-HAWORTH, 9:00 a.m. - 5:00 p.m. (EST). E-mail address: docdelivery@haworthpress.com].

http://www.haworthpress.com/store/product.asp?sku=J109
© 2003 by The Haworth Press, Inc. All rights reserved.
10.1300/J109v08n03_15

or individuals in the recent past but are now only a click away. Although many of the core services are fee-based, the amount of tax information available at no cost via the Internet continues to increase at an exponential rate. This increase mirrors a coinciding increase in the popularity of the Web and a preference for finding information in electronic format. According to a recent survey, "almost all accountants (96%) have access to the Web, as opposed to only 51% in 1996."[2]

Surfing the Web through search engines or general directories will help identify and provide access to a number of core tax titles, including Internal Revenue Service forms, publications, regulations, and bulletins; federal tax law sources in the areas of pending and enacted legislation, primary and case law, regulations and revenue rulings; state and local tax information; news, updates, and discussions; international tax sources; tax help, tips, and articles; online tax preparation and much more. A recent Yahoo! search by the author using the term "tax" resulted in 3,107 hits. Searching through a results list of this size to find specific information would be impractical, time consuming, and may or may not lead to the best source. Although numerous tax Web sites are available to researchers, they cannot be considered equal in quality and accuracy of information. The differences are important because of the need for accuracy in reporting to avoid penalties and the potential opportunities in tax-savings.

Search engines by themselves are becoming more and more inefficient in leading users to the best sources that fit their needs as the amount of tax information continues to increase on the Web and effective searching takes a lot of practice. "Probably the most significant change in the way that tax research is conducted since the advent of electronic search services is currently underway as individuals and tax professionals explore the Internet and learn to use it to their best advantage."[3] "Subject specific directories, that are maintained by tax experts and provide category listings of links to tax information, saves researchers valuable time by searching the Web for information and organizing it into a logical, concise, and practical way."[4]

The following subject specific directories are highly recommended for saving time in locating quality and accurate core tax sources, most of which do not charge for access to specific titles. They are the author's favorites, many by well-known accounting experts or associations, and have proven to be core sites in addressing a number of questions coming to the reference desk.

COMPREHENSIVE

Accountant's World.com: Taxation
(http://www.accountantsworld.com/default.aspx)

As part of the Web site name, "the community of accountants who think ahead," this site was launched in 1999 as a dynamic virtual learning community whose mission is to "give the accountant the power they will need to thrive and survive under the new dynamics that are reshaping the accounting profession . . . through the power of information, knowledge and technology."[5] The layout of the site assists the member in finding information and resources very quickly. A top menu bar, as well as a category toolbar to the left of the screen, follows the user throughout the site. After a free simple registration process, members are provided with access to numerous resources arranged into seven dynamic channels consisting of: "Accounting/Audit"; "Consulting"; "E-business"; "Financial Planning"; "Payroll/HR"; "Practice Dev."; and "Taxation."

Under the "Taxation" channel, topic areas include: "Resources"; "News"; "Tools"; and "Discussion." "Resources" consist of links to government agencies, especially the IRS, and forms links to core tax research resources, and links to specialist topics. "News" provides full-text news articles in the areas of corporate, estate and gift, individual, international, partnership, reg. and taxes, and taxation. News archives are provided although they are more conveniently browsed than searched. "Tools" provides a practical calendar, tax calculators, forms, and a privacy letter template. Multiple threaded discussion forums provided under "Discussion" are a key feature of the virtual learning community. Based on tax topics, ten active forums provide a place for members to connect with other tax professionals, discuss topics, and ask questions.

Tax and Accounting Sites Directory
(http://www.taxsites.com/)

Dennis Schmidt, a well-known tax expert at the University of Northern Iowa, has maintained this subject specific tax directory since 1995. Schmidt describes the design of the site as a "starting point for people who are searching for tax and accounting information and services."[6] Users benefit from Schmidt's expertise in identifying and organizing links to core resources saving them invaluable time. The directory is a comprehensive index of tax resources easily navigable and understood by the user since information is arranged by topic category links from two main areas, "Tax Sites" and "Accounting Sites." Twenty categories are available under "Tax Sites" and further information and links are provided based on the specific topic. Free and fee-based information and links are current, reliable, and relevant. Although Schmidt provides a simple search engine, searching is a secondary concern as the layout and design of the site leads users to relevant information very quickly.

The directory has grown in popularity over the years. Based on site stats, the directory received "10,919 page views" in January 1996 compared with "451,021 page views" in January 2002.[7] Frequently mentioned and unique topic pages include "Academia" (http://www.taxsites.com/academia.html), "Tax Policy and Reform Groups" (http://www.taxsites.com/policy.html), "International Tax" (http://www.taxsites.com/international.html), and "State and Local Tax" (http://www.taxsites.com/state.html). Based on the author's familiarity with the directory, several revisions and updates have occurred since it was launched in 1995. Links to a new "Tax Jobs" area (http://www.tax-talent.com/ts/) is now included throughout the site as well as links to more practical information such as "Rates and Tables" for the individual taxpayer.

Tax Resources on the Web
(http://taxtopics.net)

Alan G. Kalman, a tax accountant based in California, created this "site as a public service . . . to provide easy access to tax resources that are available on the World Wide Web for individual and small business taxpayers."[9] The layout and design of the site allows for the nonprofessional to easily find information they need through an extremely practical topic category arrangement. Links are current, reliable, and relevant as indicated by current dates of update on each page throughout the site. From the front page, site visitors can choose from among 132 topic links arranged within a "directory box." Below the main directory box are links to "Federal Tax Law" and "California Tax Library." Even though the site is menu/topic driven, an excellent search feature has been added to the site. Visitors can search the entire site using a number of search options such as matching (any word, all words, exact phrase, and sound-alike matching), and within fields (anywhere, title, description, keywords, body, alternate text, URL). Results can be displayed by number of results per page (5, 10, 25, 50, 100) and with or without summaries or sorted by confidence score or date.

Kalman does an excellent job of designing the site to suit the non-tax professional. The use of technical jargon has been avoided and terms are selected that will be understood by most taxpayers (e.g., deceased tax-payers vs. estate tax). A caution has been placed on the front page warn-ing visitors to check the latest tax laws (with accompanying links to those new laws) because sites that he links to may not be updated. He also warns visitors to be aware that sites he links to may be trying to sell a ser-vice and for accurate information a tax professional should be contacted.

E-COMMERCE

Tax Cybrary: Internet Taxation
(http://www.vertexinc.com/cybrary/internet/articles.asp)

Dennis Schmidt and Will Yancey, in a recent *Practical Tax Strategies* article, define the hottest issues in e-commerce to be "the state and local governments' quest to compel out-of-state sellers to collect sales and use tax when they sell into the state."[10] Enter Vertex, Inc., a multi-state sales/use tax software developer, creator of the Tax Cybrary which ad-dresses that very issue by providing "a resource for the most up-to-date in-formation on state and local taxes."[11] An excellent site design, concisely targeted and focused on state and local tax issues, allows for intuitive navi-gation and location of information from six topic categories which are out-lined on a left toolbar that follow the user throughout: "Internet Tax"; "Sales Tax"; "Telecommunications Tax"; "Property Tax"; "Useful Tax Links"; and "Free Publications." Clicking on "Internet Tax" expands the menu offering with additional resource links:

- Articles–listing of news articles focused on the issue of Internet tax legislation
- State Laws and Definitions–provides a comprehensive outline of each state's laws and/or definitions in three areas: Internet access charges; sales of goods purchased over the Internet; and informa-tion/software purchased via downloading from the Internet
- Tax Simplification Initiatives–provides information on Tax Sim-plification Model Legislation
- EC Considerations–helps provide information to help businesses answer 3 questions: What kind of e-commerce will your company conduct? How will your system be configured? How will you inte-grate the Front-Office and Back-Office calculation processes?
- Internet Tax Terms–concise glossary of Internet terms

Will Yancey's Home Page: Electronic Commerce
(http://www.willyancey.com/ecom.htm)

Will Yancy, a CPA and Independent Consultant based in Dallas, TX, is a research partner of Dr. Dennis Schmidt (Tax and Accounting Sites). Together they have co-authored a number of articles on Web resources for tax research. From his comprehensive tax subject directory (Will Yancey's Home Page http://www.willyancey.com), Yancey provides a category link to "Electronic Commerce" that offers visitors a concisely designed list of the best resources on this dynamic topic. Over ninety links are organized into the following topical categories:

- General Issues of Electronic Commerce and EDI
- Taxation of Electronic Commerce
- Ecommerce Tax References
- Tax Havens
- Vendors of Software for Ecommerce

Additional punch outs to related categories include:

- Electronic Evidence and Records Retention
- Internet Law
- Retailers on the Web
- Technology for Professional Firms in Law or Tax
- Web and Computer Resources

GOVERNMENT/LEGAL

The Digital Daily
(http://www.irs.ustreas.gov/)

The Digital Daily is a popular Web site created by the Internal Revenue Service. "The IRS is the nation's tax collection agency and administers the Internal Revenue Code enacted by Congress. Its mission: to provide America's taxpayers with top quality service by helping them understand and meet their tax responsibilities and by applying the tax law with integrity and fairness to all."[12] Recently redesigned for easier navigation, resources can be accessed with less clicking and are now organized and targeted to various customer groups through multiple access points. From a side menu bar, customer links include: "Individuals"; "Businesses"; "Charities & Non-Profits"; "Government Entities"; "Tax Professionals"; and "Retirement Plans." Under the "Tax

Professionals" link, click on the "Practitioner's Corner" for access to research links that include:

- State Law Guides
- Federal and State Court Opinions
- Government Sites
- Tax Research
- Income Tax Issues
- Offer in Compromise
- News and Events

The top menu bar provides links to the most popular site pages including "Tax Stats," "About IRS," "Careers," "FOIA," "The Newsroom," "Accessibility," "Site Map," "Espanol," and "Help." Even though information has been customized and can be accessed through multiple access points from the main page, a simple search box is provided to search all or a portion of the site. "Forms and Publications Finder" allows for visitors to search by keyword or form/publication number.

FindLaw: Legal Topics: Tax Law
(http://www.findlaw.com/01topics/35tax/index.html)

FindLaw is a popular and frequently mentioned legal subject directory that utilizes content management/personalization technologies to suit resources/features to differing customer groups. Multiple access points to site resources increases usage by suiting information retrieval to a variety of customer preferences. According to site statistics, the site has "over 42,000,000 page views and 2,000,000 unique visitors each month."[13] A top menu bar links to customer groups, legal professionals, students, businesses, and the public, directing them to appropriate channels through which they can access content especially designed for them. To further suit unique customer needs, another link on the top menu to "My FindLaw" allows users to personalize content after a simple registration process.

Resources can also be accessed through topical links, on a separate menu bar at the top of the main page, including "Cases & Code," "Forms," "Legal Subjects," "Federal," "State," "Library," and "Boards." The topic of "Tax Law" can be found under the topical link of "Legal Subjects" at the top of the page. A very concise design of the specific "Tax Law" page allows for information to be found easily. Resources are divided under four main headings: "FindLaw Resources"; "Tax Law Web Guide"; "Related FindLaw Guide Pages"; and "Related West

Group Products." The "Tax Law Web Guide" heading provides links to the most practical categories of tax law resources arranged by format. Access is also provided to topical links through a reorganized menu of textual links found at the bottom of the main page.

Prof. Spalding's List of Tax, Legal, and Regulatory Research Resources
(http://www.cis.wayne.edu/aspalding/lawlist.html)

Federal tax law research is extremely multi-faceted addressing legislative, administrative, and judicial concerns as well as differing levels of legal authority in each of those concerns. A plethora of Web sites exist that address specific aspects of each of these areas. Dr. Albert D. Spalding, an accounting professor at Wayne State University, School of Business Administration, has provided an excellent comprehensive subject directory that brings together the availability of a variety of resources.

From informational links on such topics as the basics of legal research to links to specific courts, primary and secondary law sources, as well as practical links to associations, governments, publishers, calculators, Spalding provides over 400 links organized into thirty-two topical categories. Although a search feature is not available, visitors will be able to navigate the site easily through those categories.

STATE/LOCAL

Ryan Salt Gateway
(http://www.ryanco.com/salt.html)

As Dennis Schmidt and Will Yancey point out, because of "the volume of cases, administrative determinations and publications is greater than in federal tax due to the large numbers of different jurisdictions and types of cases . . . the Web is an ideal method of disseminating State and Local Tax (SALT) information."[14] In recent years, many professional firms and organizations, government associations, research groups, and publisher and software vendors have developed SALT subject directories to assist researchers in locating key resources. Ryan & Company, a respected state and local tax-consulting firm, provides such a directory known as the Ryan Salt Gateway. The Gateway is organized into two main areas:

Jurisdictions

The "State & Local Taxing Jurisdictions" page provides links to Web resources for each of sixty jurisdictions. Based on the resources available per jurisdiction, links are provided to such areas as "Departments of Revenue," "Legislatures," "Administrative Offices," "Treasury Departments," "Tax Incentives," "Electronic Commerce Taxation," etc.

Topics in State & Local Tax

Includes the following topic links:

- Associations and Research
- Electronic Commerce Tax
- Excise and Fuels Tax
- Federal Law on State & Local Tax
- Finding People and Firms
- Income and Franchise Tax
- Payroll Tax
- Property Tax
- Sales and Use Tax
- Sampling for Audits
- Severance Tax
- Unclaimed Property

Although a search feature is not offered, site visitors will be able to easily locate specific resources for information needs due to excellent layout and design.

MULTINATIONAL

Tax World.org: International
(http://www.taxworld.org/OtherSites/International/international.htm)

Professor Thomas C. Omer, Director of Tax World, provides Tax World "as a public service to Internet users whose primary mission is providing links to tax information from state, federal, and international taxing authorities on the Internet."[15] His comprehensive subject directory provides concise navigation through a left tool bar comprised of topical category links. Of interest to multinational tax researchers:

- "Tax Information Sites: International"
  (http://www.taxworld.org/OtherSites/International/international.
  htm)
  This page provides international tax resources from private and
  government resources arranged by country.
- "The Language of Tax" (http://www.taxworld.org/Language/
  Language.htm)
  A unique resource via the Web, this page provides information
  about how the concept of taxation is expressed in languages
  around the world. A concise glossary of terms is currently provided to eighteen countries.

Sites listed were last reviewed February 15, 2002.

NOTES

1. White, G.W. & Zabel, D. (2001, Spring). The Alert taxpayer: building a taxation collection. *Reference & User Services Quarterly*, 40 (3), 214-223.

2. Covaleski, J. (2000, Oct 9-Oct 22). Survey: Accountants are enjoying their
time online. *Accounting Today*, 14 (18), 5,57.

3. Klien, K.H. & Wilmot, J. (1998, Fall). Using the Internet for tax research.
Bank Accounting & Finance, 12 (1), 50.

4. Harrington, D.L. (2000, Aug.). Tax and Accounting Sites Directory. *Journal
of Business & Finance Librarianship*, 6 (3), 63.

5. Accountants World.com, [Online]. Available at: http://www.accountantsworld.
com/mission.asp February 15, 2002.

6. Tax and Accounting Sites Directory, [Online]. Available at: http://www.
taxsites.com/info/about.html February 15, 2002.

7. Tax and Accounting Sites Directory, Site Usage Report, [Online]. Available
at: http://www.taxsites.com/info/history.html February 15, 2002.

8. About Tax Planet.com, [Online]. Available at: http://www.taxplanet.com/
pressreleases/newsrelease020100/newsrelease020100.html February 15, 2002.

9. Tax Resources on the Web, [Online]. Available at: http://pages.prodigy.net/
agkalman February 15, 2002.

10. Schmidt, D. & Yancey, W. (2001, June). Web resources for tax professionals: update 2001. *Practical Tax Strategies*, 66(6) 358.

11. Tax Cybrary, [Online]. Available at: http://www.vertexinc.com/cybrary/
default.asp February 15, 2002.

12. Internal Revenue Service, [Online]. Available at: http://www.irs.ustreas.gov
February 15, 2002.

13. FindLaw: Advertising Info, [Online]. Available at: http://company.findlaw.com/
adkit/one.html February 15, 2002.

14. Schmidt & Yancey, 355.

15. Tax World Purpose, [Online]. Available at: http://www.taxworld.org/rename.
HTM February 15, 2002.

Index

Library of Congress's Global Legal
 Information Network, 38
"Library Services and Construction
 Act," 39
Linberger, P., 103
Linus Insider, 135
List of CPA Firms, 12
LIVEDGAR, 66
LivingWageLaws.org, 232
London Business School, 241
Los Angeles Times, 176
Loyola Marymount University, 31
LPA. *See* Labor Policy Association
 (LPA)
LRA. *See* Labor Research Association
 (LRA)

Mai, B., 213
Major Laws and Regulations Enforced
 by the Department of
 Labor–U.S. Department of
 Labor, 49
Malven, Powers, and Pasucci, LLC, 51
Management, web resources for, 237-244
 About.com Guide to Management,
 238
 Bpubs, 239
 BUBL LINK, 239
 Business Management Supersite, 239
 Business Researcher's Interests,
 239-240
 The Business Search Engine, 240
 CEO Express, 240
 Continuous Quality Improvement
 Online, 240-241
 European Case Clearing House, 241
 Fast Company, 241
 Free Management Library, 241-242
 HBS Working Knowledge, 242
 introduction to, 237-238
 IOMA, 239
 Knowledge@Wharton, 242
 Management Best Practice, 242-243
 Management Link, 243

ManagerWise, 243
MIT Sloan Management Review,
 243-244
U.S. Business Advisor, 244
Working Papers in Management, 244
Management Assistance Center for
 Nonprofits, 263
Management Assistance Program for
 Nonprofits, 241
 St. Paul, Minnesota, 30
Management Best Practice, 242-243
Management Link, 243
ManagerWise, 243
Managing Training and Development,
 239
Manchester School of Management, 244
Mansfield University, Census and
 Demographics of, 104-105
*Manual for Area & Industrial
 Labor-Management
 Committees,* 234
Marien, S., 81
Marketing and advertising, web
 resources for, 245-252
 The Ad*Access Project, 249
 Adage.com, 251
 Adweek.com, 247
 American Demographics, 252
 Brandweek.com, 247
 Commarts, 249-250
 Emergence of Advertising in
 America, 248
 Fedstats.gov, 251
 introduction to, 245-246
 Larry Chase's Web Digest for
 Marketers, 250-251
 MarketingTerms.com, 250
 Mediaweek.co, 248
 Medicine and Madison Avenue,
 248-249
 PaintedCows.com, 246-247
 SALESandMARKETING.com, 248
 TechnologyMarketing.com, 248
 UTexas Marketing World, 246
 The VNU Media Group, 247
 Wilson Web, 251

Pace University School of Law,
    Institute of International
    Commercial Law of, 44
PaintedCows.com, 246-247
PayPal, 93
PC World, 143
Pearson plc, 198
PEG. *See* "Price to Earnings Growth
    Ratio" (PEG)
Penn State Population Research
    Institute, 110-111
Penn World Table, 124-125
Pennsylvania State University Schrever
    Business Library, 272
Perry-Castaneda Library, 60
Philanthropic Research, Inc., 85
*Phoenix Database of Minority
    Businesses,* 277
Pitney Bowes, 145
PKF, 170
PopNet, 111
Population Reference Bureau, 111
Population Studies Center (PSC),
    University of Michigan,
    111-112
PR Newswire, 257
Practical Accountant, 11
Practical Tax Strategies, 285
PRARS, 83-84
"Press Room," 19
"Price to Earnings Growth Ratio"
    (PEG), 166
PricewaterhouseCoopers, 11,170
PricewaterhouseCoopers Technology
    Centre, 89
Primedia, 195
Prism, 257
Prison News, 33
Privacy Rights Clearinghouse, 99
Private Securities Litigation Reform
    Act of 1995, 44
PRNewswire, 176
Product/service evaluation and opinion,
    web sites for, 100-101

Prof. Spalding's List of Tax, Legal,
    and Regulatory Research
    Resources, 288
"Professional Ethics," 26
Professional Ethics Division, 6
Profile of State Chartered Banking, 20
Prophet Finance: Java Charts, 165-166
Protection, consumer, web sites for,
    96-99
Public Citizen, 99
Public Register Annual Report Service
    (PRARS), 83-84
"Public Sector Continuous Improvement
    Site," 241
Public Services International Research
    Unit, University of
    Greenwich, 226
Purdue University, American Religion
    Data Archive of, 107

*Quarterly Review: International Banking
    and Financial Market
    Developments,* 23
"Questions to Answer Before
    Beginning," 61
Quicken, 155
Quicken's One-Click Scorecard, 166
Quintessential Careers, 76

RAI. *See* Restructuring Associates Inc.
    (RAI)
Railway Labor Act, 229
Rare Book, Manuscript, and Special
    Collections Library, Duke
    University, 248
Real estate, web resources for, 265-270
    Freddie Mac, 267
    Free-Real-Estate-Info.com, 267
    Ginnie Mae, 267
    HSN Associates, 267-268
    HUD, 267, 268
    introduction to, 265-266

For Product Safety Concerns and Information please contact
our EU representative GPSR@taylorandfrancis.com Taylor & Francis
Verlag GmbH, Kaufingerstraße 24, 80331 München, Germany

T - #0085 - 160425 - C0 - 229/152/18 - PB - 9780789020956 - Gloss Lamination